STUDYING
MILTON

Geoffrey M. Ridden

BA M PHIL (LEEDS)
Principal Lecturer in English,
King Alfred's College, Winchester

LONGMAN
YORK PRESS

Reproduction of William Faithorne's engraving of Milton
on page 8 is by courtesy of the Mansell Collection

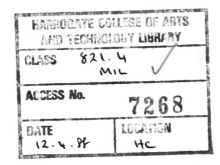
YORK PRESS
Immeuble Esseily, Place Riad Solh, Beirut.

LONGMAN GROUP LIMITED
Longman House,
Burnt Mill,
Harlow,
Essex.

© Librairie du Liban 1985

First published 1985
ISBN 0 582 79281 9
Produced by Longman Group (FE) Ltd
Printed in Hong Kong

Contents

Preface

In some respects, interest in the history and literature of mid-seventeenth-century England has never been keener than at present. Major new books have recently appeared on the political aspects of Andrew Marvell's writings,[1]* and on Milton's prose;[2] there have been new collections of revolutionary and religious pamphlets,[3] a detailed study of one of the more extreme religious sects,[4] and a new biography of Milton himself.[5] There is no longer a neat division between material which is the province of the historian and that which belongs to the literary critic, as is indicated by the fact that some of these books have been reviewed for one journal by historians and for others by critics,[6] and the general interest in the period has found its outlet in a television serial on the Civil War, and in three recent editions of the television historical magazine programme *Timewatch*.

A leading historian of the period has suggested in a recent newspaper article that the events of the mid-seventeenth century in England were 'as great a liberating experience'[7] as the French Revolution, and yet, he went on to argue, few people have an accurate impression of what actually went on. In the case of Milton's life and work this is certainly true, and the aim of this book is to counteract some of the mythologies which have grown up around Milton, and to place his work, poetry and prose, in the context of contemporary religious, political, and literary thinking. It is intended both as an introduction for the general reader and as a handbook for the student who wishes to discover the background to particular 'set' texts. It includes, therefore, not only sections on the works which might be expected to feature on examination syllabuses, but also discussion of some of the lesser-known poetry and prose, in addition to substantial introductions to Milton himself and to the development of Milton criticism.

* Notes are given on pp. 168–78.

ACKNOWLEDGEMENT

I should like to express my thanks to those who helped in the writing of this book. I have profited greatly from conversations with colleagues in the English and History departments of King Alfred's College, and I am particularly grateful to Dr Michael Jardine, Dr Roger Richardson, and Dr John Simons, who read parts of this work in draft: the errors which remain are mine, and not theirs.

I owe a debt also to the advice of Professor Jeffares, as General Editor, to the authorities of the College, who allowed me time to complete the book, and to the library staff, especially Joyce Tuffill, for responding so efficiently to my queries.

Winchester, 1984   GEOFFREY M. RIDDEN

A note on references

References to poems by Milton are to *The Poems of Milton*, edited by John Carey and Alastair Fowler, Longman, London, 1968, unless otherwise specified.

The standard edition of the prose works is that under the general editorship of Don M. Wolfe, *Complete Prose Works of John Milton*, Yale University Press, New Haven, 8 vols., 1953–82. In order to assist the less specialist reader, references to this edition (cited as *CPW*) have been made only when the passage is not included in one of the more accessible paperback collections. In every case the reference includes the title of the pamphlet as well as a page number to simplify the locating of the passage.

Gal. Faithorne ad Virum · Delin. et sculpsit ·

Joannis Miltoni Effigies Ætat: 62.
1670.

An engraving by William Faithorne (1616–91) of Milton, aged sixty-two, from *The History of Britain* (1670).

Part 1

Backgrounds

Milton's life and career

John Milton was born in Bread Street in London on 9 December 1608.
His father, also John Milton, was prosperous and cultured, a musician
with many published compositions to his credit. He was by profession
a scrivener, which involved the drafting of legal documents and also
dealing in various financial and property transactions, and he had his
own coat of arms to proclaim him a gentleman.[1] John Milton senior
had been brought up in Oxfordshire (where he maintained business
connections) but had left for London, according to an early biographer,
because of a dispute with his father over religion: Richard Milton was
a Catholic, and his son a Puritan.[2]

No such disputes, however, seem to have marred the relationship
between John Milton senior and his own sons, John and his younger
brother Christopher. Young John Milton paid tribute in a prose work
to the debt which he owed to the encouragement of his father:

> I was born at London, of an honest family; my father was
> distinguished by the undeviating integrity of his life; my mother, by
> the esteem in which she was held, and the alms which she bestowed.
> My father destined me from a child to the pursuits of literature; and
> my appetite for knowledge was so voracious, that, from twelve years
> of age, I hardly ever left my studies, or went to bed before midnight
> . . . My father had me daily instructed in the grammar-school, and
> by other masters at home.[3]

Milton had a tutor, Thomas Young, before he went to school, and he
maintained his relationship with this Scots Puritan for many years
after, dedicating a Latin poem to him in 1627 (when Young was in
Hamburg) and defending his Puritan views in his earliest English prose
works in 1641: the friendship cooled, however, when their political
beliefs started to lead in different directions.[4]

Milton's 'grammar-school' was the nearby St Paul's whose High
Master Alexander Gil had recently published a treatise on the English
language (*Logonomia Anglicana*, 1619) which might well have led
Milton to champion the cause of his native tongue in poetry and prose,
and to take particular care to indicate through his own spelling how
individual words should be pronounced.[5]

It was at St Paul's that Milton first met Charles Diodati, who was to remain his closest friend and confidant until Diodati's death in 1638. Despite their mutual affection and regard, however, the two young men proceeded to different universities: Diodati to Trinity College, Oxford, and Milton to Christ's College, Cambridge.

We do not know the reason, but Milton seems not to have been at all happy at Cambridge. Legend has it that he was beaten by his first tutor, William Chappell,[6] and Milton's enemies suggested that he had been expelled in some disgrace. Milton himself consistently maintained that there was no truth in these rumours and that he had remained on good terms with the University authorities. All that can be certainly concluded is that Milton spent some time away from Cambridge during 1626 (his first year as an undergraduate), and that he wrote a poem entitled 'Elegia Prima' to Diodati from London at this time, though this may indicate nothing more than that Milton was on vacation at that time. He did, in any case, return to Cambridge, and was placed in the tutorship of Nathaniel Tovey,[7] a friend of the Diodati family, with whom he seems to have had a more settled relationship: when Christopher Milton went to Christ's in 1631, Tovey became his tutor.[8]

It is clear, however, from Milton's own writings of the period that, whether or not he clashed with individuals at Cambridge, he found the syllabus little to his taste. In a letter to Alexander Gil, son of the High Master of St Paul's, in 1628, Milton bemoans the lack of stimulating conversation,[9] and three of the prolusions (academic exercises) delivered during his Cambridge career attack the rigidity of the syllabus. In Prolusion IV, for example, he attacks the teaching at the university as follows:

> foul Error reigns supreme in all the schools, and has seized the power, as it were, with the help of a strong and active body of supporters.[10]

One of these prolusions, however, reveals a very different side to Milton's character and to his reputation at Cambridge. Prolusion VI, on the theme that light-hearted entertainments are not prejudicial to philosophic studies, is full of bawdy innuendo and witty personal allusions, presumably to members of the original audience. The existence of this piece suggests a Milton who was called upon to speak at boisterous functions and could acquit himself admirably at them.[11]

Milton's writing at Cambridge was by no means confined to academic exercises or to prose. He wrote a considerable body of poetry in English, Italian, Latin, and in Greek. His facility in a range of languages suggests that he might have had good reason to feel oppressed by the narrowness of the academic syllabus, the more so since this corpus includes his first published poem 'On Shakespeare' which was included, anonymously, among prefatory material to the second Folio edition of Shakespeare.

In addition to the poems to Young and to Diodati, Milton's output at this point in his career includes a series of love-poems about a girl called Emilia (who may have been a real person, or merely an invention around which a series of poems could be woven), a number of poems on the deaths of well-known figures, and the companion poems 'L'Allegro' and 'Il Penseroso'. Among those whose deaths Milton commemorated were Thomas Hobson, the University carrier, subject of two witty English poems which were very popular during Milton's lifetime, and the Bishop of Winchester, Lancelot Andrewes, for whom he composed the Latin 'Elegia Tertia'. By coincidence, Andrewes had been vicar from 1588 to 1604 of the very church where Milton himself was to be buried, St Giles's Cripplegate.[12]

When Milton left the University with his M.A. degree in 1632 he did not, as we might expect, set about training for a profession. His brother had already committed himself to the law, and Milton considered following him, but did not carry through this project. Neither did he become a minister of the Church; not, as a letter of 1633 makes clear, because he disapproved of the ministry, but rather because he felt he would not be a competent preacher.[13] Instead, from 1632 until 1638 Milton lived at home, first in Hammersmith where his father had retired and later at Horton in Buckinghamshire, and devoted himself to an independent programme of studies, presumably to make up for the education which he thought he had missed at University.

In the 1633 letter referred to above Milton calls this period of his life a 'studious retirement', although this label might well evoke an image of tranquillity rather different from the reality of his life. In a Latin poem dedicated to his father ('Ad Patrem') Milton tries to reassure him that he does indeed have a vocation, and that his intention to dedicate himself to poetry is sincere and responsible. In this revealing poem Milton describes his father's generosity to him, and argues that the investment has been worthwhile (a most appropriate line of reasoning to follow in the light of his father's profession). He summarises, in a passage reminiscent of Sir Philip Sidney (1554–86), the position of poets in other civilisations, and ends with the defiant claim that his present modest fame will one day be surpassed and he will 'no longer mix with the brainless mob'.[14] We do not know the precise date of this poem, and cannot be certain therefore what Milton had produced before writing it, but despite its apparent confidence, its arrogance even, it encapsulates neatly the difficulties which he must have experienced in attempting to devote himself to study when those closest to him, parents, and neighbours perhaps, expected him to be more practical and more in keeping with his social position.

Milton made two excursions into the world of his social superiors, the gentry, during this period, to write the masques *Arcades* and *Comus*.[15] The Egerton family who commissioned both masques were probably introduced to Milton by Henry Lawes, but it is also possible that they had heard of the poet from London: the family had a house at the Barbican in Cripplegate.[16] The other major product of this period of 'studious retirement' is the elegy 'Lycidas', written on the death of Edward King, a contemporary of Milton at Cambridge who was drowned in 1637: the poem was published in 1638 as part of a memorial volume of Greek, Latin and English poems.

Although Milton was already producing works of rare distinction at this comparatively early point in his career, he felt himself unprepared as yet for major poetry, as the opening lines of 'Lycidas' indicate, and he did not put his name to any of his published compositions, despite the apparent popular success of *Comus*. The mask was published at the instigation of Lawes in 1637, without the name of its creator; 'Lycidas' appears with only the initials 'J.M.' to identify it. Milton preferred to wait and to devote himself to reading. We are fortunate in having a detailed record of Milton's reading from the Horton period, preserved in a document generally called the Commonplace Book, a notebook in which the poet listed topics of interest and associated reading from about 1635 to 1665.[17] From the Commonplace Book we can see the extent of Milton's reading during this period of preparation: it ranges across history, theology, philosophy, political theory, education, mathematics, and music, as well as including the literature of his own and of classical civilisation.[18] Milton was systematic in his recording of his reading, and this care was to stand him in good stead when he came to make use of these references in his later prose pamphlets.

Shortly after the publication of 'Lycidas' Milton made the acquaintance of Sir Henry Wotton, a traveller and poet, a former diplomat who had worked on behalf of the Earl of Essex, and who was ending a long and distinguished career as provost of Eton, not far from Milton's home in Horton. A letter from Wotton to Milton indicates that he was impressed by the young poet and by the copy of *Comus* which he had seen.[19] Furthermore, he offered advice on the forthcoming European tour which Milton was planning, and allowed the young man to use his name to effect introductions to influential people on the continent. Armed with this advice, and probably with further introductions from the Diodatis who, originally from Tuscany, had branches of the family in Paris and Geneva as well as in Italy, Milton left England in May 1638 for a tour which was to last some fourteen months.

Milton's desire to complete his education through travel, and the route which he took, were by no means unusual for gentlemen of his time, but his trip proved remarkable, both in the people he was fortunate enough to meet and in the troubles, personal and political, which he left behind him. He travelled from Paris to Florence, Rome and Naples, returning home via Geneva and France, and seems to have been warmly received everywhere by scholars and patrons of the arts. He met the lawyer Hugo Grotius in Paris (his tragedy *Adamus Exul* (1601) is among the sources Milton read for *Paradise Lost*); in Naples he met Manso (1561–1647),[20] the friend and biographer of the epic poet Tasso (1544–95); and, most impressively of all, he was able in Florence to meet Galileo (1564–1642), the distinguished astronomer who had been prepared to risk imprisonment rather than recant his assertion that Copernicus had been right and that the Earth was not the centre of the universe.

However, despite the personal benefits which he obtained from his tour, and the friendships which he maintained through correspondence long after, Milton was not able to cut himself off from events at home. The first signs of what was to become a Civil War had become apparent in the First Bishops' War against the Scots which had broken out in 1638, and, touching Milton more deeply in all probability, Charles Diodati died in August. Milton received the news of his friend's death in Naples and began the long journey back to England.

Milton honoured Diodati, his closest friend and one whose family Milton had visited on his tour, in a Latin elegy 'Epitaphium Damonis' which he completed on his return to England. In the 'Argument' which precedes the poem he describes Diodati as 'a young man extraordinary endowed with talents, learning and other gifts of a most exemplary kind'.[21] The first edition of this poem was probably published in 1640, by which time Milton was settled back in London, in a large house which he used as a private school, the pupils of which were mainly the children of his friends. Among them were John and Edward Phillips, the sons of Milton's sister Anne, who were both, in later life, to write biographies of their uncle.[22]

It was at this time that Milton became embroiled in the political and religious issues of the day. He was used to airing opinions in public which he expected to be controversial: his Cambridge prolusions give ample evidence of this. James Holly Hanford is right to assert that 'It was at Cambridge that he became a controversialist.'[23] This tendency remained through the period of retirement, emerging in an attack on the false priests in 'Lycidas' and in some rather surprising egalitarian sentiments in *Comus*. It was in the early 1640s, however, that this career as a controversialist in prose took flight, temporarily eclipsing his poetry. Although Milton himself describes this output as the product of his 'left hand',[24] a rather dismissive phrase, his corpus of prose constitutes a significant and varied body of work in its own right, and was, furthermore, the achievement for which he was best known in his own lifetime.

His first five pamphlets (1641–2) were part of the dispute over Church Government and the role of the bishops; in this controversy Milton adopted the cause of the Puritan Presbyterians against the Bishops, supporting in particular his former tutor Thomas Young. Pamphlets, however, could do nothing to stop the rift developing into war, and King Charles finally raised his standard at Nottingham on 22 August 1642.

The outbreak of war came at a time of crisis in Milton's personal life. He had gone to Forest Hill, near Oxford, in May 1642 to enquire about an outstanding debt due from Richard Powell and, to the astonishment of his young nephews, had returned home with a seventeen-year-old bride, Mary Powell. It seems that Milton had never met Mary before this visit, and the match has struck many later commentators as an odd one, the more so since there is not hint in Milton's writings immediately preceding his marriage that he was contemplating such an act.[25] By July 1642, however, the marriage was for the time being at an end: Mary returned to Forest Hill and stayed there for some three years. It is tempting to read more significance into this separation than it may in fact have. At the time when Milton expected Mary to return from Oxford (October 1642) Charles had established his headquarters there, and it may have been genuinely difficult for her to have travelled. There are few facts on which to base an impression of the married life of John and Mary Milton, not even a document of the date of their marriage, and no justification for treating their relationship as somehow symbolic of the typical strife brought on by civil war.

Milton's marriage clearly affected his writing. Pamphlets attacking the bishops were, in any case, no longer of interest, and he turned his attention instead to matters which were of greater personal moment. Between 1643 and 1645 he published four pamphlets on divorce, one on education, and a plea for freedom from the restrictions on censorship. It would be naive to maintain that there is no connection between Milton's own marital problems and his decision to write on divorce, but equally it would be wrong to assume that he was simply looking for reasons to rid himself of an unsatisfactory partner: it may even be that Milton already had grounds for divorcing Mary under existing codes without needing to raise his pen at all.[26] As A.N. Wilson has commented, 'the kind of marital discord and horror described in *The Doctrine and Discipline of Divorce* could not possibly be those of a man who was married, in effect, for only three weeks . . . there would scarcely have been time for either of them to suffer from "a drooping and disconsolate domestic captivity"'.[27] If Milton had wanted to get rid of Mary, then the obvious grounds would have been those of desertion,[28] which he does not mention in his tracts, although there seem to have been contemporary precedents for it. According to Edward Phillips, perhaps the most likely of the early biographers to know the truth, Milton considered marrying 'one of Dr Davis's Daughters' in 1645,[29] which suggests that Milton thought that he had reasonable grounds for considering his first marriage over. However, in the event, Mary returned and bore him three daughters and a son who died while still a baby: Milton never did divorce her.

Whatever we may make of the connection between Milton's writings on divorce and his own marriage, his contemporaries quickly decided that he was writing out of self-interest and the unfortunate Milton gained rapid celebrity as one who advocated 'divorce at pleasure',[30] and had written a book 'in which the bonds of marriage are let loose to inordinate lust'.[31] In fact Milton, in a studious and reasoned argument, had advocated no such thing, but that did not prevent incidental attacks, nor the publication of a full-scale reply (*An Answer to the Doctrine and Discipline of Divorce*, 1644) which failed to engage with Milton's arguments at all. To make matters worse, those who did support Milton did not appear to have read his work carefully cither, and he found himself in the uncomfortable position of being cited by those whose views were very far from his own:

> after Mistris Attaway, the Lace-woman had finished her exercise . . .
> she spake to them of Master *Milton* Doctrine of Divorce, . . .
> saying, it was a point to be considered of; and that she for her part
> would look more into it, for she had an unsanctified husband . . .
> and how accordingly she hath practised it in running away with
> another womans husband, is now sufficiently known . . .[32]

Although this particular account of Mrs Attaway comes from the pen of one of Milton's opponents and may, therefore have suffered some distortion, it cannot have been pleasant for Milton to be held responsible for licentious behaviour, especially since the label 'divorcer' stayed with him, to be brought up repeatedly by those who disagreed with any aspect of Milton's thinking. As late as 1670 John Eachard dismissed those writers who 'missing preferment in the University, can presently write you their new ways of Education; or being a little tormented with an ill chosen Wife, set forth the Doctrine of Divorce to be truly Evangelical'.[33] The rumour that Milton wrote to rid himself of Mary persists in Eachard's writing: but he was only eight at the time of Milton's divorce tracts.

Milton was not unused to attacks on his beliefs. His Cambridge prolusions indicate that he felt himself to be unpopular, and his first prose works had provoked angry attacks on his personal life and his past career. But these attacks, from the supporters of prelacy, had come from Milton's enemies and cannot have made a serious impression upon him. In contrast, ridicule of Milton's views on divorce came from the very men whom he had championed against the Bishops, men such as William Prynne who had had his ears cut off for his support of the Puritan cause. Milton's divorce pamphlets had been published just at the time when a split was occurring among those who had previously united in Parliament in opposition to the Bishops, and his views were taken by Prynne and others as indicative of the dangers that might lie ahead unless freedom of worship was abolished and an established Presbyterian church adopted. Thus Milton parted company with the Presbyterians whom he had supported; in the last of his divorce pamphlets, *Colasterion* (1645), he wrote of Prynne:

> I stood awhile and wondered what we might do to a man's heart, or what anatomy use, to find in it sincerity; for all our wonted marks every day fail us, and where we thought it was, we see it not, for alter and change residence it cannot sure . . .[34]

Few men of eminence wrote in Milton's defence: Henry Burton[35] and Henry Robinson both replied to Prynne's attack on Milton's behalf, but they were more concerned to uphold the principle of freedom of speech and of the individual conscience than with Milton's particular views.[36] Milton himself had responded to early criticism of his views on divorce by amending the title page of the second edition of *The Doctrine and Discipline of Divorce* to add a biblical allusion: 'Prov. 18.13 He that answereth a matter before he heareth it, it is folly and shame unto him.' This referred to those who had criticised his views without having read his book. He also added a preface in the form of a letter to Parliament, which he signed with his full name.

This second edition, however, with its amendments, far from ensuring a more reasoned reaction to Milton's tract, provoked extreme hostility in a sermon preached to both Houses of Parliament by Herbert Palmer on 13 August 1644:

> If any plead Conscience for the Lawfulnesse of *Polygamy*; (or for divorce for other causes then Christ and His Apostles mention; Of which a *wicked booke* is abroad and *uncensured*, though *deserving to be burnt*, whose *Author* hath been so *impudent* as to *set his Name* to it, and *dedicate it to your selves*,) . . . will you grant a *Toleration* for all this?[37]

Members of Parliament, it would appear, were more impressed by Palmer's sermon than by Milton's prefatory letter to them. Censorship and the regulation of printing were subject to greater restriction, and an instruction was issued: 'diligently to inquire out the Authors, Printers, and Publishers of the Pamphlet against the Immortality of the Soul, and concerning Divorce'.[38]

Thus, in the midst of his work on divorce, Milton changed course once again to defend freedom of speech in his best-known and most admired prose work, *Areopagitica* (1644). It is an indication of the talent of this remarkable man that in a single year, 1644, he published the second edition of *The Doctrine and Discipline of Divorce*, a translation of the writings of the German theologian Martin Bucer on divorce, *Areopagitica*, and a short pamphlet, *Of Education*, indicating that Milton believed that a liberal education system was an essential prerequisite for a healthy democracy. This was also the year when Milton first began to notice that he was losing his sight: he was to become totally blind by 1652.[39]

In 1645, in addition to completing his writings on divorce through two further pamphlets, *Tetrachordon* (an examination of biblical references to marriage, again with a prefatory letter to Parliament), and *Colasterion* (an abusive response to the anonymous *Answer to the Doctrine and Discipline of Divorce* mentioned above), Milton also had his first collection of poems published, generally known by the title *Poems 1645*. Prefacing the title page to this volume is an engraving by William Marshall which is so incongruous as to be grotesque. Its label suggests that it is based upon a portrait of Milton at twenty-one, but it is either a malicious or an incompetent piece of work, and he evidently hated it.[40] He did, however, have the last laugh, for he had Marshall engrave a Greek epigram beneath the portrait which has been translated as follows: 'You would say, perhaps, that this picture was drawn by an ignorant hand, when you looked at the form that nature made. Since you do not recognise the man portrayed, my friends, laugh at this rotten picture of a rotten artist.'[41]

Poems 1645 included all the poetry noted above, with pride of place given to *Comus*, as well as the letter from Sir Henry Wotton and commendations from Italian friends. Its publisher, the bookseller Humphrey Moseley, prefaced the collection with a letter to the reader in which he made a generous comparison between Milton and the great Elizabethan poet Edmund Spenser (1552–99). The collection was, he said, 'as true a birth as the Muses have brought forth since our famous Spenser wrote; whose poems in these English ones are as rarely imitated as sweetly excelled'.[42] Despite this letter and the use of Wotton's name, despite even the notoriety of Milton as 'the divorcer' in 1645, the collection was not an immediate popular success and, as A.N. Wilson remarks, it was fifteen years before the first edition looked like selling out.[43]

The years from 1646 to 1649 were quiet in terms of Milton's publications, especially in comparison with the activity of the preceding three. Mary returned and the Miltons started a family: both Richard Powell and John Milton, senior, died, and this, coupled with a change of house, must have involved Milton in a good deal of domestic responsibility and activity. He published a sonnet to Henry Lawes in 1648, but other poems of the period remained unprinted. Many of these show a keen interest in contemporary events: he celebrated the victory of General Fairfax over the royalists at the siege of Colchester, and hoped that this military triumph would lead to victory over the financial chaos caused by the war, and to freedom for truth. These sentiments echo feelings expressed in two other poems of this period. One ('On the New Forcers of Conscience') attacks the Presbyterians for continuing to attempt to impose their form of worship on everyone. The second ('A book was writ of late') censures those who ridiculed his divorce tracts.

Milton had not withdrawn altogether from political issues during this period: he was working on *The History of Britain* and on *The Character of the Long Parliament*, a digression from the *History* in which Milton expressed his bitter disappointment with the Presbyterians. The opinions which Milton advances in this attack seem, at times, close to those of the Levellers, a group who were urging Parliament, and the Army, to take more decisive action, but it is unlikely that Milton would have sided with the Levellers in their demands for votes for every freeborn Englishman in 1647. During that year of intense pamphleteering Milton stayed silent, and did not publish his attack on Parliament during his lifetime.

In April 1648 Milton translated nine psalms from Hebrew into English, a testament to his range of accomplishment. It is tempting to read these translations as comments on the state of England in that year, especially since it was common to think of England as a new Israel,[44] favoured by God's special providence. Psalm 82, for example, calls for those in power to bring about social justice:

How long will ye pervert the right
  With judgement false and wrong
Favouring the wicked *by your might*
  Who thence grow bold and strong . . .[45]

This is very close in its sentiments to Milton's sonnet to Fairfax.

Political turmoil increased in late 1648, leading to the trial and execution of Charles at the beginning of 1649. This was a crucial event in the development of the English Revolution, because, whilst there were many who approved of the attempts to curb the power of the King and the Bishops, far fewer were in favour of the execution of the

King, which seemed to some the inevitable outcome of the uncertainties of the late 1640s. Milton, however, was in no doubt where his sympathies lay, and he published, within two weeks of the execution, a pamphlet called *The Tenure of Kings and Magistrates*, arguing that a King was as accountable as any other individual to the law of the land. It includes the quotation from the Roman tragedian Seneca:

> There can be slain
> No sacrifice to God more acceptable
> Than an unjust and wicked king.[46]

It attempts to argue the basis for the accountability of kings from biblical and historical precedent. Milton takes care not to write too directly about the particular circumstances of Charles's execution (and indeed much of it may have been written before the execution took place). He refers to the King only to castigate those who withdrew from their obligation to carry through the Revolution:

> He who but erewhile in the pulpits was a cursed tyrant, an enemy to God . . . and so to be fought against, is now, though nothing penitent or altered from his first principles, a lawful magistrate, a sovereign lord . . . not to be touched, though by themselves imprisoned . . .[47]

Milton's concern is not with Charles but with monarchy in general, tyranny more especially, and with attacking Presbyterians who had, he felt, betrayed their cause, shirking their responsibility for reform. He does not attempt to argue the case for Charles's guilt, nor to assert that the majority of people favoured the execution: he limits himself to defending the right of the people to try their king and, if necessary, to depose him. The tract was the most personally successful of all Milton's prose, for he was invited in March 1649 to become Secretary of State for Foreign Tongues, a post he filled for the next six years, until his health made it impossible for him to continue. His responsibility was to write on behalf of the Council governing the country, supporting its policies both at home and abroad.

His first major task was to write again on the execution, not a general work such as *The Tenure of Kings and Magistrates* had been but a book very much concerned with Charles and in reply to a particular defence of the king. On the day of the King's burial a book entitled *Eikon Basilike*, commonly called *The King's Book*, had been published which purported to be Charles's own account of his dispute with Parliament and his eventual trial. The book presented Charles as a man who had made mistakes, but who had been, for all that, a pious and Christian king with his people's best interests at heart, bullied and threatened by an avaricious Parliament hungry for power and position. It was immensely successful as a piece of propaganda for those who supported the monarchy: it evaded the censorship regulations, perhaps because of its Greek title, and was reprinted thirty-five times in 1649 alone. With its engraved frontispiece of Charles at his prayers it fuelled the cult of Charles as a martyr and thus undermined the position of the Council among the people at large. *Eikon Basilike* made no attempt to offer political debate; instead it played upon the sentimentality of the people, and it had to be refuted.

Milton published his reply, *Eikonoklastes* (Image breaker), in October 1649, refuting the *King's Book* chapter by chapter. Whereas an early refutation had worked from the premise that *Eikon Basilike* had not been written by Charles, and had used this as the cornerstone of its argument, Milton assumes that the king was indeed the author, and attempts to discredit the portrait Charles paints of himself.[48] He points out that one of the prayers included in *Eikon Basilike* as an example of Charles's spontaneous devotions came in fact from a secular prose romance: so much for the saintly king! *Eikonoklastes* presents a detailed account of the events leading up to the execution (presumably supplied to Milton by officials of the Council) but it failed to prevent the impact of *Eikon Basilike*, and it fails also to stir the interest of the modern reader. This is partly because its structure is not of Milton's own choosing but is determined by the structure of the work which he is attacking, but it is also a result of the fact that some of the assertions made in *Eikon Basilike* about the corruption of the Long Parliament are uncomfortably close to those which Milton expressed himself in *The Character of the Long Parliament*. Milton's *Eikonoklastes* proved to be in some respects the equivalent of a modern political manifesto: it appeared to identify faults in the government of Charles I which would be avoided in a republic. It was referred to in the 1650s by radicals who felt that these promises of a republic superior to monarchy had never been realised.[49]

Milton's next task as official apologist brought him into contest with his most celebrated adversary, and won for him an international reputation as a scholar and a controversialist. It was, of course, as necessary for the Council of the Commonwealth of England (established after the execution of the King) as for any modern regime after a *coup d'état* to achieve international recognition, and the Council looked anxiously, therefore, for European reactions to the execution. There was some diplomatic activity (the severing of relations by Russia) and the ambassador sent by the Commonwealth to Spain was murdered by exiled royalist supporters, but no attempt at military intervention: most European governments had problems of their own to think about, and whilst expressing horror at the execution were prepared to wait until the policies of the new Commonwealth became clearer. The Spanish and French ambassadors even went so far as to buy up some art treasures from the collection of the dead King. The King's son, however, who was later to become Charles II, commissioned an eminent French scholar, Salmasius (Claude Saumaise), residing at that time in Holland, to write a defence of the royalist position, the *Defensio Regia*, to discredit the new government. Intended for a wide European audience, the *Defensio Regia* was written in Latin, the international language of scholarship and diplomacy. Salmasius had a formidable reputation, having published some eighty learned books, the first of which dates from the year of Milton's birth (1608).[50] He had received offers of university positions in many countries, but had chosen to settle in Holland, in a republic rather than in a monarchy. During the early part of the Civil War he had been consulted for advice by both sides and now, in late 1649, he produced a formidable piece of royalist propaganda, an enquiry into the rights of kings, drawn from Old and New Testament sources, working through ancient and modern history as well as surveying the basis of kingship in England. Its thesis was that the monarchy was independent of the control of Parliament, and it concluded with a description of the trial and execution of Charles I and a eulogy of his personal qualities.

Milton was commissioned to write a reply to Salmasius, and his *Pro Populo Anglicano Defensio* (February 1651) accomplished that task most efficiently. His 'Defence of the English People' was considered dangerous enough to be banned and burned in parts of Europe governed by Royalist sympathisers, and this in itself was sufficient to ensure that it was widely sought for. As a news-sheet of the time records, in Toulouse

> It is so farr liked and approved by the ingenious sort of men, that all the Copies, sent hither out of the *Low-Countries* were long since dispersed, and it was designed here for the *Press*; whereof notice being taken, it is made *Treason* for any to print, vend, or have it in possession; so great a hatred is born to any piece that speaks liberty and Freedom to this miserable people.[51]

The same news-sheet recorded in the months following the gradual disgrace of Salmasius, and his loss of reputation and favour. He died in 1653, without completing the reply he had promised to Milton's attack.

Although Milton's pamphlet won him fame, he appears to have gained no financial reward from the Council, nor is the work of any great interest. It adds little to our sense of Milton's developing ideas, consisting of quotations which refute Salmasius's quotations, and of personal attacks upon the writer and upon Charles I. There are, however, two points of note: firstly that Milton had now made a complete break with monarchy, condemning not merely tyrants but all kings; secondly, that Salmasius set Milton a major problem by arguing that those who executed Charles I did not represent the majority of the English people. Milton is driven to reply that 'the act of the better, the sounder part of the Parliament, in which resides the real power of the people, was the act of the people.'[52] Milton was beginning to argue for a restricted franchise, for a government in which only the better part of the people have a voice.

Milton's next piece of propaganda, again in Latin, is of much greater interest, partly because it includes a long autobiographical digression. A Royalist answer to Milton's *Defensio* had eventually been published in 1652, though not by Salmasius. *The Cry of the King's Blood* was written by Peter du Moulin, although Milton thought it by Alexander More and based his reply on that assumption, including some abuse of More's personal life which is often witty and amusing and occasionally borders on the obscene. Although its title, *Defensio Secunda* ('Second Defence', 1654) suggests that this is a sequel to Milton's response to Salmasius, it is a work of a very different character with much less of the air of a commissioned piece. It defends neither the English people (not even the restricted group so identified in the previous pamphlet) nor republicanism. It is fundamentally a defence of Milton's own career which it reconstructs to follow a uniform and consistent set of principles. It aroused little interest (except for denials from Alexander More that he had written *The Cry of the King's Blood*), and yet it demonstrates very clearly what Milton thought about the government of the day and includes advice for its future policy.

Milton's dispute with Salmasius and his general views on kingship were given careful consideration by one contemporary writer, Sir Robert Filmer, who, although an ardent royalist, treats Milton's views with restraint and respect in his *Observations Concerning the Originall of Government*.[53] This is possibly the most rational analysis of Milton's views on monarchy before the nineteenth century, but Milton made no reply, perhaps still waiting for that Salmasius pamphlet which was not to come until after the Restoration.

The man who had become leader of the Army, who had brought Charles to execution and was to become Protector of England after dismissing the elected Parliament in 1653 was Oliver Cromwell, whom Milton clearly greatly admired. It may be that they had never met before Milton acquired his official position in 1649, but Milton's views on Cromwell are well documented. He wrote a sonnet to Cromwell in 1652, urging him not to allow either an established Church in England or the payment of clergy from taxes, and in his *Defensio Secunda* Milton included a lengthy address to Cromwell, written after he had assumed the Protectorship. Milton's feelings about Cromwell were somewhat ambivalent: on the one hand he was essentially opposed to the dominance of any leader, and was always more interested in principles rather than in personalities (he makes no mention, for example, of Cromwell in *The Tenure of Kings and Magistrates*); on the other hand, Cromwell seemed uniquely fitted for the task in hand, and he manifested the quality of self-control which Milton felt to be essential to personal and national government.

Milton devoted a considerable portion of the *Defensio Secunda* to a defence of Cromwell's position and, in particular, to a justification of Cromwell's assumption of the office of Protector. This was difficult for Milton in the light of his condemnation of the individual rule of Charles I, but he tried to emphasise Cromwell's reluctance in accepting the task, and to suggest that Cromwell, far from elevating himself by becoming Protector, in fact debased himself:

> But since, though it be not fit, it may be expedient, that the highest pitch of virtue should be circumscribed within the bounds of some human appellation, you endured to receive, for the public good, a title most like to that of the father of your country; not to exalt, but rather to bring you nearer to the level of ordinary men; the title of king was unworthy the transcendent majesty of your character.[54]

Milton's emphasis here is carefully placed: he suggests that there is a real difference between the office of Protector and that of King, and he asserts that Cromwell assumed the title 'for the public good'. Many of the public, however, disagreed with Milton on the rightness of the Protectorate. John Bradshaw, who had conducted the trial of Charles I, refused to recognise Cromwell's right to dissolve Parliament: he was Milton's friend, and the *Defensio Secunda* includes a glowing tribute to him which, sitting alongside the defence of Cromwell, emphasises the paradox in which Milton found himself. The work ends, not with a defence of Cromwell's past or present actions, but with advice for the future, for Cromwell and for the country as a whole. Milton offers Cromwell a list of those who he feels will advise him, a list which includes names of those who opposed the Protectorate but supported Milton's own favourite causes. He urges these causes, too, at the end of the piece: the separation of Church and State; the reduction in the number of laws; the abolition of censorship; the need for improved educational provision. Cromwell, of course, had to listen to advice and petitions from many other sources, and was not in a position to effect all the reforms which Milton would have liked: Milton made no further public reference to Cromwell during Cromwell's lifetime, but he was to feel, at the end of the 1650s, that the Protectorate had been an unsuccessful experiment in government.[55]

If the *Defensio Secunda* illustrates nothing else, it indicates forcefully that Milton remained very much his own man during his period as Secretary, and was no mere lackey, parroting official opinion. This is also borne out by his brief period as licenser (an ironic office for one who had written so eloquently on censorship, but one which he felt he could undertake in all conscience).[56] He approved the publication of a work of which Parliament disapproved, and claimed, in his defence, to have done so as a gesture of his disagreement with the practice of licensing. He was not called upon to license any further books.

In February 1653, before the Protectorate had forced Bradshaw into political exile, Milton wrote to him recommending for State employment a young man called Andrew Marvell. Although the friendship between Milton and Marvell blossomed, it was not until 1657 that Marvell became Latin Secretary to the Council of State, the man who was to walk beside Milton at Cromwell's funeral. Marvell, some thirteen years younger than Milton, was already a poet of some accomplishment. He, too, wrote about Cromwell, and his poems provide a useful yardstick for Milton's views on Cromwell.[57] Marvell was also to prove a faithful friend to Milton when, after the Restoration of the monarchy in 1660, Milton was in great personal danger.

Milton's personal life had not been untroubled during his period of official employment. His sight had deteriorated, and his blindness had become total in 1652. His wife Mary and his son John had both died in that same year, leaving him with three daughters to care for, one deformed, the youngest a few months old. He considered agonising medical treatment in an attempt to save his sight,[58] but all to no avail, and he was never to see his second wife, Katherine Woodcock, whom he married in November 1656, and who died in February 1658. The sonnets which he wrote during this period are a testimony to these private griefs.

Milton returned to prose pamphleteering in 1659 when, after the death of Oliver Cromwell and the accession of his son Richard as Protector, the Restoration of monarchy was favoured by an increasing number of people. Typically, however, Milton did not join at once in the debate on this most pressing political and constitutional issue: instead he took the opportunity of a reconvened Parliament (Richard Cromwell having abdicated) to urge once more his concern for religious liberty and the freedom of the individual conscience. In February 1659 he published *A Treatise of Civil Power in Ecclesiastical Causes*, arguing for the separation of Church and State and for freedom of worship for all (with the exception of Catholics, partly because they represented a political threat to the state). In August 1659 he published *Considerations Touching the Likeliest Means to Remove*

Hirelings out of the Church, advocating a system of clergy serving without material rewards, supported only the voluntary contributions of parishioners. It was not until 1660, when the restoration of Charles II seemed inevitable, that Milton wrote of politics and of the constitution. He produced two editions of a pamphlet called *The Ready and Easy Way to Establish a Free Commonwealth* in rapid succession; the second, published a month before Charles's return, was printed at his own expense because no bookseller would put his name to such an inflammatory piece of writing.[59]

Although there are considerable differences between the two versions of the tract, to take account of the rapidly changing political situation, both are essentially concerned with drafting a detailed plan for a republican system, and with indicating how a republic might be maintained in the face of pressure to return to monarchy. Other writers of the time were preoccupied with the effects of the Restoration on trade and on the economy, but Milton continues to attack the institution of monarchy on moral and on religious grounds, and to suggest instead a kind of democracy in which those who are 'rightly qualified will have a vote'.[60]

Milton's views were attacked, implicitly from the pulpit and explicitly in print. Worse still, Milton's life seemed to be in danger when the Restoration eventually did take place, in May, and those responsible for the execution of Charles I were punished. He went into hiding and two of his books were burned and banned by Parliament.[61] It became clear as the year went on, however, that Milton was unlikely to be executed and, although he was imprisoned and fined, he was released after about a month. Others, more closely involved with the execution, did not escape so lightly: nine were hanged, disembowelled and quartered, and the bodies of Cromwell, Ireton and Bradshaw were disinterred from Westminster Abbey, exposed all day on the gallows at Tyburn and, at sunset, beheaded.[62]

In these circumstances Milton may be considered to have escaped lightly, although he was cruelly ridiculed by Royalist pamphleteers. Nevertheless he protested, through Andrew Marvell, about the size of his fine, and an investigation followed: in December 1660 he was officially pardoned.[63]

In the early years of the Restoration Milton continued to live in London, tutoring a young man called Thomas Ellwood, marrying for a third time in February 1663 (his new wife was Elizabeth Minshull), and composing his major epic poem, *Paradise Lost*. We know little of the exact date of the composition of Milton's three major poems or of his theological treatise, although two of the early biographers say that *Paradise Lost* was written over a four- or five-year period between 1658 and 1663.[64] Ellwood claims to have seen the completed epic in

1665. By this time the Milton family had been forced to leave London because of a plague epidemic, and had taken a house, arranged by Ellwood, in the Buckinghamshire village of Chalfont St Giles. The house, the only one of Milton's many residences still standing, is now the Milton museum and visitors to it gain a vivid impression of how hard it must have been for Milton, a blind man, to have moved from his familiar London to such cramped conditions. It is against this background that rumours about Milton's being on bad terms with his daughters must be set.[65]

Milton returned to London in 1666 and suffered a further misfortune, financial this time, when his most substantial piece of property, the house in Bread Street, was destroyed by the Great Fire of London. Heavy taxes during the war, fines after it, and now this fire conspired to make Milton comparatively hard pressed for money. Part of his library was sold and, although he never earned a living from his writing, he strove to publish as much of his work as he could.

Paradise Lost was published in August 1667 and sold quite successfully. Two prose works, *Accidence Commenced Grammar* (1669) and *The History of Britain* (1670), followed, the latter with the first new portrait of Milton since the Marshall fiasco of 1645. In 1671 Milton published *Paradise Regained*, his 'brief epic', and *Samson Agonistes*, modelled on Greek tragedy, although there is a considerable dispute about the date of composition of this second work. They were the last of his major poems to be published, although a new collection of his shorter poems appeared in 1673, and a revised second edition of *Paradise Lost* in 1674. In the last years of his life Milton's letters and prolusions were published, his *Art of Logic*, and his final pamphlet on religion, *Of True Religion*. In this last tract it is clear that none of Milton's fighting spirit has ebbed: he is equally fierce in his defence of toleration for Protestants and in his denunciation of Catholics.[66]

Milton died of gout in early November 1674 (the exact date is not known). He was buried in the church of St Giles, Cripplegate, where his father had been buried, Cromwell married, where Lancelot Andrewes had been vicar, and the Egerton family had worshipped. Ironically, in 1790 when the effects of another Revolution, this time in France, were being felt in England, a body, assumed to be that of John Milton, was disinterred from the church and its bones sold off as relics.[67] A memorial bust to the poet was erected in the church in 1793 (made by John Bacon and paid for by the brewer Samuel Whitbread) and a further monument was placed in Westminster Abbey in the 'poets' corner' in 1737.

Milton's biographers

It is probably true, as James Holly Hanford declares, that 'The life of Milton is known to us in far more fullness of detail than that of any other major English poet before the eighteenth century'.[68] But the material which we have may not always be accurate, and there are, moreover, crucial details of which we know nothing. Where and when, for example, did he marry Mary Powell; why did Marshall produce so bad a portrait; why did Milton not publish *The Character of the Long Parliament*; when did he write *Samson Agonistes*; was it his body which was dug up in 1790?

Milton's prose, however much it may be disliked by some readers, includes three lengthy passages of autobiography;[69] and his personal letters reveal his opinions and his range of friends. Biographers of the poet date from as early as 1681.[70] It would be a mistake, however, to take all of this early material at its face value. The three pieces of prose autobiography were all prompted by attacks upon Milton by his antagonists, and there is clear evidence of his tailoring his accounts of his life in order to appear at all times respectable and consistent. Thus, for example, he excludes from the account of his Italian acquaintances the author of a sequence of obscene sonnets, even though that sequence was dedicated to him and he corresponded with the author on his return to England.[71] After the misunderstanding of his motives in writing on divorce, Milton was even more anxious to safeguard his reputation, to the extent that his account of the circumstances which led to his writing *Areopagitica* omits all mention of the sermon preached by Palmer or the threat of Parliamentary action being taken against him.[72] Frank Kermode reports a comment by a fellow-critic to the effect that if Milton had been Adam he would have eaten the apple and then written a pamphlet in defence of his action:[73] this may well be true, but we would not be able to trust in the accuracy of that pamphlet. If we knew of Milton only through his own writing our impression would be significantly different from the truth.

Although early biographies of Milton were written either by those who knew him or were in a position to talk to those who had known him, they are not the products of modern scholarly rigour and include some surprises. Not all of the early biographers, for example, bothered to interview his widow,[74] or his brother,[75] and thus a number of legends have been created that might have been killed at birth. It is, however, fortunate that there is comparatively little difficulty in establishing the chronological sequence of most of Milton's work, and thus being able to trace with some certainty the developments in his thought. The works of Andrew Marvell, for example, have a far more uncertain chronology and partly for this reason his political allegiances have always been more difficult to establish than those of Milton.

It may be, nevertheless, too tempting to pin down Milton's opinions on the basis of his published writings. There is, for example, a tendency for critics to support their views on Milton's thinking by reference to his Commonplace Book despite the problems of dating entries in that journal. Sometimes, also, even the most sensitive of critics will assume that Milton's public face, in prose or poetry, conveyed the absolute truth of his private feelings. It may be a useful exercise in critical appreciation to place side by side, as Mary Ann Radzinowicz does, Milton's account of his own blindness in *Paradise Lost* Book III (and the sonnets of the early 1650s might have been included) and Samson's lack of acceptance of blindness in *Samson Agonistes*, but it is surely going too far to speak of 'the sublimation Milton himself drew upon for courage in his own personal lyric lament at blindness'.[76] A.N. Wilson describes the desperate lengths to which Milton was prepared to go in order to try to save his sight, and this looks far from patient sublimation of his suffering.[77] If there is such a disjunction in the treatment of Milton's physical feelings, the difficulty in establishing his intellectual views is huge.

There is a strong temptation to create fictions about and around Milton, partly because of his involvement in the political issues of his day, partly because of his mysterious first marriage, and to interpret his poems as if they were all glosses on the conflicts of his own life. Thus, Satan in *Paradise Lost* has been seen to reflect both Charles I and Cromwell by different critics,[78] Dalila and Eve can be seen as reflections of Mary Powell, Manoa as Milton's father, Harapha as Salmasius, Samson as Milton himself, or as Galileo. Some of these possible parallels have been developed into full-scale fictional accounts of Milton's life (in some senses the early biographies are themselves close to fiction) and the poet features in a dozen or so novels, as well as in plays, poems and films.[79] These works do have a role, if they whet the appetite for the reading of Milton, but they are dangerous if they are accepted as factual, accurate, and free from bias. Robert Graves's novel, *Wife to Mr Milton*,[80] presents a most unsympathetic view of Milton's relationship with Mary Powell, emanating from the premise that Milton was, in fact, a fascist. In contrast, Anne Manning in *Deborah's Diary* produced a beautiful, lyrical account of Milton in the mid-1660's, sensitive to the difficulties of blindness and financial struggle.[81] Since any novel worth the name ought to be more memorable than a straightforward biography, it is undoubtedly true that many students of Milton harbour impressions of 'facts', such as meetings with Cromwell and Marvell or performances of *Comus*, which derive ultimately from fiction.

As Christopher Hill, a recent Milton biographer, has remarked, 'each critic can create his own Milton',[82] partly because of Milton's own interests were so wide-ranging, and partly because the issues of his day involved, as we shall see below, a complex combination of social, political, religious and economic disputes. It is possible, therefore, to set Milton against any of these contexts, and different biographers will place their emphasis according to their own inclinations (it is noticeable, for example, that American writers on Milton tend to stress Milton's relationship with Roger Williams,[83] founder of Rhode Island, whereas the most recent English biographer of Milton makes no reference to Williams at all).[84]

Of the modern biographies of Milton the two-volume work by William Riley Parker[85] is comprehensive (its index is almost encyclopaedic) although its dating of *Samson Agonistes* is now disputed by all but a handful of Miltonists. Christopher Hill's *Milton and the English Revolution*, although at times extreme in the claims it makes for Milton's radicalism, is provocative, and likely to prove an indispensable point of reference for all serious students of Milton.[86] A.N. Wilson's biography is well-written, as might be expected from a novelist of some repute, and very readable, as long as the reader is on guard against its prejudices and bias: at least Wilson is honest enough to parade these openly.[87]

Milton's personality

Milton's personal reputation has suffered badly because of the belief that he mistreated women in general and his own wives and daughters in particular, and from the modern tendency to regard anyone who could be labelled 'Puritan' as therefore odious and repulsive. Neither of these beliefs can pass unchallenged.

Milton had a genuine regard for the physical beauty of women, which he displays in the revealing first elegy to Charles Diodati. He writes tenderly of his love for 'Emilia' in his Italian sonnets and his *canzone*, at least one of which, were it in English,[88] could come appropriately from a Shakespearean hero; from the mouth of a Benedick from *Much Ado About Nothing*, or a Berowne from *Love's Labour's Lost*: Shakespeare is never accused of hating women.

His English poetry also suggests that Milton knew about love, and of its pleasures. The love-making of Adam and Eve before the Fall for example, is treated joyfully. One instance is Adam's delight in Eve at the beginning of *Paradise Lost* Book V:

> he on his side
> Leaning half-raised, with looks of cordial love
> Hung over her enamoured, and beheld
> Beauty, which whether waking or asleep,

Shot forth peculiar graces; then with voice
Mild, as when Zephyrus on Flora breathes,
Her hand soft touching, whispered thus. Awake
My fairest, my espoused, my latest found,
Heaven's last best gift, my every new delight,
Awake, the morning shines, and the fresh field
Calls us . . .

(V.11–21)

It could even be argued that Milton treated women with greater respect than many of his contemporary poets. The court of Charles I and Henrietta Maria had a reputation for sexual permissiveness, where the Queen herself was known to act in plays.[89] Milton disapproved of such promiscuity and of an attitude to women which smacked of idolatry, any form of which Milton opposed. The pure love of *Paradise Lost* is explicitly divorced from such behaviour:

Here Love his golden shafts employs . . .
                        not in the bought smile
Of harlots, loveless, joyless, unendeared,
Casual fruition, nor in court amours,
Mixed dance, or wanton mask, or midnight ball,
Or serenade, which the half-starved lover sings
To his proud fair, best quitted with disdain.

(IV.763–70)

The courtly pose of the half-starved lover was never sincere, and not particularly flattering to women. It is a pose which Milton makes Satan adopt in order to seduce Eve, and one which he had rejected as early as 1642:

if I found those authors anywhere speaking unworthy things of themselves, or unchaste of those names which before they had extolled, this effect it wrought with me, from that time forward their art I still applauded, but the men I deplored; and . . . preferred . . . [those] who never write but honour of them to whom they devote their verse, displaying sublime and pure thoughts, without transgression.[90]

There is every indication that Milton did treat women honourably. He seems not to have been lacking in female companions, and his emphasis, in the divorce tracts, on intellectual compatibility in marriage suggests a liberal and enlightened attitude far removed from those who condoned arranged matches. It is true that he did not write in those tracts about the provision to be made for children of dissolved marriages or of the division of property and the maintenance of the former wife, and a contemporary response was quick to point this out.[91] But this need not be interpreted as indicating Milton's callous, male chauvinist indifference to these matters: he simply was not concerning himself with the practical consequences of divorce, but was addressing himself to the theoretical basis for it. As Christopher Hill observes:

> to criticize Milton because he stated a theory of male superiority is like criticizing him because he did not advocate votes or equal pay for women. No one, to my knowledge, in the seventeenth century claimed that women were wholly equal to men.[92]

William Riley Parker makes a similar point, with particular reference to the role of Dalila in *Samson Agonistes*:

> There is nothing misogynous, nothing unusual in Samson's hatred of the particular woman who has wronged him. Nor can we call misogynous Milton's ideas on the place of women in marriage. These ideas may be obsolete in Western civilization, may seem to us deplorable, but they are no more 'misogynous' than was our ancestors' acceptance of slavery 'misanthropic'.[93]

Despite these persuasive arguments, attacks on Milton's views on women continue.[94]

Milton was, throughout his life, opposed to intolerance and to any restriction in the free flow of ideas. He may well have been a difficult person, especially in later life, but his blindness and his financial problems in part account for this, and the failure of successive modes of government to bring about the reform he hoped for makes his impatience the more comprehensible.

A.N. Wilson describes Milton's autobiographical references as a 'self-obsession',[95] and this may be unjust. Misinterpreted early in his career, Milton had to work hard to win an audience, hence the frequency of his prefatory letters to Parliament; and if he was proud, and convinced of his own talents, he was justified in holding that opinion. His early poems reveal a love and appreciation of life and his approval of its pleasures, including music and the theatre. His letters and poems to Diodati show him warm in his affections, and this loyalty in friendship continued throughout his life, and included his defence of Bradshaw. His physical attractiveness earned him the nickname, the 'Lady of Christ's'; he is said to have smoked, and the addresses which he delivered at Cambridge were certainly sometimes bawdy. Both his poetry and prose are full of a delight in puns, some of which strike the modern ear as extreme but would have been much to the taste of a contemporary audience. This is an attack, for example, on Alexander More, in which Milton is suggesting that More has had a love affair with a servant girl (which for Milton represented the epitome of licentious behaviour):

> the neighbours had frequently observed them enter together a small lodge in the little garden. This amounts not, it may be said, to adultery ... he might have been talking with her, for example, on the subject of gardening ... might have been allowed no other liberty than to engraft a mulberry in a fig, thence to raise, with the utmost dispatch, a line of sycamores – a most delectable walk. Then he might have taught the woman the art of engrafting.[96]

The sexual innuendoes in this passage are all the more pointed if you appreciate that Milton is playing with the name of his opponent (More, hence 'a line of sycamores') and that that name is the root of a Latin word meaning 'mulberry'. Milton extended little charity to his opponents in his writing, but he researched his abuse very carefully, and, however offensive he may appear when writing of Hall or More or Salmasius, we need to bear in mind the conventions of the prose of his time, and the cruelty with which Milton himself was treated by others: it was all too easy for his blindness to be used by his enemies as an instance of God's punishment of the wicked, and some of these references are offensive in the extreme.[97]

Political, religious and economic context

Accordingly to L.P. Hartley, 'The past is a foreign country: they do things differently there'.[98] To Englishmen in the early seventeenth century the reverse must have seemed to be true: their country, which had progressively asserted its Englishness throughout the reign of Elizabeth I, seemed in danger of losing that distinctiveness under James I and Charles I, and of becoming swamped by foreign influences and customs. Whatever the disputes between historians about the cause and the effects of the crisis in the mid-seventeenth century, that crisis clearly involved different responses to the issue of what it meant to be English.[99]

The established Church of England was in its infancy, to the extent that Charles I was the first monarch to be brought up as a member of that Church.[100] Elizabeth I had inherited an established Catholic Church and the new Church of England which she introduced in its place was by no means totally devoid of Catholic influence. From the time of Elizabeth onwards there was conflict between those who wished to 'purify' the Church more thoroughly of the rituals which they associated with a foreign religion, and the attempts of those in authority to impose conformity to the practices of the official Church of England.

Those who looked for this 'purification' (who were known as Puritans) saw a twin threat in the possibility of a resurgence of Roman Catholicism in England. In the first place it would prejudice England's political independence, as Milton continued to assert as late as 1659: 'Their religion the more considerd, the less can be acknowledgd a religion; but a Roman principalitie rather, endevouring to keep up her old universal dominion under a new name'.[101] Secondly, they believed that Roman Catholicism denied the individual the opportunity to exercise his own powers of reason and discrimination, since, they claimed, it consisted of a series of received truths, passed down from the priest to the people which the latter were required to believe: there was no room for debate or for personal discovery. Thus, a discussion of Puritanism moves very rapidly from theology to the nature of education, and Puritan reformers were anxious to emphasise that developments in education in England made the country uniquely fitted to establish liberty for the individual, for the Church and for the State. Such ideas, however, were very dangerous for the establishment because, as Don M. Wolfe points out, 'The poor and lowly, when they could read at all, found in the Bible ideas of society disturbingly unlike those of the prayer book and the parish minister'.[102] After the conflict was over, the Duke of Newcastle advised Charles II on education:

> Bishops, he said, are 'the most effective guards against the dissemination of wrong opinions among the people', and so must be selected with great care. Too much preaching is a bad thing, and should be replaced by the reading of homilies. . . . There should be less education, and books on controversial subjects should be printed in Latin only, 'for controversy is a civil war with the pen which pulls the sword out soon afterwards'.[103]

It was essential for the ruling class to suppress Puritanism, because of its political dimension, and to establish a state Church which was hierarchic and elitist: in other words, one which mirrored the governmental system. Elizabeth I had seen the danger and had warned her successor:

> the Puritans 'wold have no kings but a presbitrye'. 'Yea, looke we wel unto them,' she wrote to him. 'Whan the have made in our peoples hartz a doubt of our religion, and that we erre if the say so, what perilous issue this may make I rather think than mynde to write. I pray you stop the mouthes . . . of such ministers as dare presume to make oraison in their pulpitz for the persecuted in Ingland of the gospel. . .'[104]

It would be an exaggeration, however, to describe the crisis of the seventeenth century as if it were solely a conflict between Puritanism on the one hand and the establishment on the other. Clarendon, in his contemporary account of the crisis, described it as a 'rebellion', which is indicative of the Royalist attitude. In contrast, nineteenth-century historians termed it the 'Puritan Revolution' and saw the Puritans (whom they equated with Parliament) as the forerunners of their own nonconformity in religion, and of constitutional parliamentarianism. This view is now regarded as an oversimplification and modern historians, although they may argue about the origins of the crisis or about its significance in later political and intellectual developments, agree in using the terms 'Civil War' to refer to the military encounters, and 'English Revolution' for the wider economic, social, and religious upheaval.

The modern connotations of the word 'puritan' are unhelpful to the student of the English Revolution: seventeenth-century Puritans were by no means sour, grave, and repressive. On the contrary, they strove for liberty of conscience and freedom of speech, and many left this country for America rather than be persecuted for these beliefs or conform to systems which they thought inhibiting. Milton was conforming absolutely to the Puritan tradition in arguing for a free press in *Areopagitica* and would hardly have agreed, therefore, with present-day 'Puritans' who wish to have certain plays and television programmes banned because they may corrupt others.

Some of the discontent which brought about the English Revolution had begun, as we have seen, before the end of the reign of Elizabeth, and had she lived another twenty-five years the Revolution might still have taken place: the increase in the population of London, where Puritan preachers influenced a rising middle-class, would still have gone on. But the foreignness of James I and his son Charles I aggravated the situation. James was a Scot, and spoke with a broad Scots accent, and he showed his failure to understand the ways of the English in advocating a marriage between Charles and the Infanta of Spain. This, he hoped, would ensure peace between two countries who had been hostile for so long, but it failed to take account of the extent of anti-Spanish and anti-Catholic feeling. Charles himself ended the negotiations on this marriage, but his own choice, Henrietta Maria, daughter of the King of France, was still Catholic, still foreign, and felt to exercise a powerful influence over her husband. Thus the English court took on an increasingly continental air and the gap between court and country grew. James hated crowds and so avoided large-scale public pageantry, spending his money instead on private court entertainment. Charles followed his father's lead: 'He did not organize patronage to influence cultural trends beyond the Court because the administrative work and the political calculation such a task would have demanded were alien to him'.[105] The unpopularity of the monarchy therefore grew: 'In 1627 London failed to honor the King's birthday only two days after it had rung its bells and lit bonfires to observe the anniversary of Elizabeth's accession'.[106]

The administration of the country also took on an unfamiliar foreign air. The court did not draw upon (and look after) a broad base of advisers who received royal patronage; it was reliant upon a few favourites who were, as a result, heartily disliked. The established Church too, which could have remained open to a wide range of beliefs, became hierarchic and repressive, with many of its priests making fortunes by holding more than one living simultaneously. To make matters worse, one of Charles's chief ministers was, at the same time, both Archbishop of Canterbury and Charles's principal adviser, thus symbolising plurality of office and the interdependence of Church and State. It was the reactionary authoritarianism of Charles and Laud which turned Puritans into revolutionaries and made their interests coincide with those of Parliament. As Merritt Y. Hughes remarks: 'Charles made the mistake of solidifying everything that was revolutionary in the English Church against himself'.[107]

The Parliament of the seventeenth century was very different from that of our own day. There was, for example, no constitution, and therefore no regulation of how often a Parliament should meet, how long it should serve, or whether it should be called at all. A Parliament was an event, not an institution, and would be called in response to a specific situation not as a matter of form. Charles found himself unable to agree with his Parliament, and tried to govern without it for some eleven years, raising the necessary finance by means of unpopular taxation. Worse still, he added to his revenue by transporting Spanish troops in English ships to fight against the Protestant Dutch. The end to this unpopular experiment in government without Parliament came when Archbishop Laud's attempts to force the Scots to accept the established mode of the English Church brought Charles into a war against Scots rebels which he could not afford to pay for. He needed an army to fight the rebels and thus he had to summon Parliament again in November 1640. Once summoned, this Parliament was naturally intent on ensuring that personal government could never be attempted again. Blame for the mistakes of the previous decade was placed not upon the shoulders of the King, for all those writing and speaking in the early 1640s emphasise that they are concerned with the best interests of both King and country, but on his counsellors, especially Laud and Strafford, both of whom were prosecuted. It was now a question of whether the King would continue to make further concessions to Parliament, or whether he would resist. Charles attempted to arrest the leaders of the Parliamentarians and, having failed, withdrew to prepare for war.

Although we can say with some certainty what Parliament felt and what the Puritans felt in the years leading up to the outbreak of war, it is more difficult to assess the feelings of the people as a whole. The King was the largest landowner in the country and proved unpopular with his tenants by disputing their right to use common land, a traditional source of income:

> Laud's role makes clear how interwoven were political religious and economic forces. Though best known for his high-church views . . ., Laud was perhaps most unpopular for his efforts to stop the enclosure of open fields for cattle raising.[108]

This kind of intervention can have done as little to win over the people to Charles's side as interference in their mode of worship:

> It was one thing to have restored the beauty of holiness in our sanctuaries; but did every parish want it? One old lady in Norwich, seeing her . . . parson standing at the holy table in scarlet mass-vestments asked why the mayor was officiating in church . . . In the seventeenth century, far more than in our own day, people were very little aware of what the government was up to in London, whether they had a good King or a bad King. But they were all aware of what was happening in church.[109]

The scale of neutralism during the Civil War itself reinforces this impression that regional concerns frequently outweighed national concerns, but irritation at the interference of central government with regional autonomy was growing.

It would be easy, however, to overemphasise the coherence of the movement which was to bring about war and, ultimately, the death of the King. Milton, whose prose tracts of 1641 and 1642 show him clearly a Puritan (and at that time the term still had some meaning) was not opposed to entering the priesthood on any political or doctrinal grounds in 1633; as the letter to a friend makes clear, he simply did not feel he would be good at the task. In the years following those in which Milton was composing Latin elegies for dead bishops, poets were praising the serenity of the English court compared with its war-torn European neighbours,[110] and the peaceful environment of England was celebrated in a masque as late as 1637:[111] in that same year Charles declared himself 'the happiest King in Christendom'.[112]

These contrasts might be taken to indicate how swift the eventual move to war was, or how well the court had insulated itself from reality. They might, on the other hand, be interpreted as signs of how little planning lay behind the outbreak of war. There was no meeting in 1640 of a group of men who planned a revolution in the knowledge that Charles I would have to be executed and that he would be replaced as head of state by Oliver Cromwell. Like Milton in *Of Reformation*, Parliamentarians would claim to be acting in the best interest of the King to bring about a situation where:

> under a free and untutored monarch, the noblest, worthiest, and most prudent men, with full approbation and suffrage of the people, have in their power the supreme and final determination of highest affairs.[113]

For a brief time the interests of Parliament, Puritans, the people at large, and the Parliamentary Army seemed to coincide and, after some early military success, the Royalist armies were decisively beaten and the King taken prisoner by the middle of 1645. By this time the original Parliamentary leaders were dead and, by the time of the King's execution in 1649, another prominent Army leader was preparing to resign. The Revolution did not develop tidily towards a goal which had been agreed at the outset, but developed through a series of divisions and alliances between groups with a wide range of social, political, and religious ambitions.

It was possible, in the early years of the English Revolution, for a whole range of different ideas to find an audience. As Sarah Wintle has recently written:

> In each of the years 1642, 43, 47 and 48 over a thousand political and religious pamphlets and treatises were printed . . . and the figure excludes newspapers or diurnals, which in 1648, for example, were on occasion being printed at the rate of over ten a week.[114]

In such circumstances it would have been surprising if the interests of all these writers had coincided: they did not and, after 1642, the term 'Puritan' ceases to have a meaning specific enough to be useful. Many different factions continued to use the label, claiming that they represented the true spirit which had given the impetus to the Civil War. This fragmentation led to a situation whereby there were not only Royalist lampoons ridiculing the division of opinions among what had been the Puritans,[115] but also serious guides by those who continued to oppose the King explaining the precise points of difference between these sects.[116]

Just as there was no foreign intervention on behalf of either monarchy or republicanism, so the fighting in England itself was sporadic and by modern standards hardly deserves to be called a war. It started as an armed negotiation and never affected the whole country. Having opened in confusion the war provoked mixed reactions in the counties, which were overwhelmed with demands for support from both King and Parliament. Many remained neutral and concentrated on trying to keep fighting out of their particular area.

Even when Parliament tried to organise local armies into larger units (Associations) the attempt was unsuccessful in most cases because the local interest of these Associations extended only to defence, whereas Parliament needed an instrument of aggression. Hence the New Model Army was formed in 1645, a national army under direct Parliamentary control. Its success was not only a victory over the Royalist army, it was also a triumph for centralised government over regionalism. It also altered the direction of the English Revolution, making the Army and not Parliament the pace-setter, and opening up the possibility of a more radical social revolution than the Parliamentary leaders had imagined or desired. As Don M. Wolfe points out, those who supported the Parliamentary cause in the early 1640s 'embraced no far-reaching political objectives: their aim was the purification of the church and the protection of Parliament's prerogatives'.[117] The Parliamentarians and their supporters were themselves men of property, irritated at the erosion of their wealth caused by the King's taxation, and it would be wrong to see the English Revolution as a peasant uprising. Parliament was interested in removing particular individuals from office but, in order to do this, they needed the support of the Army, which included men of a different class:

> what comes over most powerfully [in the late 1640s] is the soldiers' sense that they themselves who had helped to defeat the Royalists were going to be betrayed by the gentry attitudes of their own commanders in negotations with the King. The feeling [was common] that those whose efforts had won the war had, whether landowners or not, a right to a say in the future.[118]

Before discussing this debate within the Army, however, we must consider the development of the religious aspect of the English Revolution. Merritt Y. Hughes has observed that 'Our habit of regarding the Puritan Revolution as the beginning of civil liberty and modern constitutional government in England makes us forget its originally ecclesiastical, and perhaps genuinely religious, nature'.[119] It is perhaps worth emphasising that the original disputes were more to do with modes of worship and with the relationship between Church and State than doctrinal arguments over particular routes to salvation. What Milton was most concerned with in his writings against the bishops in 1641 and 1642 was their avarice and corruption, and their failure to allow freedom of worship. This was of more significance than the issue of whether virtuous action on earth did or did not have an effect on the salvation of the soul. There were disputes on that issue, but opinions tended not to harden into political factions as they did in matters of Church government and toleration.

Although he himself denied it, the doctrine which Archbishop Laud wished to impose on England was, in fact, that of Arminianism, which held that salvation was open to all who led virtuous lives, and differed therefore from Calvinism, the earlier branch of Puritanism, a doctrine in which the elect were specified from birth. This is not to say, however, that all those who opposed Laud and the King were opposed to Arminianism, and all their supporters in favour of it; Milton himself increasingly moved towards Arminianism, although he was bitterly opposed to Laud and his bishops. The crucial issue is that whereas Milton, and some other radicals, believed that all men could be saved, he placed emphasis on individual freedom of choice and the exercise of reason: these took priority over the ceremonies of the church, or even over attendance at church. For Laud, the priorities were reversed: the Church came first, salvation could only come through its sacraments, and the individual conscience was fettered.

It was the corruption and the enforcement of Laud's Church which made it unpopular rather than the path to salvation which it preached, and a passage from a novel by Rose Macaulay neatly sums this up: 'the Archbishop . . . hates Popery as much as he fonds the Arminians. You know the jest – "What do the Arminians hold?" Answer: "All the best bishoprics and deaneries." '[120] In the early years of the Civil War, with Laud and his Church gone, it seemed as if freedom of worship was at last going to be available, but that freedom did not come, as the Presbyterian movement attempted to impose its own doctrine as the official Church of England. Church and State had become intertwined once again.

Milton was bitterly disappointed with the Presbyterians, partly because they failed to allow religious toleration, partly because they were so scathing about his writings on divorce, and he attacked them at length in *The Character of the Long Parliament* (1648) and, more succinctly, in the poem 'On the New Forcers of Conscience' (1646) in which he alleges:

> they shall read this clearly in your charge
> New *Presbyter* is but old *Priest* writ large.

(lines 19–20)

Although Milton's sense of betrayal is understandable, the Presbyterians had good reason to oppose freedom of worship at that particular moment. It was essential for all those writing or speaking in the cause of freedom in the 1640s to appear to be respectable, hence the frequency of supporting references from Scripture and history, and the claims of both Parliament and the Royalists to have God on their side. The Parliamentary cause could, however, be fatally weakened if it appeared that they counted among their allies those for whom liberty meant sexual excess or political communism. There were those, for example, who believed that Christ's atonement was sufficient to save all men, and that everyone therefore lived on earth in a state of grace. If men were already saved then there were no constraints on human behaviour and no human institution, monogamy for example, or property, is beyond question. The Parliament's case could appear ludicrous if it allowed such sects to thrive (and Royalist propaganda emphasised the alliance between Parliament and 'dangerous' sects) and its conservative base for support would crumble: hence the plea for a State Church and for curbs on publishing mounted by the Presbyterians.

The effect of Presbyterian conservatism upon Milton was twofold: firstly, he distanced himself from the fanatics, the lunatic fringe, and the libertines:

> That bawl for freedom in their senseless mood,
> And still revolt when truth would set them free.
> Licence they mean when they cry liberty;
> For who loves that, must first be wise and good . . .
>
> (Sonnet XII, 1646)

Secondly, he took pains to ensure that he maintained an image of absolute correctness and respectability in all his subsequent published work. This, in part, explains Milton's traditionalism in his choice of poetic forms: the notion of 'original' as a positive term indicating freshness, vitality, and novelty dates only from the middle of the eighteenth century, and for Milton's contemporaries originality (the word itself did not exist for them) would have looked dangerously close to anarchy. The turning point for Milton seems to have come in the mid-1640s when he not only found that the gospels did not appear to say what he wanted them to say on the subject of divorce, but was also pilloried in print for his divorce tracts. Milton had to re-establish his respectability and, in *Tetrachordon*, find fresh biblical sanction for his views. He needed also to re-possess the imagery through which he could assert traditionalism of his position. The Bible provided him with this image, in the first epistle of St Paul to the Corinthians; chapter 13 begins: 'Though I speak with the tongues of men and of angels, and have not charity, I am become as sounding brass, or a tinkling cymbal'. The image of musical harmony as the metaphor of order, and of cacophony for disorder was an attractive one for Milton. He introduces harmony into his 'Hymn on the Morning of Christ's Nativity' (1625):

> She knew such harmony alone
> Could hold all heaven and earth in happier union.
>
> (lines 107–8)

and in 'Lycidas' (1637) the Puritan pastors appropriate the harmony, whilst their Laudian counterparts are most unmusical:

> And when they list, their lean and flashy songs
> Grate on their scrannel pipes of wretched straw . . .
>
> (lines 123–4)

However, in 1645, Daniel Featley, in *The Dippers Dipt* (which is particularly critical of divorce tracts), attempted to win back the image of harmony for a different purpose, suggesting that those in favour of control and censorship are harmonious and that the sectarians a discordant rabble:

> thou hast heard a Harmony, listen not to discords; thou hast heard a consort of silver Trumpets, hearken not to a single oaten-pipe, or the harsh sound of Rams hornes; thou hast heard the suffrages of all the learned Divines in the Reformed Churches; regard not the votes of a few illiterate Mechanicks, much lesse the fancie and dreames of fanaticall Enthusiasts.[121]

Milton's response was to publish his first collection of poems, demonstrating his own command of the harmony of words, reprinting 'Lycidas' and, in the words of Thomas Corns:

> The abiding impression . . . of any browser selecting this volume in Moseley's bookshop early in 1646 must surely have been of the eminent respectability of its author . . . the volume declares his wealth, his establishment connexions, his contact with European culture, and his scholarship.[122]

It was perhaps this concern with his reputation that kept Milton silent during the pamphleteering which centred on the debates within the Army between 1647 and 1649. Although he might have sided with the Levellers (the radical side in this debate) about censorship and modes of worship, he could not have supported their bid for universal suffrage, and for the Levellers, primarily a political rather than a religious group, this was the cornerstone of their policy. Milton never took up his pen to write in support of causes which the majority already espoused (his antiprelatical tracts were obviously against the *status quo*, his divorce pamphlets individual in their viewpoint, and the tracts after the execution of Charles increasingly defended an unpopular cause). It could be that Milton's silence during the Army debates is an indication of the fact that, finding that he could not write in support of the radical side, he preferred to say nothing at all.

The radical Leveller wing within the Army was forcibly suppressed, demonstrating that the generals were as conservative after victory as the Presbyterians had been in Parliament. The English Revolution lurched to its next crisis over what should happen to the imprisoned King. Although there was strong popular support for sparing him, many astute politicians were aware that Charles continued to threaten everything which they had won so far: the Earl of Manchester had declared in 1644:

> If we beat the king ninety and nine times, yet he is king still, and so will his posterity be after him; but if the king beat us once we shall all be hanged.[123]

Charles had a right to bring his subjects to justice, but it was by no means accepted that the people could try the King. No faith could be placed in the attempts at negotiation which went on in the late 1640s and, after attempting to escape from Army custody, Charles I was brought to trial, still King of England, and was condemned to be executed on 30 January 1649. Such was the confusion over the legal and constitutional validity of this act that the execution itself had to be delayed so that Parliament could pass legislation which made it illegal to proclaim Charles II successor to his father: the country was still a monarchy.[124] The trial of the King had caused division within the Army and between the Army and the Presbyterians, and the execution provoked a reaction which the regicides could do little to control: 'On both sides . . . the King's death was . . . a religious event . . . either a holy martyrdom (for this is what all the royalists started to claim) or . . . the righteous deposition of a tyrant, a divine act'.[125]

The discussion above has indicated how successfully the Royalists managed this propaganda war, principally because the dead Charles was a more eloquent and potent symbol than the live King had ever been: any attack upon him appeared tasteless and base, and Charles himself was safe from making further blunders. Significantly, the Army inflicted no further indignity on the body of Charles after the execution: it was not dismembered but allowed a decent burial next to his predecessor Henry VIII at Windsor. The treatment of those responsible for this execution after the Restoration a dozen years later makes a marked contrast.

After the execution, the personality of Cromwell became the dominating factor in the running of the country. Royalist military resistance was ended in 1651 at the Battle of Worcester, but the struggle over how the country should be governed continued between the Army and Parliament, a Parliament which was now very different from that which had first met in 1640, and which could hardly claim to be representative. Increasingly Cromwell assumed individual control, and, when granted the power to nominate his own successor, looked King in all but name.

Unfortunately for the Protectorate, Cromwell's gifts for maintaining

a balance of power were unique to him. He could mediate between the Army and Parliament and could keep local interests under central control. After his death, however, opposition to the expensive standing Army increased, and there was pressure to decentralise government and to return control to the counties. Through expediency, rather than through a commitment to royalism, and because commercial interests believed that it might be good for continental trade, Charles II was restored to the throne in 1660, promising that the Army would be disbanded and their arrears of pay would be settled, that an acceptable land settlement would be imposed, that rebels would be pardoned, and that a measure of religious toleration would be granted.

It is easy to exaggerate the divisions within communities caused by the Civil War and its aftermath, as many fictional accounts of the period do, and to suggest that the effects of the war were long lasting. T.S. Eliot claimed that: 'the Civil War of the seventeenth century, in which Milton is a symbolic figure, has never been concluded'.[126] And he was right in the sense that there are still serious rifts within society and that Milton is still wheeled out as a spokesman in the cause of liberty. Nevertheless, those rifts are by no means identical to those which caused the Civil War, or the subsequent debates on liberty, franchise, and the constitution. Indeed, many of those who would press for 'liberty' at the end of the twentieth century, quoting the Levellers as their political ancestors, would also vociferously oppose militarism itself. At a personal and individual level, it is clear that the Civil War ended very quickly indeed. Christopher Milton worked for the King during the war, although there is every reason to suppose that he remained on good terms with his brother John, who seems to have sheltered Christopher's family as he did the Powells (also Royalists). Although Milton's loyalty to friends and family is well-attested, there is no indication that he was unusual in placing family loyalties before ideology. Christopher Milton may have become a Catholic late in life, but he, like his brother, the notorious defender of the Puritan cause against the established Church, was eventually buried in an official Protestant church.[127] Even Richard Cromwell, whose abdication from the Protectorate had made the Restoration possible, was able after a period of exile on the continent to return to his Hampshire estates (where local legend says he was frequently visited by Charles II) and to be buried in the family tomb of the local church.

Although many cruel comments were published about Milton at the Restoration he was quickly rehabilitated as a literary figure, not only, as might be expected, by those in sympathy with his radical or liberal views, but by the Royal family itself: Queen Caroline donated £50 to an appeal for Milton's daughter Deborah in 1727;[128] Prince Albert

commissioned paintings of scenes from *Comus* for the garden pavilion at Buckingham Palace in 1841; and a text from Milton was sung during the signing of the register at the wedding of Prince Charles and Princess Diana in 1981.[129]

The English Civil War was certainly a very different phenomenon from its apparent counterpart some two centuries later in the USA. The difference between the Northern and Southern States had been apparent for some seventy-five years before war broke out in 1861, and the divisions are still emphasised today in separate cultural identities.[130]

Milton's literary background

The autobiographical references in Milton's prose, his letters, his Commonplace Book, and the allusions to other writers throughout his work give an indication of the range of reading which Milton undertook in his commitment to become a poet. We shall never have a complete list of Milton's reading, but the selection we know of makes the study of his writing, the poetry in particular, a daunting task, and scarcely a year goes by without a new source being discovered for one of his works.

Milton was well versed in classical literature, as well as in the more recent literature of the continent and of England. Specific sources for particular works will be dealt with in Part 2 below, and this section will concentrate upon general influences, on Milton's attitude to literature, his own role as national poet and a 'true poem', and on the choices available to him in the literature of his own day.

From a twentieth-century perspective Milton can appear something of a conformist, a reactionary writer. He invented no new poetic forms, and even in his prose, where it might be assumed that there was scope for formal innovation, Milton adopted traditional rhetorical modes whenever possible. However, we should bear in mind not only the particular political circumstances which led Milton to present himself as a respectable, establishment figure writing within an accepted tradition, but also that Milton left none of these traditional modes untouched by his own originality. The epic, the tragedy, the masque, the pastoral elegy and the sonnet are all shaped by Milton to fresh ends, and concepts such as heroism, victory, and defeat are re-defined. Milton's attitude to tradition is typified in a comment by Mary Ann Radzinowicz on Milton's use of Aristotle, the accepted source of guidance on poetic practice: 'Milton's Aristotle . . . was . . . a text he felt free to set aside . . . Aristotelian rules were conditional, subject to appeal to the higher rules of nature, discerned by experience of art and by judgement'.[131]

For Milton, traditions were rather like the Sabbath: there to be used by man, rather than to prescribe his behaviour. Milton undertook rigorous personal preparation in becoming a writer, having found the syllabus at Cambridge deficient for his needs. Having prepared himself for a life as a priest, he found that the practices of the Laudian Church were abhorrent to him and thus devoted himself to training as a poet, only to find that events forced him to join the pamphleteering war. Milton, however, saw no grave inconsistency between priesthood, poetry, and prose writing. There is little fundamental distinction for him between prose and poetry,[132] and indeed some passages from his prose read with the fervour and inspiration of poetry:

> Then, amidst the hymns and hallelujahs of saints, some one may perhaps be heard offering at high strains in new and lofty measure to sing and celebrate thy divine mercies and marvellous judgement in this land throughout all ages . . .[133]

In the passage above, from *Of Reformation*, Milton is writing of the development of England as a nation and of his role as poet in celebrating that triumphal movement towards reformation. In his early Latin poem to his father, 'Ad Patrem', Milton catalogues the attributes and magnificences of poetry. Poetry was, for Milton, not only part of the educational curriculum for the cultured man, it was also a product of that education, and thus poetry meant not a retirement from the issues of the world into pretty fancies, but an engagement with them and an attempt to mould minds and opinions through the power of words.

In *The Reason of Church Government* Milton sets out his views on the roles of poet and priest, and on the differences between good and bad poets. He says, of the gifts of poetry:

> These abilities . . . are the inspired gift of God, rarely bestowed, but yet to some (though most abuse) in every nation; and are of power, beside the office of a pulpit, to inbreed and cherish in a great people the seeds of virtue and public civility, to allay the perturbations of the mind, and set the affections in right tune . . . to deplore the general relapses of kingdoms and states from justice and God's true worship.[134]

The poet, therefore, ranks equally with the priest as an instructor, and Milton seems to feel rather as his near-contemporary George Herbert (1593–1633) did, that 'A verse may find him, who a sermon flies,/ And turn delight into a sacrifice'.[135] Good poetry is to be distinguished from bad poetry not on the grounds of technical deficiency (although it may be distinct in that respect too), but on the grounds of its moral content:

the writings of libidinous and ignorant poetasters; who, having scarce ever heard of that which is the main consistence of a true poem . . . do for the most part lay up vicious principles in sweet pills to be swallowed down, and make the taste of virtuous documents harsh and sour.[136]

In 'Lycidas' the virtuous and worthy characters are associated with the music of true, moral poetry:

> Who would not sing for Lycidas? he knew
> Himself to sing, and build the lofty rhyme.
>
> (lines 10–11)

and harmony is equally associated with virtue in *Comus* and in 'L'Allegro' and 'Il Penseroso'. As Milton explains in *An Apology for Smectymnuus*:

he who would not be frustrate of his hope to write well hereafter in laudable things, ought himself to be a true poem; that is, a composition and pattern of the best and honourablest things; not presuming to sing high praises of heroic men, or famous cities, unless he have in himself the experience and practice of all that is praiseworthy.[137]

Thus, throughout his career, Milton is careful to present himself as a true poem, a virtuous man whose views are therefore worth listening to, and to attack the views of his opponents because they are not true poems:

while pluralities greased them thick and deep to the shame and scandal of religion more than all the sects and heresies they exclaim against – then to fight against the king's person . . . was good, was lawful.[138]

For Milton, the validity of an argument depended upon the integrity of the person who advanced it, and to teach this lesson was one of the functions of poetry. In this respect he was following in the direct line of writers such as Sidney and Spenser, both of whom emphasised that the educational aspect of poetry was more important than its power to entertain. As will be evident in the next section, Milton was a great admirer of Spenser, whom he mentions in *Areopagitica* as 'our sage and serious poet',[139] and *Poems 1645* was advertised, as we have noted above, as an imitation of Spenser. Spenser's declared aim in writing his epic *The Faerie Queene* seems close to that of Milton: 'The generall end therefore of all the books is, to fashion a gentleman or noble person in vertuous and gentle discipline'.[140] Spenser, however, was able to do this without risking giving offence to those in power; Milton had to take much greater risks to get across his educational message.

Milton did not have to follow in the line of Sidney and of Spenser; he could have done as Herbert did before him and Marvell was to do after him: he could have written in the 'metaphysical' style of John Donne. This witty, detached manner of writing, which became suddenly fashionable again among critics in the early part of the twentieth century, was available to Milton for the expression of personal, political, or religious ideas, but Milton did not adopt it. Raymond Williams has recently characterised the difference between Milton's position and that of the metaphysical poets, and the implication of those critics who praised the latter whilst reviling Milton:

> On the one side, you have a man who totally committed himself to a particular side and cause, who temporarily suspended what you call literature, but not in fact writing, in that conflict. On the other, you have a kind of writing which is highly intelligent and elaborate, that is a way of holding divergent attitudes towards struggle or towards experience together in the mind at the same time. There are two possibilities for any highly conscious person in a period of crisis – a kind of commitment which involves certain difficulties, certain naïvetés, certain styles; and another kind of consciousness, whose complexities are a way of living with the crisis without being openly part of it.[141]

By the time the political crisis was at its height, Donne and Herbert were dead, but the poems which they wrote describing their crisis of faith were very different from Milton's religious poems both in character and in function. They were private expressions of their individual relationships with their God, sometimes uncertain, often passionate. They are striking and dramatic and, in the case of Herbert, often deceptively simple. In neither case was Donne or Herbert writing for a public platform and, indeed, neither found a publisher for their religious verse in their own lifetime. Milton, on the other hand, feels that the situation of the moment demands either celebration or explanation, and is far less concerned with his own relationship with God than with the larger issues of determining what is God's will for his people. It is ironic that Milton should be associated in the popular mind with egoism when there is far less self-interest in his poetry than in that of many of his contemporaries. Some of Milton's characters may express doubts (Satan, for example, or Samson) about the ways of God, and there may be shifts and even inconsistencies in Milton's views from work to work, but each individual poem or prose pamphlet attempts to convince its readers of Milton's own absolute certainty on theological issues. When, for example, in 1649, the point at issue is whether a King has a relationship with God different from that of his subjects, Milton delivers his opinion confidently: 'all men naturally were born free, being the image and resemblance of God himself, and were, by privilege above all the creatures, born to command, and not to obey'.[142]

Milton, however, could also write in the manner of Herbert; he could investigate his own faith more personally. The sonnet 'When I consider how my light is spent', which he left unpublished for over twenty years, provides an intimate insight into Milton's private uncertainties and the way in which he resolved them.[143]

Part 2

Milton's works

Poems 1645

Milton's first collection of poems was published at the end of 1645, with the masque *Comus* given pride of place. The collection introduces a poet of great technical skill with a complex mind already prepared to tackle controversial themes. This section will concentrate mainly upon three English poems from the collection (*Comus*, 'Lycidas', and the twin poems 'L'Allegro' and 'Il Penseroso'), which demonstrate Milton's mastery of form and structure and his contribution to the literary mode of pastoral: two aspects of his work which are of continuing significance throughout his poetic career.

Pastoral poetry

The pastoral mode has a long history in literature and indeed in other art forms. The poet and critic Alexander Pope (1688–1744), writing at the beginning of the eighteenth century, felt that, by his time, the mode had badly degenerated: 'There are not, I believe, a greater number of any sort of verses than of those which we called Pastorals, nor a smaller, than of those which are truly so'.[1] In the popular imagination, incompetent or tasteless manifestations of pastoralism are likely to have more impact than works which follow the mode more decorously and more faithfully: the attempt by Marie Antoinette, for example, to fashion a pastoral world in miniature in the grounds of the Palace of Versailles, is a striking illustration of how the pastoral influence can go astray. Pope's critique, however, is useful as an index to the characteristic features of the pastoral mode, and its place in literature:

> A Pastoral is an imitation of the action of a shepherd, or one considered under that character. The form of this imitation is dramatic, or narrative, or mix'd of both; the fable simple, the manners not too polite nor too rustic. . . . The expression humble, yet as pure as the language will afford; neat, but not florid; easy, and yet lively.[2]

This defines the subject of pastoral, the action of shepherds or shepherd-like figures, and its manner of operation, dramatic or narrative, thus drawing our attention to the possibility of debate as the backbone of the mode. It is also inherently unreal and idealised, as Pope goes on to say:

> pastoral is an image of what they call the Golden age. So that we are not to describe our shepherds as shepherds at this day really are, but as they may be conceiv'd to have been: when the best of men follow'd the employment.[3]

Pastoral is part of the process of idealising the past, and of looking back in admiration for that Golden Age when man lived in a state of prosperity and happiness. Furthermore, as Pope indicates, pastoral poetry is not about real shepherds, neither is it written by them or for them:

> We must therefore use some illusion to render a Pastoral delightful; and this consists in exposing the best side only of a shepherd's life and concealing its miseries.[4]

Pastoral, according to Pope, shows only the attractive aspects of the shepherd's life and describes only the time when the best of men were shepherds: by no stretch of the imagination, therefore, is it proletarian literature.[5]

The origins of the pastoral mode lie in the works of Theocritus, a native of Sicily writing in the fourth century BC who composed short poems for a sophisticated Greek audience which describe the attractions of the rural life, and of rural occupations, in contrast to the corruption of the life of the city. In these poems there is at least some link with reality in that Theocritus is describing a way of life which he himself might have witnessed in his childhood, and he did live in a climate where the life of the shepherd could be pleasant: as the mode became popular, however, it was increasingly adopted by those who knew little of the countryside and who lived in the cold, wet northern European countries where the shepherd's lot was often miserable. As Hughes, an early editor of Spenser, points out, pastoral

> is a wonderful Amusement to the Imagination, to be sometimes transported, as it were, out of modern life, and to wander in these pleasant Scenes which the Pastoral Poets provide for us, and in which we are apt to fancy ourselves reinstated for a time in our first Innocence and Happiness.[6]

In order to be transported, the audience for pastoral poetry must have a non-pastoral, urban starting point, and the mode depends upon tensions between the ideal world which it describes and the reality in which its audience actually lives. Pastoral is, then, an urban form composed by urban artists.

When the poems of Theocritus were imitated by later classical and neo-classical writers, the mode became increasingly removed from reality, and the conventions of the mode rapidly became established: pastoral was associated with the innocence of the Golden Age, when human nature was better:

> 'Twas in such wise, methinks, they lived whom the primal age produced, in friendly intercourse with gods. They had no blind love of gold, no sacred boundary-stone, judging betwixt peoples, separated field on the spreading plain; not yet did rash vessels plough the sea; each man knew only his native waters.[7]

The pastoral world was one of contentment, free from the ambition and bustle of the contemporary world: a place of stasis where time and progress stood still, even though the passage of time seemed to be marked by the cycle of the seasons. The quotation above comes from the Roman tragedian Seneca (*d.* AD65), but the values it expresses were to be of great relevance to philosophers and writers in England sixteen hundred years later, and to Milton in particular.

Among the most influential medieval pastorals were those written by Johannes Baptista Spagnola (1448–1516), who was known as Mantuan. His pastorals were written in a Latin simple enough to be used for school translations. This simplicity, coupled with the fact that some classical poets (Virgil included) had begun their careers with pastoral poems and then moved on to other genres, led to the use of the mode by Renaissance poets as a training exercise, a stage through which they needed to pass in order to embark on more ambitious forms. Thus both Spenser and Milton write pastoral poetry early in their careers, before attempting the epic form; yet neither entirely abandons the pastoral, each weaving elements from pastoral into the fabric of their epic.

Renaissance pastoral was more explicit about the faults of contemporary urban civilisation (such criticism in classical pastoral was there only by implication). Higher motives were imputed to shepherds than to courtiers, and, when the two classes met, the shepherds were made to seem the wiser. In Spenser's *The Faerie Queene*, for example, the knight Sir Calidore spends some time in the pastoral world in Book VI and has this to say to the shepherd Meliboe:

> How much (sayd he) more happie is the state,
> In which ye father here doe dwell at ease,
> Leading a life so free and fortunate,
> From all the tempests of these worldly seas,
> Which tosse the rest in daungerous disease;
> Where warres, and wreckes, and wicked enmitie
> Doe them afflict, which no man can appease,

That certes I your happinesse envie,
And wish my lot were plast in such felicitie.

(Canto IX, stanza 19)

Thus, by concentrating upon incidents in which representatives of the courtly world and the pastoral world can meet, Renaissance pastoral becomes an alternative to the heroic life of action. At its best, in the hands of poets like Spenser and Milton, and dramatists like Shakespeare, the pastoral is presented not as separate from the active life, but as complementary to it. Given the alternatives suggested earlier (p. 47) for writers to cope with the crises of the seventeenth century, pastoral poetry assumes a particular pertinence. Marvell withdrew to a rural retreat during the English Revolution and composed pastoral poems; Milton, whilst never advocating a withdrawal from political commitment, suggests in *Paradise Regained* (after the Restoration) that a period of pastoral-like contemplation is the necessary accompaniment to any political action.

At an early stage in the development of pastoral the shepherd figure had become frequently employed as a means of representing the poet. Within the pastoral convention the writing of poetry is expressed as the singing or playing of songs, and the poets themselves become shepherds, acquiring stylised names. Mantuan carried this process a stage further by making allusions to his friends and fellow-poets in his pastorals, using conventional names. Spenser followed this tradition by referring to Chaucer in the February eclogue of *The Shepheardes Calender* (1597) as Tityrus, and Spenser himself becomes Meliboeus in Milton's *Comus* (line 821). It is, of course, a very short step to move from pastoral allusion as a form of compliment, as in these cases, to pastoral allusion as an oblique attack, as Spenser does in this catalogue of poets at the court of Queen Elizabeth I in *Colin Clout's Come Home Againe*, not all of whom can be identified with certainty:

There is a good *Harpalus*, now woxen aged
In faithfull service of faire *Cynthia*:
And there is *Corydon* though meanly waged,
Yet hablest wit of most I know this day . . .
There eke is *Palin* worthie of great praise,
Albe he envie at my rustick quill;
And there is pleasing *Alcon*, could he raise
His tunes from laies to matter of more skill.[8]

The pastoral mode allows Spenser to suggest that 'Corydon' is underpaid, that 'Palin' is talented, even though he has been disparaging of Spenser, and that 'Alcon' has not yet found an adequate genre in which to write. If rigid censorship was in force, as it was for most of

Milton's career, the oblique mode of reference available in the pastoral would be particularly attractive.

There is one further feature of Renaissance pastoral which distinguishes it from its classical ancestry, and which has a significant bearing upon its development. Christian readers of pastoral would quickly see analogies between the innocence of the Golden Age and the perfection of unfallen man in the Garden of Eden, and these would be reinforced by the presence of the shepherd as a Christian symbol for the pastor or priest, caring for his congregation. Francis Bacon (1561–1626), writing in the early seventeenth century, asserts the superiority of the shepherd over all other occupations in Christian theology:

> We see . . . an image of the two estates, the contemplative state and the active state, figured in the two persons of Abel and Cain, and in the two simplest and most primitive trades of life: that of the shepherd (who, by reason of his leisure, rest in a place, and living in view of heaven, is a lively image of a contemplative life,) and that of a husbandman: where we see again the favour and election of God went to the shepherd, and not to the tiller of the ground.[9]

Hence, Milton's use of the pastoral mode as a means of carrying his attack upon false priests is, in a sense, a logical outcome of the way in which the pastoral had developed in the hands of Christian writers: if 'shepherd' could be used as a metaphor for poet, and pastoral used to attack bad poets, then, when 'shepherd' meant priest and teacher, pastoral could be used to attack corrupt clergy and bad teaching. But there was a danger that the pastoral mode, which had originally been concerned with escapism and the portrayal of ideal (and idealised) communities, might eventually be submerged beneath the weight of carrying contemporary satire. It was not this development, however, which arrested the growth of the pastoral and led to the state of affairs lamented by Pope. It was rather that the desire for the ideal community associated with the pastoral world expressed itself more forcefully in the seventeenth century through other media. Firstly through philosophical works, which developed the principles which Sir Thomas More (1478–1535) set out in *Utopia* (1516), and secondly through political action when, during the English Revolution, groups such as the Levellers and the Diggers attempted to do away with the divisions caused by property ownership and land boundaries: some of their tracts echo remarkably closely the passage from Seneca cited above. The ideas of the Levellers and the Diggers were too radical to succeed, and their failure effectively prevented the continued portrayal of the ideal community in pastoral poetry: the mode had to develop in new directions.[10]

Milton's use of pastoral owes a considerable debt both to Spenser (1552–99) and to Shakespeare (1564–1616), both of whom extended the existing conventions, sometimes to comic effect. Spenser's *The Shepheardes Calender* is a series of twelve poems, one for each month of the year, in which shepherds either debate or deliver monologues on subjects which are appropriate to the seasons. Thus Spenser moves beyond the restrictions of the convention which dictated that only the pleasant side of the rural life could be portrayed: his shepherds feel the pain of winter, which matches the pain of love:

> now is come thy wynters stormy state,
> Thy mantle mard, wherein thou maskedst late.
> Such rage as winters, reigneth in my heart,
> My life blood friesing with unkindly cold . . .[11]

In *The Faerie Queene*, similarly, Spenser demonstrated that a rural world need not be idyllic, and his forests can be places of danger, the haunts of bears and tigers. By employing the pastoral mode in this narrative poem, Spenser is able not only to describe the attractions of the rural life, but also to introduce into that environment courtly characters, suggesting the strengths and limitations of both worlds.

Shakespeare exploits the pastoral to similar effect in *As You Like It* (1599) and *The Winter's Tale* (1610). This passage looks at first glance thoroughly conventional in its condemnation of the court and its praise of the pastoral life:

> Are not these woods
> More free from peril than the envious court?
> Here feel we but the penalty of Adam,
> The seasons' difference; as the icy fang
> And churlish chiding of the winter's wind,
> Which when it bites and blows upon my body,
> Even till I shrink with cold, I smile and say
> This is no flattery . . .
>
> (*As You Like It*, II.i.3–10)

If this were an isolated lyric we should have no difficulty in identifying its stock characteristics: courts are full of envy and flattery, woods may be uncomfortable, but they are at least honest. However, this is not an isolated lyric but a speech from a play and Shakespeare is fully exploiting the dramatic context in which the speech is placed. This passage is delivered by a Duke who is in temporary exile in the forest, but who still continues to live very much as a Duke should, hunting, feasting and commanding his men, and, at the end of the play, despite these fine words on the superiority of forest over court, he wastes no time in returning to the court when given the opportunity.

The pastoral mode, then, is an oblique one in which poets are, in effect, employing disguises. They may appear to be writing of shepherds but they are, in fact, writing of and for the court. The very language given to 'shepherds' in the pastoral mode is far removed from that used by their real counterparts. Shakespeare exploits these particular conventions by placing within his pastoral world courtly characters who are literally disguised, either by choice or by fate, and setting them alongside rustics who speak in a far less sophisticated manner. Since these rustics are themselves the products of Shakespeare's invention, as well as operating within other constraints of the convention, the audience is left to ponder what the real world might be. Corin, Silvius, and Phebe, for example, in *As You Like It* seem to be genuine natives of the Forest of Arden, and are contrasted with the courtly characters who arrive in disguise. However, they prove to be equally subject to convention in the manner of their courtship, and are given verse, not prose, in which to talk of their love: are they, therefore, any more real than the disguised Rosalind? As we shall see below, Milton was able to profit from the example of Shakespeare in exploiting pastoral conventions in a dramatic context in *Comus*.[12]

'L'Allegro' and 'Il Penseroso'

This pair of poems seems to date from 1631 and demonstrates Milton's command of metre, structure and poetic debate. The two poems have closely parallel structures: each opens with a dismissal of the contrasting emotion, followed by a welcoming of the mood which is to be the subject of the poem, a description of its ancestry, and the introduction of appropriate figures to accompany that mood. Each includes a walk in a country landscape and allusions to the theatre, and each closes with a reference to the power of music. The imagery of the two poems is similarly paralleled, the emphasis in each being upon the sounds of the countryside, especially birdsong, and the visual appeal of the landscape and sky.

It is tempting to regard these two poems as presenting competing states or ways of living, and to focus attention upon determining which state Milton advocated. E.M.W. Tillyard, arguing for an early date for the poems, pointed out that they are similar to one of the prolusions which Milton delivered at Cambridge, and therefore suggested that they constitute a poem about day and a poem about night: a further polarising of the pair.[13] In fact the two poems do not present such contrasting or mutually antithetical positions. Together they represent the product of a synthesis of active and contemplative states (a product also of the kinds of debate found in pastoral poetry, especially in Spenser's *The Shepheardes Calender*) and are, therefore, complementary rather than competing poems: each is highly dependent on the other, and neither can stand adequately alone.

One problem for the reader who is less than fully attentive is that one poem seems to be totally concerned with day, the other with night, and each seems to dismiss in its opening nine lines the emotion which is celebrated in its partner-poem. To take the second illusion first, it is clear on close reading that Milton is deliberately exploiting the ambiguity of the terms Melancholy and Mirth. Melancholy to the modern reader has exclusively negative connotations and will be associated with mental depression; for Milton, however, two quite different meanings were in current use, and both senses of the word are employed in *Comus*. Comus, speaking to the Lady, uses the word in its current sense:

> 'tis but the lees
> And settlings of a melancholy blood . . .
>
> (lines 808–9)

whereas the Attendant Spirit uses the word in a positive context:

> began
> Wrapt in a pleasing fit of melancholy
> To meditate my rural minstrelsy . . .
>
> (lines 544–6)

Melancholy could imply nothing more sinister than a period of quiet contemplation: a similar case of a word being capable of two apparently incompatible meanings occurs in modern use of 'the blues', which can mean, on the one hand, a state of depression, on the other a pleasant kind of popular music. At the beginning of 'L'Allegro' Milton is banishing the negative aspect of melancholy, which leaves man disordered; at the beginning of 'Il Penseroso' he is welcoming the positive, contemplative sense of melancholy, which improves man through its discipline.

In his use of the term Mirth, Milton observes the same careful distinction which he is to make throughout his career as a thinker and writer, between innocent pleasure and licentious vice. Milton came to acquire the unfortunate reputation of libertine, and it may well have been the desire to counter that charge that led him to include in the *Poems 1645* this pair of poems which make his position quite clear. The Mirth which he welcomes in 'L'Allegro' is the innocent capacity to enjoy 'unreproved pleasures free' (line 40), pleasures which are utterly blameless. The Mirth which is dismissed at the beginning of 'Il Penseroso' is the dangerous temptation of excessive pleasure which can stupefy man and prevent him from achieving his full potential. It is this temptation of licentious behaviour which Milton rejects in the second poem, and he continues to confront and to overcome temptation through all of his major poems.

To return to the illusion that one poem deals with day and the other with night, the fact is that neither has this exclusive preoccupation. Each poem encompasses both day and night, and may, indeed, be intended to suggest a number of days rather than a single twenty-four-hour cycle. The emphasis is different, however, in the two poems, 'L'Allegro' focusing upon the daylight hours and 'Il Penseroso' upon the night.

This is why the ordering of the two poems is so significant: Milton intends us to work through 'L'Allegro' before we attempt 'Il Penseroso', just as in life the activities depicted in the first poem are a necessary preparation for those of the second. Although there are many respects in which the pair of poems are comparable to twin pictures, the verbal medium imposes a substantial difference: our eye is not allowed to stray from one self-contained picture to the other and back, evaluating their comparative merits; Milton's poems are given an argument and a definite order. This is evident in the constrasting ways in which music is introduced at the conclusion of the two poems. In 'L'Allegro' the music is relaxing, a Lydian air which recalls to the poet the legend of Orpheus:

> That Orpheus' self may heave his head
> From golden slumber on a bed
> Of heaped Elysian flowers, and hear
> Such strains as would have won the ear
> Of Pluto, to have quite set free
> His half-regained Eurydice.
>
> (lines 145–50)

This passage indicates the delights and the limitations of the music, or poetry, of the world of 'L'Allegro'. Orpheus, the poet of Greek legend, attempted to bring back his wife, Eurydice, from Pluto after her death. However, he failed because he looked back at her, and the music of 'L'Allegro' is similarly deficient: it can rouse the man who has been suffering from depressive melancholy, and make him human once more, but it cannot turn his thoughts any higher. The youthful, lyric poetry celebrated in the first poem is pleasant but limited, and is replaced by poetry of a superior kind which is presented at the end of 'Il Penseroso':

> There let the pealing organ blow,
> To the full-voiced choir below,
> In service high, and anthems clear,

As may with sweetness, through mine ear,
Dissolve me into ecstasies,
And bring all heaven before mine eyes.
And may at last my weary age
Find out the peaceful hermitage, . . .
Till old experience do attain
To something like prophetic strain.

(lines 161–73)

Music and poetry have acquired a different significance, and the legend of Orpheus has become just one instance in the middle of 'Il Penseroso' of possible subjects for reflection; it is no longer the climax. This second poem closes with poetry which allows the mind to reach heaven, and with a poet, in old age, who can teach others through his gift of prophecy.

Together, therefore, 'L'Allegro' and 'Il Penseroso' constitute a manifesto of Milton's intentions for his career as a poet, encompassing the depiction of rural scenes in the sociable, pleasant life of a pastoral poet, and the solitude and reflection necessary to produce mature, prophetic poems. In some respects the two central figures in these poems are more remarkable for their similarities than for their differences: although they may choose to walk at different times of day, the one 'not unseen' ('L'Allegro', line 57), the other 'unseen' ('Il Penseroso', line 65), they are both primarily observers and listeners rather than participants, poets of different schools using life, legend, and reading in their search for material. In his *Elegia Sexta* written to Charles Diodati not long before the composition of these two poems, Milton had drawn a similar distinction between the pleasant occupation of writing elegiac poetry and the rigours of more serious writing, showing no distaste for the former and no reluctance to accept the responsibilities of the latter:

while the ivory plectrum dances over the strings and the crowd of merry-makers, keeping time with it, fills the perfumed ballroom, you will notice Phoebus creeping silently into your heart, like a sudden warmth flowing through your bones. Girls' eyes and girls' fingers playing will make Thalia dart into your breast and take command of it . . . So grand banquets are quite all right for elegiac poets, . . . but the poet whose subject is, one minute, the holy counsels of the gods above, and the next, those deep-buried kingdoms where a savage dog barks – let this poet live frugally.[14]

Milton accepted from an early age what it meant to live his life as a 'true poem' (see p. 46 above), although he could not have anticipated that his later poetry would be progressively concerned with individuals like Abdiel in *Paradise Lost* who are isolated politically, not through their choosing a life of poetic austerity: this was to be Milton's fate too.

Critics have commented on the fact that in his later poems Milton places a typically Puritan emphasis upon the active life: 'the Puritan emphases on the active life, the idea of vocation, the virtue of discipline . . . are not just religious ideas; they are ideological and psychological weapons in the hands of men who are transforming English society.'[15] Milton may not have begun his attempt to transform society at the time he was writing 'L'Allegro' and 'Il Penseroso', but there is ample evidence in these poems of his early emphasis upon activity, vocation, and discipline. It is all too easy to read the poems as if they were advocating the avoidance of engagement, a life of ease on the one hand and of retirement on the other, yet the reverse is true: Milton is anticipating a life of long, hard work:

> let my lamp at midnight hour,
> Be seen in some high lonely tower . . .
> let my due feet never fail,
> To walk the studious cloister's pale . . .
> ('Il Penseroso', lines 85–6, 155–6)

The life of a poet presented in these two poems is as taxing, and as respectable, as that contained in 'Ad Patrem', dedicated to his father a year or so later (discussed above on p. 11): in each case Milton is presenting a defence of his chosen career, and associating poetry with vocation.

This conception of poetry is also closely associated with moderation and temperance. The quotation from *Elegia Sexta* above linked elegiac poetry with feasting and revelry whilst committing the serious poet to a frugal, ascetic life. Milton's poetic career is a testament to this belief in the need for temperance: in a sonnet written in the early 1650s, a similar image occurs:

> What neat repast shall feast us, light and choice,
> Of Attic taste, with wine, whence we may rise
> To hear the lute well touched, or artful voice
> Warble immortal notes and Tuscan air?
> He who of those delights can judge, and spare
> To interpose them oft, is not unwise.[16]

Milton is far from advocating the total avoidance of all forms of pleasure, indeed the very language of this sonnet expresses joy in pleasures of the senses. The distinction which he is drawing is between temperate enjoyment and luxurious over-indulgence: the distinction between liberty and licence. It is this middle course which Milton is presenting in 'L'Allegro' and 'Il Penseroso', the delight of 'the spicy nut-brown ale' in the first poem (line 100) giving way in the second to: 'calm Peace, and Quiet,/Spare Fast, that oft with gods doth diet' (lines 45–6).

According to Raymond Havens, some two hundred and seventy-five poems were influenced by 'L'Allegro' and 'Il Penseroso' in the period 1760 to 1800 alone,[17] but none of those introduced so appropriately the style and preoccupations of a major poet.[18]

Comus

The masque which we know as *Comus* was almost certainly Milton's second excursion into the world of courtly, complimentary drama. In 1632 or 1633 he had written *Arcades*, a pastoral masque of just over one hundred lines as part of an entertainment in honour of the Dowager Countess of Derby, then an old lady, but who had been the subject of complimentary verse from the time of Spenser onwards. It is likely that the composer Henry Lawes (1596–1662) was associated with the music for *Arcades*, and certain that he composed the music for the songs and dances of *Comus*, which was acted for the first time at Ludlow Castle on the Welsh border on 29 September 1634.

Lawes was the music teacher to the Egerton children, grandchildren of the Dowager Countess, and it may be that he was instrumental in suggesting that Milton should be commissioned to write *Comus*. The Egerton family had recently suffered some disgrace as well as public honour, for in 1631, whilst one of the Countess's sons-in-law was made President of the Council of Wales, another, the Earl of Castlehaven, was tried and executed for crimes of sexual perversion against his wife and family.[19] In those circumstances, therefore, the family might well have been looking for a poet who could not only celebrate the promotion of the Earl of Bridgewater, but also present the family as a whole in a respectable light: Milton could do both.

It may seem that the masque was an odd genre for Milton, since it is essentially associated with the aristocracy, for which he felt no sympathy.[20] It was a private form of theatrical entertainment, making full use of music, song and dance, as well as of elaborate (and expensive) stage machinery for special effects. A recent book on the theatre before the outbreak of civil war has suggested that some writers of masques used the medium to carry political attacks on the establishment, which the courtiers were too dull to perceive,[21] and yet *Comus*, with its more abstract theme of Chastity and its generally youthful cast, does not seem to fit this category of subversive masques.

Arcades is in many ways more typical of the masque genre than *Comus*, because the verse is clearly not the principal focus of the entertainment, there is no plot to speak of, and the whole piece is entirely ephemeral, existing for and relevant to a single evening when the Dowager herself was present. There would be little point in attempting to re-stage *Arcades* for the benefit of a contemporary audience, because a good deal of its original interest, like that of most masques, derived from the awareness of the audience that the Countess herself was playing a central role. In contrast, *Comus* has been regularly revived: it has a firmer plot than most masques, it is certainly more rhetorical, and it can be appreciated without a detailed awareness of the relationship between the audience and the members of the Egerton family who performed in the original production. However, such a detailed awareness may help to explain what Milton was attempting to do with the masque form.

The masque is inherently artificial, perhaps more so than any other type of drama. It is theatrically as well as socially distinct, in that it presumes a different relationship between audience and actor than that found elsewhere in drama. Most theatre presumes that the audience watching a play will forget the real identity of the actor and become preoccupied with the role which he is playing: we may sometimes go to the theatre especially to see a famous actor, but it is the job of that actor to make us forget his name and his public fame, and to make us believe that he is Lear, or Hamlet. The masque, on the other hand, sets out to break down the barrier between audience and actor, partly by involving members of the aristocracy as actors and by creating a counterpoint between their public lives and their roles on stage, partly by involving the audience in the entertainment at the end of the masque, moving from a play into a public dance. There is a well-known example of this phenomenon at the end of *As You Like It*, where Shakespeare has the characters from the masque of Hymen reunited in dance and song with their fathers and their suitors. *Comus*, too, ends with a dance in which cast and audience participate, and in which those members of the Egerton family who have acted are reunited with those who have watched, just as the Attendant Spirit promised in the masque.

There is, then, in the masque form, a complex interplay between illusion and reality which Milton exploits to its full effect. Masques do not have to be based upon pastoral subjects, but both of Milton's masques have pastoral themes, and a further level of possible ambiguity: we have actors, who are really young aristocrats, looked after by a shepherd, who, according to pastoral convention, is not really a shepherd at all but a poet, or a pastor. To add a further stage of unreality, there are constant references in the masque to an outdoor setting with woods, stars, sky and darkness, and yet, in all probability, the Ludlow performance took place inside, in an artificial wood.[22]

Milton makes good use of these multiple levels of illusion from the very start of his masque in his presentation of the Attendant Spirit. This character is a superior being descended from the sky to care for mere mortals, a servant of the household (and therefore Henry Lawes himself, who played the role), a shepherd, a poet, and a representation of Milton, controlling and shaping the narrative. In opposition to the Attendant Spirit, who is armed with Lawes's harmony, is Comus, the false shepherd, whose crew produce discordant music and riotous behaviour:

> the sound
> Of riot, and ill-managed merriment,
> Such as the jocund flute, or gamesome pipe
> Stirs up among the loose unlettered hinds . . .
>
> (lines 170–3)

Comus, himself, however, is far from being an obvious representation of Vice, so revolting that anyone would run in fear. He, like the Attendant Spirit, adopts the disguise of a shepherd, and is so well versed in the language of pastoral poetry that the Lady, played by young Alice Egerton, mistakes the convention for reality:

> *Comus*:   I know each lane, and every alley green
> Dingle, or bushy dell of this wild wood, . . .
> I can conduct you lady to a low
> But loyal cottage, where you may be safe
> Till further quest.
> *Lady*:   Shepherd I take thy word,
> And trust thy honest-offered courtesy,
> Which oft is sooner found in lowly sheds
> With smoky rafters, than in tap'stry halls
> And courts of princes, where it first was named,
> And yet is most pretended . . .
>
> (lines 310–26)

This comes close to being a dramatic parody of the pastoral convention, for the Lady is essentially saying that she recognises Comus as one of the honest, trusty shepherds from pastoral poetry and is therefore prepared to go with him.

In Milton's masque, therefore, the Lady not only has to encounter and overcome whatever dangers lie in the wood, but also pass through the illusion and the temptation of the masque-world itself. Comus relies upon 'blear illusion' (line 155) such as drama itself uses, but, whereas in other masques there is the danger that central figures will be forced to assume undignified or unseemly roles, Milton's Lady passes unscathed through her theatrical ordeal. The central theme of this masque is the triumph of the Lady over temptation, and we may wonder why it is that she is ever exposed to temptation at all, and why the Attendant Spirit does not arrange for the Lady and her brothers to avoid these dangers altogether. On a very simple level, of course, exposure to danger is vital because it provides the dynamic for the whole drama: if Comus is not encountered then there is no play. However, the necessity to encounter temptation and not merely to avoid it is also part of Milton's system of beliefs, which underpins his arguments for a free press and for religious toleration. As far as Milton is concerned it is essential that virtue and faith are constantly tested and reaffirmed by being exposed to evil and temptation. This is affirmed by the Elder Brother in *Comus*:

> Virtue may be assailed, but never hurt,
> Surprised by an unjust force, but not enthralled,
> Yea even that which mischief meant most harm
> Shall in the happy trial prove most glory.
>
> (lines 588–91)

and by Milton himself in *Areopagitica*, written shortly before the first version of *Comus* to bear Milton's name was published:

> I cannot praise a fugitive and cloistered virtue, unexercised and unbreathed, that never sallies out and seeks her adversary, but slinks out of the race, where that immortal garland is to be run for, not without dust and heat. Assuredly we bring not innocence into the world, we bring impurity much rather; that which purifies us is trial, and trial is by what is contrary.[23]

The virtue which is celebrated in *Comus* is chastity, not a 'fugitive and cloistered' doctrine of total sexual abstinence but the temperate channelling of passion through marriage. The choice for the Lady is not between succumbing to the seduction of Comus or entry into a nunnery: she has the option of moderation, and the exercise of temperance in this one respect is to be taken as representative of other instances, political, religious, and moral, when man must encounter temptation and choose for himself the right path. Although it would be unwise to treat *Comus* as specifically allegorical, there is no doubt that the journey through the wood and its successful conclusion are designed in part to make us reflect upon a journey through life, or a journey towards salvation, avoiding false religious dogma. In *Areopagitica* Milton paints a graphic portrait of the religious consequences of the failure to seek purification through trial:

> A wealthy man, addicted to his pleasure and to his profits, finds Religion to be a traffic so entangled . . . that of all mysteries he cannot skill to keep a stock going upon that trade . . . What does he

therefore, but resolve to give over toiling, and to find himself out some factor, to whose care and credit he may commit the whole managing of his religious affairs . . .[24]

The result of such an action would be to allow the priests total control over doctrinal matters, with the congregation merely appearing on Sundays to participate in ceremonies determined by others. This is not the action advocated in *Comus*, in which, even in the very business of watching a masque, the audience are reminded to take care of their souls:

Love Virtue, she alone is free,
She can teach ye how to climb
Higher than the sphery chime . . .

(lines 1018–20)

This particular group of wealthy men, as much addicted to their wealth and pleasures as those Milton wrote of in *Areopagitica* no doubt, are not flattered in this masque, despite elegant compliments to the Egertons. They are not given a comforting message that their wealth will assure them of salvation; on the contrary, they have to listen to this radical speech from the Lady:

If every just man that now pines with want
Had but a moderate and beseeming share
Of that which lewdly-pampered Luxury
Now heaps upon some few with vast excess,
Nature's full blessings would be well-dispensed
In unsuperfluous even proportion,
And she no whit encumbered with her store,
And then the giver would be better thanked,
His praise due paid, for swinish gluttony
Ne'er looks to heaven amidst his gorgeous feast,
But with besotted base ingratitude
Crams, and blasphemes his feeder.

(lines 767–78)

The sentiments of this passage are remarkably close to those expressed by Seneca in the passage from *Hippolytus* cited on p. 51 above. Their appearance in such an aristocratic form as the masque is unusual, to say the least.

It has been suggested that Milton was embarrassed at having written a masque, that this led to his refusal to put his name to the first edition, and that a quarrel may have arisen between the poet and his father.[25] There is slim evidence for any of this. We know tantalisingly little about that first performance, not even whether Milton himself was present, and nothing about further performances during the poet's lifetime. Milton failed to put his name to the first edition of 'Lycidas' as well, so an unnamed *Comus* is scarcely clear evidence of a desire to disown a work that might taint him as a Royalist sympathiser. The two parties could hardly be said to exist when the masque was first performed, but when, in 1645, the parties not only existed but had fought a war, Milton gladly acknowledged the masque as his own. The reason can only be that Milton felt that the masque expressed ideas on freedom, temperance, and self-respect which were entirely compatible with his prose writings in support of the Puritan cause. The central scene, the dispute between Comus and the Lady, expresses these values very evidently.

This scene is an exercise in the use of poetic convention, in which Milton allows Comus to use a tradition of great antiquity, but one which is undermined not only through the speeches of the Lady but by the very situation itself. The tradition, which derives from the Odes of the Roman poet Horace (65–8BC), notes the brevity of life and uses this as an argument for seduction. The tradition, known as *carpe diem* (seize the day), can be expressed within the pastoral mode, as in this lyric by the English poet Marlowe (1564–93):

> Come live with me and be my love,
> And we will all the pleasures prove,
> That valleys, groves, hills, and fields,
> Woods, or steepy mountain yields.
>
> ('The Passionate Shepherd to his Love')

or in this well-known example by Herrick (1591–1674):

> Gather ye rosebuds while ye may,
> Old time is still a-flying;
> And this same flower that smiles today
> Tomorrow will be dying.
>
> ('To the Virgins, to make Much of Time')

As isolated lyrics these appeals seem harmless enough, and may even appear convincing. However, their limitations were made evident in a number of ways. Ralegh (1552–1618) wrote a reply to the Marlowe poem, pointing out that it is not always spring and that old age and bitterness too quickly follow youth and love. Spenser includes a version of *carpe diem* in *The Faerie Queene*:

> Gather therefore the Rose, whilest yet is prime,
> For soone comes age, that will her pride deflowre;
> Gather the Rose of love, whilest yet is time,
> Whilest loving thou mayst loved be with equall crime.[26]

But this occurs in the final canto of Book II (The Book of Temperance) as an instance of the kind of seduction which the hero, Sir Guyon, must overcome in order to demonstrate his self-control: in this song love is a crime.

Both Shakespeare and Jonson (1572–1637) exploit the potential of setting a *carpe diem* lyric in a dramatic context. In *Twelfth Night* (1601) Shakespeare pokes gentle fun at the ridiculous, debauched Sir Toby and Sir Andrew by including a scene (II.iii) in which Feste, the jester, sings a song encouraging them not to let youth slip by: advice which is much too late to do them any good. Jonson's *Volpone* (1606) uses the convention in a way which most nearly anticipates Milton's practice in *Comus*, and which almost becomes sinister. Volpone, having lured Celia into his bedroom through a complicated intrigue by which she believes him to be nearly dying, suddenly leaps upon her, and accompanies his physical attack by singing a lyric in the *carpe diem* tradition:

> Come, my Celia, let us prove,
> While we can, the sports of love,
> Time will not be ours for ever,
> He, at length, our good will sever . . .
>
> (*Volpone*, II.vii)

Both Shakespeare and Jonson realised that lyrics which sound pleasant in isolation, or delivered by a young lover to his lady, could become either ludicrous or vicious in a different context.

Milton follows in the line of Shakespeare and Jonson in his use of *carpe diem* in *Comus*. His seducer is no young Leander using the tradition to persuade a girl who loves him already: Comus has physically imprisoned the Lady and has fixed her to her chair. It is the horror of that situation as much as the Lady's arguments for freedom of choice, which undermines Comus's assertion that

> If you let slip time, like a neglected rose,
> It withers on the stalk with languished head.
>
> (lines 742–3)

To surrender to the temptations of the arguments of *carpe diem* represented for Milton abandoning temperance, dignity, freedom of choice, and self-respect. The *carpe diem* tradition was also, incidentally, much used by the poets associated with the court of Charles I, of whom Herrick was one: Comus's defeat could, therefore, be seen as a defeat for Cavalier poetry.

It is obvious that Milton's *Comus* is a sophisticated example of the ways in which traditional modes and genres can be developed, sometimes in surprising directions. It also places great emphasis on the power of song, and therefore of poetry. Comus is almost won over before he even speaks to the Lady by the very beauty of her singing, and, when other remedies seem lost, the singing of Sabrina frees the Lady from her seat. Milton places his work in a larger context of poetry by referring to the classical legend of Circe in the opening speech, thus giving himself the status of a British Homer, and also by using Spenser's legend of Sabrina to provide the final solution, thus making himself Spenser's heir too. This is comparable to the allusions to Orpheus and to the great English poet Geoffrey Chaucer (1345–1400) in 'L'Allegro' and 'Il Penseroso': poetry is universal and Milton sees himself as part of a tradition which includes classical, European, and British poets. For Milton, allusion to poets implies his own inclusion in their ranks.

'Lycidas'

Of all the poems included in the 1645 anthology, none is more clearly an imitation of Spenser than 'Lycidas', which draws upon the May, October, and November eclogues of *The Shepheardes Calender* as well as upon the elegy *Astrophel* which Spenser wrote for Sir Philip Sidney. 'Lycidas' is also the most difficult of Milton's shorter poems, because of the number of conventions to which the reader must become attuned.

'Lycidas' is a pastoral elegy, a memorial to Edward King, a Cambridge Fellow who died in 1637 whilst crossing the Irish Sea. Since King was both a poet and training for holy orders, 'Lycidas' provides Milton with the opportunity to reflect upon poetry and the priesthood, and thus to make full use of the dual symbol of the shepherd. Milton's poem was given pride of place in the anthology of memorial verses published in 1637, and is markedly superior to the other poems which are included, not least in the way in which King's death is treated as the focus of other, wider issues.

The opening eight lines of 'Lycidas' give a foretaste of the subjects with which the poem is to be concerned, as well as the complexity of its operation. This introduction appears to be an *apologia*, in which the poet is reluctantly agreeing to write a poem before he feels himself ready. Thus, the lines seem to be concerned with Milton himself and the place of 'Lycidas' in his own poetic career: he is acknowledging the fact that the writing of this poem has broken into his period of preparation for the great poetry of which he felt himself capable. However, the image which Milton selects to convey this *apologia* allows him to weave another level of meaning into this introduction. He describes himself as a hand plucking berries which are as yet unripe: this is a perfectly appropriate image of the striving for the rewards of poetry whilst still unprepared, but it also evokes the sense of the poet as a death-like figure, bringing a premature end to these young plants. In this second sense Milton is matching his own actions with the death of Edward King: King was 'plucked' whilst still unripe, before he had reached his full maturity, his 'season due'. Milton's immature poem is therefore presented from the outset as a fitting memorial for the death of a young, unfulfilled poet, and the poem as a whole is to contain many examples of images of premature death.[27]

The major line of development within the poem is from the early assertion (line 8) that:

Lycidas is dead, dead ere his prime

to the consolation in line 166:

For Lycidas your sorrow is not dead

That consolation is derived from the argument that Lycidas has won salvation for himself through his goodness on earth, and involves the progressive development of three strands of images: those in which Milton argues that not all water is harmful; those associated with sinking and rising, and those associated with music.

These are the images which give the poem its unity and coherence, and which balance the tendency of the poem to become sectionalised. All three images occur in this passage (lines 10–14) which follows the *apologia*:

Who would not sing for Lycidas? he knew
Himself to sing, and build the lofty rhyme.
He must not float upon his watery bier
Unwept, and welter to the parching wind,
Without the meed of some melodious tear.

Lycidas himself is associated with music and must be commemorated through music, so that, although water brought about his death, the tears of mourning will be melodious. Moreover, although he now floats upon the surface, the rhymes of Lycidas were lofty, and this poem will ultimately effect his ascent:

So Lycidas sunk low, but mounted high,
Through the dear might of him that walked the waves;

(lines 172–3)

So far in this discussion of 'Lycidas' it has been assumed that Milton and the poet-figure are one and the same, and the movement of the poem encourages this association. Milton, like the poet-figure, is writing under compulsion: he knew King just as the poet-figure knew Lycidas, and shared the concerns with the relation between clergy and congregation which dominate the centre of the poem. Yet, in the closing lines of the poem, it becomes clear that this association has not been entirely true, because the first-person mode of address of the poet-figure gives way to this description:

> Thus sang the uncouth swain to the oaks and rills . . .
> At last he rose, and twitched his mantle blue . . .
>
> (lines 186, 192)

We have not, therefore, been listening to Milton directly at all, and the whole poem has been mediated through the Miltonic fiction of an 'uncouth swain'. This is not dissimilar to the device employed by Spenser in the November eclogue of *The Shepheardes Calender* in which the lament for Dido, sung by Colin, is embedded in a dialogue between Colin and Thenot. The significant difference is that the embedding is quite obvious in Spenser, whereas in 'Lycidas' we are unaware of it until the very end of the poem. It is, however, a necessary device, because the poem is not concerned only with the salvation of Lycidas but with larger contemporary issues. Whilst complimentary references to Cambridge and to tutors there may have been safe enough within the pastoral convention,[28] Milton's attack on the clergy, put into the mouth of St Peter, might have needed the extra protection of the fictional swain.

In this section of the poem (lines 113-31), Milton develops for St Peter a distinctive voice quite different from the other characters who speak in the poem, drawing upon the dramatic skill which he had used in *Comus*, and anticipating the technique of *Samson Agonistes*. St Peter's tone is angry and bitter, and is expressed in short, pithy words, mostly of Anglo-Saxon origin:

> What recks it them? What need they? They are sped;
> And when they list, their lean and flashy songs
> Grate on their scrannel pipes of wretched straw . . .
>
> (lines 122–4)

What Milton is attacking in the clergy is not their particular doctrinal position, nor even the fact that their ceremonies seemed dangerously close to those of the Roman Catholic Church. He is attacking their greed, their intolerance, and their failure to guide their congregrations adequately. Their lack of care, and their lack of music, is in marked contrast to the earlier description of the life of the true shepherds, in tune with nature and looking after their flocks:

> we were nursed upon the self-same hill,
> Fed the same flock; by fountain, shade, and rill . . .
>   both together heard

What time the grey-fly winds her sultry horn,
Battening our flocks with the fresh dews of night . . .

(lines 23–9)

The attack on the clergy comes in the middle of the poem, however, not at its climax.[29] Despite the corruption of the clergy, it is still possible for Lycidas and for other individuals to win salvation, through a personal faith in Jesus Christ (line 173), and through living one's life as a 'true poem' (see p. 46 above). The temptation to give up this life and to choose instead a less rigorous one (represented by elegiac poetry, line 69) is rejected early in the poem: salvation is made to depend directly upon good deeds on earth:

As he [Jove] pronounces lastly on each deed,
Of so much fame in heaven expect thy meed.

(lines 83–4)

At the outset of the poem, Milton, in the guise of the 'uncouth swain', anticipates his own death and hopes:

So may some gentle muse
With lucky words favour my destined urn,
And as he passes turn,
And bid fair peace be to my sable shroud.

(lines 19–22)

To some extent Dryden performed this task in comparing Milton to Virgil and Homer in the edition of *Paradise Lost* produced by Jacob Tonson (1656–1736) in 1688. Ironically, however, it is a poem by William Cowper (1731–1800) in 1790 which most nearly approaches the spirit of 'Lycidas', and which begins with a translation of three lines from Milton's Latin poem 'Mansus'. This poem by Cowper does not commemorate Milton's death; it is a complaint about the desecration of his grave in St Giles's, Cripplegate.[30]

Latin and Italian poems

Among the Latin and Italian poems in the 1645 collection, three are of special interest: the elegies to Diodati and Thomas Young ('Elegia Prima' and 'Elegia Quarta') and the Italian Sonnet IV.

'Elegia Prima' was probably written in the spring of 1626, and gives a clear indication of Milton's zest for life. Not only is he pleased to have the friendship of Charles Diodati, but he also revels in the delights of London, its theatres, its books, and its girls. This poem confirms the impression given in 'L'Allegro' and 'Il Penseroso' that Milton not only approved of the theatre but was himself a keen theatre-goer. Milton describes the ingredients of typical comedies and tragedies, ending the section on tragedy with the tender lines:

> Often, too, there is a young girl who is surprised by a warmth of feeling she never felt before, and falls in love without knowing what love is.[31]

In contrast, the concerns of 'Elegia Quarta' are indicative of Milton's early political interests. The elegy, written in 1627, is addressed to his former tutor Thomas Young, who was at that time living with the English protestant exiles in Hamburg. Milton deplores the intolerance of Puritanism which has forced men of conscience to emigrate:

> O native country, hard-hearted parent, more cruel than the white cliffs of your coastline, battered by foaming waves, is it fitting that you should expose your innocent children in this way? Is this the way you treat them, iron-hearted land, driving them onto foreign soil and allowing them to search for their food on distant shores, when God Himself has sent them to you in His providence; when they bring joyful news to you from heaven . . .[32]

As early as 1627 Milton was writing of England as a chosen nation, uniquely favoured by God to carry through the Reformation to its ultimate conclusion. He was also, however, indicating that he had misgivings about the ability of that nation to undertake that task:

> You really deserve to live shut up in hellish darkness and to die of a never-ending hunger of the soul!

Spiritual ignorance is represented here as darkness (like the 'blind mazes' of the wood in *Comus*, and the tangled wood of doctrinal dispute in *Of True Religion*), and the absence of an adequate clergy represented by hunger (as in 'Lycidas'). Ironically, Young himself did not remain true to what Milton regarded as the true spirit of Puritanism, and the two seem to have ended their friendship in the mid-1640s.

Sonnet IV, probably written late in 1629, is a delightful example of what Milton was able to achieve whilst working within an established convention. It is impossible to know whether Milton really had fallen in love with a beautiful girl, or whether he was simply imagining himself in that situation in order to explore this poetic convention. He certainly draws not only upon situations from Petrarchan sonnets, but also upon techniques from Shakespeare's plays and poems. The sonnet is addressed not directly to the lady, but to his friend, Diodati, and thus the poem becomes an opportunity for the poet to unburden himself and to confess that he appreciates how ridiculous he must appear. Diodati's role is merely to listen to this confession and the sonnet is, therefore, similar to a soliloquy in a play where the character reveals his personal feelings to the audience. It is strikingly similar to this passage from Shakespeare's *Love's Labour's Lost* (1594) spoken by Berowne, a young man who has also made a habit of scorning love and laughing at its snares:

> And I, forsooth, in love; I, that have been love's whip;
> A very beadle to a humorous sigh; . . .
> What! I love, I sue, I seek a wife . . .
> And I to sigh for her! to watch for her!
> To pray for her!
>
> (II.i)

Like Berowne, Milton has not fallen in love with a conventional beauty, but with one who expresses a 'new idea of loveliness', and the sonnet examines with wit and delicacy exactly how this new beauty has overcome him.

Milton's prose

It is possible to write intelligently and sensitively about Milton's poetic achievement without making reference to his prose, but it would be dangerous to assume that such an account could deal adequately with the development of Milton's ideas. There is a real difficulty in establishing Milton's political and religious opinions from his poetry alone, and not merely because the precise dating of the poetry is problematic (although that obviously does present a problem in an age when ideas could become outmoded so rapidly). The principal difficulty is in penetrating the conventions and the *personae* adopted by the poet, which intervene between the reader and the ideas of the writer. In a novel by Iris Murdoch, a critic misleads his student by suggesting that Shakespeare's sonnets are autobiographical: that kind of critical blindness can lead to similar distortions in the interpretation of Milton's poetry. We cannot assume that, because Milton wrote poems about his love for a girl called Emilia, such a love and such a girl actually existed. Without Milton's private correspondence we might assume that his poetic statements on blindness are to be taken as representing the truth of his feelings, and that he accepted his lot with equanimity: the letters tell a different story.

If we cannot take Milton's autobiographical references in his poems at their face value, then interpreting his political allusions is all the more difficult. In his major poems in particular he is constantly alluding to contemporary historical, political and ecclesiastical issues but his major task lies elsewhere, in the telling of a fable, and a fable with a non-contemporary setting. Whatever Milton may appear to be saying about political loyalties in *Samson Agonistes*, or about the role of individual endeavour in the pursuit of salvation, the world which he is describing within the poem is an Old Testament world in which a different standard of behaviour obtained from that of his own day, and in which certain modes of thought and action were unavailable. A.N. Wilson points out that Milton was well aware that it was simply impossible to 'live now in the new dispensation as the patriarchs lived in the time before the old law was established'.[33]

Milton observes a fundamental distinction between what was once possible:

> prime Nature made us all equall, made us all coheirs by common right and dominion over all creatures.[34]

and the inequalities imposed by God on Man after the Fall:

> hee suffer'd propriety to divide all things by severall possession, trade and commerce, not without usury . . . some to bee undeservedly rich, others to be undeservingly poore.[35]

In the face of this distinction, studies of the political organisation of the angels in *Paradise Lost* in terms of seventeenth-century groups appear unconvincing. It is for this reason, if for no other, that the study of Milton's prose is so significant in determining the development of his thought and in providing a context for his poetry. Although we cannot rely absolutely and in every case upon the prose tracts to give objective information about Milton's beliefs, they are often more revealing than the poems.

The study of Milton's prose is difficult, not least because the works themselves are not readily available. A cheap anthology cannot include all of Milton's major prose, and may include only one or two pieces at their full length. Some editions lack adequate footnotes and thus, given the range of allusions in the tracts, are almost incomprehensible. Historians of the English Revolution have done much to illuminate the study of Milton's prose, both in elucidating the meaning of individual passages and in setting the tracts in the context of contemporary thinking and opinion. What this work, together with that of scholars such as Wolfe, Barker and Parker, has revealed is that Milton's prose was neither particularly successful in its own day nor politically brilliant. Too often, Milton's views were misinterpreted by his contemporaries, and the causes which he defended were either unpopular (such as his defence of regicide) or not central political issues of the day (for example, he chose to write on divorce and on freedom from censorship when the principal political issue was the effort of the Presbyterians to establish an orthodoxy).

As a political thinker Milton was limited, ironically, by his own desire to be politically involved. He could not keep out of the fray of controversial pamphleteering, and was not therefore able to refine and develop a consistent political philosophy. Whilst others were able to retire from public life in order to produce considered statements of their views, Milton was constantly in print, defending his causes, or himself, from some new attack. As a recent critic has pointed out, Milton's presentation of his political views in the *Second Defence* suggests a greater consistency in the development of his thinking than is there in practice.

Milton's prose is an odd mixture of visionary idealism and personal interest. On the one hand, he looked forward to an ideal state, considering history in the long view and refusing to write on the day-to-day politics of his time. On the other, he tended to emphasise issues which touched him personally, whether or not these issues were in the centre of current debate. He may or may not have been writing about Mary Powell in the divorce tracts, or about the suppression of those tracts in *Areopagitica*, but the issues of divorce and a free press were certainly not those which were dividing the country in 1644. This is one of the respects in which fictional accounts of Milton's life fall so wide of the mark. Their writers wish to make Milton famous among his contemporaries and, if they cannot depict him as a famous poet, they will cast him as a central political figure of the 1640s, whose advice was sought by all leading Parliamentarians. This is truer of Milton's opponent Salmasius than it is of the poet himself.

In an early prose tract, Milton looked forward to a time when he would have the attention of his readers, with no distractions:

> I may one day hope to have ye in a still time, when there shall be no chiding; not in these noises, the adversary, as ye know, barking at the door . . .[36]

There was never to be such an opportunity and, after the earliest of the anti-prelatical tracts, in which we can feel confident that we are reading the measured and objective opinions of the writer, his prose all too often obscures those views and veers between brilliant reasoning and personal abuse of his opponents. We are increasingly aware that the later prose tracts are conditioned, either in that Milton is driven to respond to a particular attack, or that he feels the need to present himself as especially respectable in order to win his audience to his side.

Given these constraints which impinged upon Milton's prose, it is scarcely adequate to talk about his 'prose style' as if it were uniform and unchanging over the thirty years in which he was a controversialist. His prose needed to be flexible and adaptable to meet the range of purposes for which it was to be employed, all the more so since Milton himself frequently attacked his opponents by attacking their style. In *An Apology*, for example, he expresses regret that the cause which he supported

> should thus lie at the mercy of a coy flirting style; to be girded with frumps and curtal gibes by one who makes sentences by the statute, as if all above three inches long were confiscate.[37]

Elsewhere he attacks the repetition and foreignness of the diction of his opponents. Milton's own preference is for lengthy sentences (although a recent study of his prose suggests that this was not unusual among contemporary pamphleteers), through which he could convey complex argument and also give the impression that he had thoroughly considered his position before committing pen to paper.[38] The opening sentence of *Of Reformation*, for example, is almost one hundred and fifty words long, and is a careful introduction which suggests that the reader is a God-fearing Christian, receptive to Milton's argument, that he is willing to think deeply about his faith, and not merely accept what he is told to think, and that the Reformation of the Church has followed a similar course to the career of Christ himself.

Although Milton may have favoured this kind of prose, especially in the opening sections of his pamphlets, he could write much more crisply to condemn an opponent, and, when occasion demanded, succinctly sum up his argument in a single phrase. Thus, in defending the principle of regicide in *The Tenure of Kings and Magistrates*, he writes:

> it is not, neither ought to be, the glory of a protestant state never to have put their king to death; it is the glory of a protestant king never to have deserved death.[39]

Thomas Corns's study of the development of Milton's prose style has revealed that the brilliance of the early tracts, with their striking imagery and wide range of diction (much of it invented by Milton himself) gives way to a plainer, more repetitive style in the later pamphlets, lacking this kind of vivid description of the dangers of episcopacy:

> that before all our eyes worsens and slugs the most learned and seeming religious of our ministers, who no sooner advance to it, but, like a seething pot set to cool, sensibly exhale the reek out the greatest part of that zeal and those gifts which were formerly in them, settling in a skinny congealment of ease and sloth at the top; and if they keep their learning by some potent sway of nature, it is a rare chance, but their devotion most commonly comes to that queazy temper of lukewarmness, that gives a vomit to God himself.[40]

One particular change which Corns emphasises is that Milton's citation of biblical quotations becomes much more rigorous and systematic. This is no doubt connected with developments both in Milton's thinking and in the reception of his pamphlets. He assumed in his early pamphlets that the Scriptures provided such clear support for his viewpoint that accurate citation was unnecessary. However, when he came to write on divorce, he found that the New Testament did not seem to say what he wanted it to say, and he was thus forced to use his Bible much more carefully, especially when accused by his opponents of advocating ungodly behaviour.

Recent criticism of Milton's poetry is taking increasing account of the context provided by the prose, not only in illuminating the early poems, but also in charting the course of his developing religious ideas. Earlier critics assumed that Milton's break with the Presbyterians at the time of his divorce tracts was the only turning point worth recording, or that his progressive lack of confidence in 'the people' as a whole could be seen as a political development devoid of religious connotations. Within the last decade, however, critics and historians have come to realise how much the prose tracts reveal of Milton's move towards Arminianism and away from the Calvinist belief in election. When God's chosen people have apparently failed in their revolution, explanation must be sought in political and religious terms to account for this failure. Milton finds this in increasing emphasis on the need for virtuous behaviour, and this has significant implications for the interpretation of Milton's major poems.[41]

Of all Milton's prose works, the most celebrated is *Areopagitica*, addressed to Parliament in 1644 as a plea for unlicensed printing. This pamphlet, parts of which have already been quoted above, incorporates many of Milton's central tenets: the danger of accepting customary practices without question; the need to be purified through the trial of temptation; the potential for Reformation in England; and the role of choice and reason in freedom. The general nature of the subject matter of *Areopagitica* has led to its frequent citation by later writers working in support of liberty, as W.R. Parker remarks: 'After more than three centuries of continuing struggle for freedom of the written word, the steady admiration of humanity has placed Milton's *Areopagitica* above my praise'.[42] Such passages as the following are memorable, impressive and appealing:

> unless wariness be used, as good almost kill a man as kill a good book. Who kills a man kills a reasonable creature, God's image; but he who destroys a good book, kills reason itself, kills the image of God, as it were in the eye. Many a man lives a burden to the earth; but a good book is the precious life-blood of a master spirit, embalmed and treasured up on purpose to a life beyond life.[43]

Areopagitica is also a powerful supporting document for the study of *Paradise Lost*, dealing as it does with the nature of good and evil, and one recent edition of the poem includes extracts from *Areopagitica* in its appendix.[44] However, it is worth tempering enthusiasm for the evident strengths of this tract with the consideration that even this, the pamphlet most praised by posterity, was politically ineffective, and that the Parliamentary Order against which it was arguing continued to be enforced.

Paradise Lost

Composition and publication

At the beginning of Book IX of *Paradise Lost* Milton refers to the time he has spent in selecting a subject for his epic:

long choosing, and beginning late;
Not sedulous by nature to indite
Wars, hitherto the only argument
Heroic deemed . . .

(IX. 26-9)

When Milton was only twenty years old he had composed a poem for an undergraduate audience in which he had expressed his intention to write of 'kings and queens and heroes old' ('At a Vacation Exercise', line 47) and thus combine two of the prime objectives of a Renaissance poet: to excel in a classical genre, and to employ his own vernacular language. Some ten years later, in his Latin poem 'Mansus', Milton specifically identifies the story of King Arthur as his intended epic subject:

if ever I bring back to life in my songs the kings of my native land, and Arthur, who set wars raging even under the earth, or tell of the great-hearted heroes of the round table . . .[45]

Although the plan to write about Arthur may have been abandoned quite early in Milton's career, his reference in *The Reason of Church Government* (1641) to a search for a 'king or knight, before the conquest' who might be chosen to 'lay the pattern of a Christian hero' strongly suggests that Milton harboured for a long time the notion of writing a national epic very much along the lines of Spenser's *Faerie Queene*. *Paradise Lost*, however, is far from being a national epic; it specifically condemns earlier epics which took warfare as their subject, and it has puzzled readers for centuries by apparently having for its hero Satan, the enemy of God and mankind.

We know little of the composition of *Paradise Lost*, and cannot even be sure whether Milton wrote the epic sequentially from beginning to end, or whether he had already completed what are now the central books before composing the description of the fallen angels in Hell. One of Milton's early biographers, Edward Phillips, claims to have seen a speech by Satan (now IV.32–41) some years before the publication of *Paradise Lost*, intended by Milton to comprise part of a tragic drama, and there is a manuscript extant containing drafts for such a tragedy which probably dates from 1640. Nevertheless, despite the fact that the greater part of the composition of *Paradise Lost* must have taken place after Milton became totally blind, and would therefore have involved his dictating passages to a number of amanuenses, the details of that process remain a matter for speculation.

The poem was published as an epic in ten books in 1667, and shows evidence of having been carefully checked by its author, despite his blindness. After the first three issues of this edition, some preliminary material was added, including a statement from the Printer (Samuel Simmons) to the Reader, the Argument (Milton's prose summary of the narrative line of the epic), and an explanation by the poet of his decision to use blank verse rather than rhyme. A second edition appeared a few months before Milton's death in 1674, and this has come to be regarded as the definitive text for modern editions. It includes poems by Samuel Barrow (1625–82) and Andrew Marvell in praise of *Paradise Lost*, and redistributes the epic into twelve books, with the Argument split into twelve sections to precede each individual book. Barrow's verse, less frequently quoted than that of Marvell, observes that Satan 'walks hardly less great than Michael himself' and asks why any reader should read *Paradise Lost* without reading it in its entirety. It might be claimed, therefore, with some justice, that Barrow began the critical debate over *Paradise Lost* (see Part 4 below) and that there was a Milton controversy even before Milton's death.

Triumphal action

Milton believed himself to be a divinely inspired writer, and had imagined himself from his youth capable of employing that inspiration in a magnificent and celebratory work. Although the epic which he eventually wrote declares itself to be concerned with the disobedience, and hence the folly, of man, it also predicts the restoration of mankind through the sacrifice of the Son, and can thus claim to incorporate a subject which is both tragic and majestic:

> I thence
> Invoke thy aid to my adventurous song,

That with no middle flight intends to soar
Above the Aonian mount, while it pursues
Things unattempted yet in prose or rhyme.

(I.12–16)

The originality of Milton's poem is considerable: earlier poems had included descriptions of infernal regions, and there is a poem on the subject of the fallen angels which dates from the tenth century. *Paradise Lost*, however, encompasses not only Hell, but also Eden, Heaven, and all the regions between. Even Spenser, the greatest English epic poet before Milton, had felt that the description of Heaven was too demanding a task:

earthly tong
Cannot describe, nor wit of man can tell;
Too high a ditty for my simple song . . .

(*The Faerie Queene*. I,x,55)

Milton, however, does not shy away from the task, and there are constant reminders of his engagement with the problems posed by this undertaking. For example, in the Argument to Book I, Milton draws attention to the fact that he has placed Hell 'not in the centre', because he is aware that he must avoid the logical flaw of locating Hell in relation to the earth which has not yet been created, let alone accursed; similar instances of his attention to the logical and theological implications of the details of his descriptions can be found throughout the poem.

The Hell of *Paradise Lost* is presented initially from the viewpoint of Satan:

At once as far as angels' ken he views
The dismal situation waste and wild,
A dungeon horrible, on all sides round
As one great furnace flamed, yet from those flames
No light, but rather darkness visible
Served only to discover sights of woe . . .

(I.59–64)

However, although Satan is able to perceive the misery of this location, he still attempts to argue in the opening books of the poem that the situation is not really so bad, and Milton allows us to be swayed by these arguments, and to be impressed by the apparent magnificence of the structure which the fallen angels can build in Hell:

Anon out of the earth a fabric huge
Rose like an exhalation, with the sound
Of dulcet symphonies and voices sweet,

> Built like a temple, where pilasters round
> Were set, and Doric pillars overlaid
> With golden architrave . . .
>
> (I.710–15)

This magnificence is entirely superficial, however, much like the splendour which Milton disapproved of in some of the churches of the day.[46] In both cases, the effort which had gone into the construction of the building masked the uncertainties of those who met within. Whatever the fallen angels might attempt to build in Hell, it remains Hell, and they remain conscious of what they have lost. Although they debate in public about the possible alternatives which the future may hold, they are constantly aware, as we are, of their own ignorance. They have experienced the wrath of God, but have no idea what the full extent of that wrath might be, or what their own capacity might be to withstand that wrath. The opening books become an index to the terrible power of imagination, in which the fallen angels, having lost the certainty and security of the love of God, attempt to predict the future on the basis of their experience of the war in Heaven. Satan's first exchange with Beelzebub indicates the delusions harboured by the fallen angels. Beelzebub suggests that God might have left them alive:

> Strongly to suffer and support our pains,
> That we may so suffice his vengeful ire,
> Or do him mightier service as his thralls . . .
>
> (I.147–9)

Satan, on the other hand, imagines that this respite in the war, which may or may not be permanent, can only be the outcome of God's malice:

> Let us not slip the occasion, whether scorn,
> Or satiate fury yield it from our foe.
>
> (I.178–9)

Neither of them can conceive of the possibility of repentance or of God's forgiveness, and thus, whilst they might disagree over the details of how God's malice might manifest itself, there is no real dispute of principle between them.

This is one of the ironies of the brilliant debate in Pandemonium in Book II: the speakers are sharply delineated, each a memorable individual in his own right, and yet the debate is not really a debate at all, since no advocate of God's mercy emerges. Thus the argument between Moloc, Belial, and Mammon about the merits or disadvantages of open warfare against Heaven, is essentially hollow, since none of the speakers can imagine God in any role other than that of antagonist. Each of the speeches includes a reference to God which clarifies the speaker's attitude to Him. Moloc speaks of:

> Turning our tortures into horrid arms
> Against the torturer . . .

> (II.63–4)

Belial is uncertain whether God can grant the fallen angels the peace of death, but convinced that He will not use such a power for their good, if he possesses it:

> who knows,
> Let this be good, whether our angry foe
> Can give it, or will ever? How he can
> Is doubtful; that he never will is sure.

> (II.151–4)

He imagines a God who is thoroughly spiteful and vengeful:

> He from heaven's highth
> All these our motions vain, sees and derides;
> Not more almighty to resist our might
> Than wise to frustrate all our plots and wiles.

> (II.190–3)

Mammon, like the other speakers, avoids naming God directly, preferring instead to describe Him by some negative epithet:

> while he lordly sits
> Our envied sovereign, and his altar breathes
> Ambrosial odours and ambrosial flowers,
> Our servile offerings?

> (II.243–6)

Our impression of this debate is likely to be further undermined when we realise that its entire shape has been contrived by Satan, in association with Beelzebub, to win for Satan the false glory of volunteering to ruin mankind. The debate has offered no alternative to hatred of God, based as it is upon His imagined tyranny. Hell is therefore presented as a state of mind in *Paradise Lost*, as Satan himself comes close to admitting in the opening book:

> The mind is its own place, and in itself
> Can make a heaven of hell, a hell of heaven.

> (I.254–5)

and he comes to realise the consequence of this definition as he approaches Eden in Book IV: he is not out of Hell, however far away it may physically be:

Which way I fly is hell; my self am hell;
And in the lowest deep a lower deep
Still threatening to devour me opens wide,
To which the hell I suffer seems a heaven.

(IV.75–8)

Nevertheless, this emphasis upon the internal torment suffered by Satan is not used by Milton as a way of avoiding physical description, either in Hell or outside of it. Satan's descent to Hell is described with both force and economy.

Him the almighty power
Hurled headlong flaming from the ethereal sky
With hideous ruin and combustion down
To bottomless perdition . . .

(I.44–7)

The alliteration and the rhythm combine here with a striking inversion of conventional word-order to make this a particularly memorable passage.

Satan's voyage to Eden includes within it further opportunities to describe other locations, one of which is turned by Milton to satiric and comic effect:

then might ye see
Cowls, hoods and habits with their wearers tossed
And fluttered into rags, then relics, beads,
Indulgences, dispenses, pardons, bulls,
The sport of winds: all these upwhirled aloft
Fly o'er the backside of the world far off
Into a limbo large and broad . . .

(III.489–95)

He chooses to list the various items associated with Roman Catholicism, in order to emphasise the extent of its involvement with ceremony and ritual, and then to end the descriptions with the anticlimax of these items disappearing over the 'backside of the world', as worthless as toilet paper.

One particularly vivid example of Milton's use of magnificent descriptive effects occurs at the end of Book IV when Satan is given a warning of his ultimate defeat:

The eternal to prevent such horrid fray
Hung forth in heaven his golden scales, yet seen
Betwixt Astrea and the Scorpion sign,
Wherein all things created first he weighed,
The pendulous round earth with balanced air

In counterpoise, now ponders all events,
Battles and realms: in these he put two weights
The sequel each of parting and of fight;
The latter quick up flew, and kicked the beam . . .

                                                                (IV.996–1004)

The gradual increase in the seriousness of this description, as we learn of the significance of the golden scales, gives way to the speed of the final line: parting and fight are not even approximately equal courses for Satan, since fighting is demonstrably hopeless.

Although the examples selected above come from the early books of *Paradise Lost*, similar instances could be cited from all sections of the epic. Book XI, for example, includes the vision of the lazar-house presented by Michael to Adam:

Dire was the tossing, deep the groans, despair
Tended the sick busiest from couch to couch;
And over them triumphant death his dart
Shook, but delayed to strike, though oft invoked
With vows, as their chief good, and final hope.
Sight so deform what heart of rock could long
Dry-eyed behold? Adam could not, but wept . . .

                                                                (XI.489–95)

Adam's reaction is unsurprising in the light of this fine and affecting description. Appropriately, this vision is presented as an allegorical portrait in the manner of Spenser's *The Faerie Queene*, and it has proved an inspiration for later illustrators of Milton.

Milton's sense of the appropriateness of verbal effect is particularly evident on those occasions when we expect a dramatic event only to find that its absence is even more impressive. For example, by the time Eve reaches to take the fruit in Book IX, our attention has become entirely focused upon serpent, fruit and woman, so that the larger reaction to her sin comes as a surprise:

So saying, her rash hand in evil hour
Forth reaching to the fruit, she plucked, she ate:
Earth felt the wound, and nature from her seat
Sighing through all her works gave signs of woe,
That all was lost.

                                                                (IX.780–4)

Another poet might have gone much further with this indication of the universal implication of Eve's action, but Milton leaves it underplayed, so that Eve is not brought too quickly to a realisation of her guilt, and so that we can concentrate upon the immediate protagonists. The sighing of the Earth gives way to the fate of the serpent: 'Back to the thicket slunk/The guilty serpent' (IX.784–5). Eve's absorption is so extreme that she notices neither the sighing of the Earth nor the departure of the serpent. For the reader, however, these two very different events serve to emphasis the significance of this moment.

As a final instance of Milton's skill in manipulating the reaction of the reader, we might consider the description of the scene which ought to have been Satan's greatest triumph, his announcement to the fallen angels of his victory over mankind. Satan's speech moves to a rousing climax, and the reaction he provokes is as unexpected to the reader as it is to Satan himself.

> So having said, a while he stood, expecting
> Their universal shout and high applause
> To fill his ear, when contrary he hears
> On all sides, from innumerable tongues
> A dismal universal hiss, the sound
> Of public scorn . . .
>
> (X.504–9)

On the earlier public occasions in Hell, the audience of fallen angels have been led by the specious logic of Satan's rhetoric to applaud unworthy actions. On this occasion they are similarly powerless, but this time through the direct intervention of God, who has seemed to be absent from the epic for two books, which affects Satan no less than the other fallen angels:

> he wondered, but not long
> Had leisure, wondering at himself now more;
> His visage drawn he felt to sharp and spare,
> His arms clung to his ribs, his legs entwining
> Each other, till supplanted down he fell
> A monstrous serpent on his belly prone,
> Reluctant, but in vain, a greater power
> Now ruled him . . .
>
> (X.509–16)

In a work which deals so much in free will and choice, this manifestation of the power of God is all the more striking.

Milton's Heaven is defined less by its physical details than by its security and harmony, in sharp contrast to the uncertainty in Hell. The angels in Heaven do not have their reactions moulded and swayed by a persuasive orator: they produce spontaneously the harmony of worship which Milton had associated with Heaven in 'Lycidas' and in his first prose tract, *Of Reformation*:[47]

> The multitude of angels with a shout
> Loud as from numbers without number, sweet

As from blest voices, uttering joy, heaven rung
With jubilee, and loud hosannas filled
The eternal regions . . .

(III.345–9)

Thus the ordering of the books in the epic leads the reader from the hatred of Hell to the harmony of Heaven, and ultimately to the pastoral innocence of Eden and the love of Adam and Eve. One of Milton's greatest challenges is to write of this innocence in a manner which does not suggest naivety, and he accomplishes this by carefully establishing a context of order and tranquillity around his central protagonists:

to their supper fruits they fell,
Nectarine fruits which the compliant boughs
Yielded them, sidelong as they sat recline
On the soft downy bank damasked with flowers;
The savoury pulp they chew, and in the rind
Still as they thirsted scoop the brimming stream;
. . . About them frisking played
All beasts of the earth, since wild, and of all chase . . .

(IV.331–41)

Whereas the description of the lazar-house could be straightforwardly translated into a visual representation, there are details of this passage which can only be adequately expressed through a verbal medium. The very branches of this garden co-operate with Adam and Eve, yielding them fruit compliantly, just as the ground and the stream provide their own comforts. The description as a whole is powerfully suggestive of harmony, peace and order, a perfect context for Milton's hymn to love:

Hail wedded love, mysterious law, true source
Of human offspring, sole propriety
In Paradise of all things common else . . .
Here Love his golden shafts employs, here lights
His constant lamp, and waves his purple wings,
Reigns here and revels . . .

(IV.750–65)

Thus Milton is able to deploy a variety of different styles to equal effect, from descriptions of magnificent grandeur to quiet lyricism, from persuasive rhetoric to hymns of faith.

On a larger scale, he shows a particular skill in ordering the various episodes which together comprise the epic. Satan's temptation of Eve, for example, the central and climactic incident in the poem, is carefully prepared for. By the time that Satan arrives in Eden in Book IV he has already been proved a skilful and persuasive rhetorician: not only has he dealt with the meeting of the fallen angels in Pandemonium, he has also encountered Sin and Death, and Uriel, thereby displaying his cunning, bravura, and guile. However, having whetted the appetite of the reader in this manner, Milton delays the temptation until Book IX, and the impetus of the principal narrative line seems to be suspended. Yet those readers who feel frustrated at those middle books fail to appreciate the contribution made by those books, not least to the development of the characterisation of Satan. Milton contrives, firstly, to isolate Satan in Eden, and to give him, apparently, the time and opportunity to choose whether to pursue his plan to ruin mankind. Satan's three soliloquies, two in Book IV and one in Book IX, indicate even more clearly than his public speeches in Hell the extent of his confusion, and yet his final resolution remains to destroy the happiness of Adam and Eve. Furthermore, in the midst of this inner conflict within the mind of Satan, a conflict which is made to seem independent of any intervention from God, Milton places the visit of Raphael, whose account of the war in Heaven allows the reader another perspective on the character of Satan. In this account Satan emerges not merely as proud and rebellious, but his struggle against God looks petty, futile and laborious, and thus calls into question his strategy against Adam and Eve. By delaying the impetus of the central narrative in these middle books, therefore, Milton is able to counterpoint Satan's own mental conflict with the larger narrative of Raphael, and thus to juxtapose the war in Heaven, the creation of the Earth, and the fall of man in successive books in the middle of his epic.

Epic and history

Two writers of very different temperaments, united in their dislike of Milton, have provided similar statements on the relationship between epic and history. Samuel Johnson wrote in 1783 that an epic

> relates some great event in the most affecting manner. History must supply the writer with the rudiments of narration, which he must improve and exalt by a nobler art, animate by dramatic energy, and diversify, by retrospection and anticipation.[48]

The American poet Ezra Pound in 1961 put the same idea more succinctly: 'An epic is a poem including history'.[49] The notion of this link between epic form and historical content is one which has persisted from the beginnings of the genre through to the current use of the term epic in popular prose: a novel such as *Gone with the Wind* or *East of Eden* will be labelled 'epic', not merely because of its length but because it embraces a wide sweep of history and because its central characters are to be regarded somehow as representative of the particular stratum of society. Even when the term is used of a sporting encounter, a soccer match which remains unresolved after two replays or a fifteen-round heavyweight boxing contest, it is not length alone that leads to this usage, but the suggestion that this event has been memorable enough to merit a place in the folk-mythology of the town or country of which the protagonists are representative.

Traditionally, the epic has a historical subject, which implies that it is written to celebrate the past triumphs of a nation or tribe, and a central hero, who is representative of that race. Alexander Pope, writing a parody of a definition for the epic, neatly summarises its essentials:

> Take out of any old Poem, History-books, Romances, or Legend ... those Parts of Story which afford most Scope for long Descriptions ... Then take a Hero, whom you may chuse for the Sound of his Name, and put him into the midst of these Adventures: There let him *work*, for twelve Books;
>
>   *For the Moral and Allegory.* These you may Extract out of the Fable afterwards at your Leisure: Be sure you strain them sufficiently.[50]

and yet Milton dismisses the kind of epic based upon historical adventure constantly throughout *Paradise Lost*: that has become, for him, mere 'fable', a term which Milton tends to employ pejoratively. Milton has chosen not to follow the example of European poets like Camoens (1524–80) who, in *Os Lusiadas*, celebrated the history of the Portuguese people, nor that of Spenser's *Faerie Queene*, a panegyric for the England of Elizabeth I. Milton is employing poetry in his epic not to celebrate history but to explain it, and, at times to suggest that the interpretation of recent events by his contemporaries was flawed. In part, however, Milton's reasons for selecting a subject for his poem not drawn from English history would be similar to those of Cowley, who wrote in the preface to his own epic on the life of David (1656):

> It is not without grief and indignation that I behold that *Divine Science* (*Poesie*) employing all her inexhaustible riches ... in the wicked and beggerly *Flattery* of great persons.[51]

The traditional epic implied an association between the aspirations of the poet and that of the nation which he was celebrating and, as in the case of *The Faerie Queene*, could hardly avoid some measure of flattery of the head of that nation. Milton could not, therefore, compose a traditional epic after the failure of his hopes for a revolution: the English nation of the Restoration was not a possible subject for his celebration, and thus his epic sets out to denigrate traditional notions of nationhood and individual achievement:

in those days might only shall be admired,
And valour and heroic virtue called;
To overcome in battle, and subdue
Nations, and bring home spoils with infinite
Manslaughter, shall be held the highest pitch
Of human glory . . .
Destroyers rightlier called and plagues of men . . .

(XI.689–97)

This is a radical redefinition of the central concern of traditional epics, the victory in battle of one race over another: this is, in Milton's terms, manslaughter and destruction, and therefore no true heroism. Milton's epic differs from Spenser's not simply because it succeeds it in time and is therefore able to build upon it, nor even because Milton is a better poet than Spenser (although few would dispute that he is), but because the social and historical changes which had occurred between Spenser's time and that of Milton made it impossible for Milton to develop the epic within the Spenserian nationalistic tradition.

The conventional epic, like the pastoral, is inherently retrospective, rehearsing the earlier triumphs of a nation in order to reassure its present citizens. Milton changes this perspective drastically, and in consequence alters the whole thrust of the narrative, by setting out to go beyond the task of merely explaining how things came to be the way they are, and suggesting instead that the history has not yet been completed, and that things may yet change. *Paradise Lost* describes the continuing failure of mankind, the blindness of the majority, and celebrates the providence of God, which has yet to be totally realised. Milton chooses not to celebrate the triumphs of his chosen race, mankind, up to a fixed point in history, but implies instead that there is no fixed point: thus the Restoration of the monarchy can be accounted for and accommodated within Milton's scheme as a purely temporary phenomenon, a further instance of the error of the majority. *Paradise Lost* implies that the error of Restoration will eventually be reversed, but that reversal, like the Redemption of man by the Son, lies outside of the scope of the history of the poem. The decision to treat history in this manner has an effect on the narrative perspective of *Paradise Lost*, described by one critic in these terms:

Our vision of history becomes for the time being that of the Creator 'whose eye Views all things at one view' (ii.189–90); like him, we are stationed on a 'prospect high Wherein past, present, future he beholds'.[52]

One result of this technique, discussed in more detail below, is that it is virtually impossible to read the narrative line of *Paradise Lost* as if it had a beginning, a middle, and an end, as, for example, Empson's interpretation (see p. 93) would imply.

History in *Paradise Lost* is either distorted or telescoped and startling effects are produced, such as the combination of epic and pastoral conventions when Satan reaches Eden. Milton's pastoral setting is not, as it might have been conventionally, on the periphery of the poem, a place of temporary solace for a battle-weary warrior, it is the central location of the poem, and the place to which we all must aspire. Thus, at the beginning of Book IV, having involved ourselves in the conventional ambition, aspiration, movement, and activity of Satan, who seems to possess the dynamism of the typical hero, we find that true beauty lies not in activity but in the stasis of the garden. The closer Satan gets to Eden, the further he is from God, whereas Adam, the father of mankind, is never closer to God than he is in the garden. Satan arrives in Eden as a result of his own misreading of history. In Hell he had needed to evaluate his status, and had done this by inventing a heroic past in which he and his followers had fought bravely and magnificently against the tyranny of God. This version of the past is celebrated, as Satan leaves Hell, in its own form of poetry:

> Others more mild,
> Retreated in a silent valley, sing
> With notes angelical to many a harp
> Their own heroic deeds and hapless fall
> By doom of battle; and complain that fate
> Free virtue should enthral to force or chance.
> Their song was partial . . .
>
> (II.546–52)

This 'partial' song seems, taken from its context, the stuff of conventional epic, and Milton leaves the reader to draw his own conclusions about the morality of this satanic epic at this stage of the poem. It becomes clear, however, from Raphael's account of the war in Heaven much later in the poem, that the battle was far from glorious, and that it was, if anything, somewhat ridiculous and pointless: in Satan's own epic he is a hero, whereas the true history shows him to have been vain and self-absorbed. One lesson to be drawn might be that Milton intended his readers to equate the satanic view of history with that of the Royalists, and to decide that the apparent victory of the Restoration would eventually be proved to have been an illusion.

Paradise Lost is a great poem, but it is also a disappointing poem, and quite deliberately and consistently so. Just as Satan's invention of a glorious past is frustrated by the reality of the war in Heaven, and his ambition of victory over mankind gives way to the bathos of deception by an apple (an irony which even Satan finds amusing), so the reader's expectations and hopes are continually frustrated by a poem which denies glory to activity and substitutes instead the primacy of obedience, an attribute which includes being obedient enough to do nothing if the need for inaction should arise. Milton is continually asserting the futility of action throughout the poem. The crisis of the world is not going to be resolved by a single, gloriously flamboyant military victory, any more than the issues of the Civil War were settled at Naseby or at Worcester. The conventional epic reassures its readers with just that fiction: it operates through a narrative in which military heroism on the part of a minority can overcome evil for the majority who abdicate their problems to these heroes. The majority will be happy to abdicate responsibility for their fate in this way, and conventional epic reinforces this desire by rewarding the reader with stories of those who will fight on the reader's behalf. *Paradise Lost* does not do this: nobody secures victory for the reader, and he is left only with the promise that Christ will one day return.

Again and again in the poem it seems that some decisive and interesting conflict is to take place: that Satan is going to fight Sin, that Gabriel is going to fight Satan, that the war in Heaven is going to prove decisive, and, even at the end of the poem, Adam, our representative, still looks for a spectacular victory by the Son over Satan and needs to be instructed by Michael:

> say where and when
> Their fight, what stroke shall bruise the victor's heel.
> To whom thus Michael. Dream not of their fight,
> As of a duel . . .

(XII.384–7)

Even those characters within the poem who, like Abdiel, seem to conform to Milton's definition of true heroism:

> that suffering for truth's sake
> Is fortitude to highest victory,
> And to the faithful death the gate of life . . .

(XII.569–71)

do not immediately prosper as a reward for their obedience. The angels who choose not to revolt with Satan have a difficult time, as do the virtuous men cited by Michael in his survey of world history in the last two books of the poem. Milton cannot allow angels or men to become ,proud or complacent in their own virtue. As Stanley Fish observes: 'The desire to serve God is a particularly subtle form of pride if it is in fact a desire to feel needed and important. Milton is especially aware of this danger'.[53]

Milton is so far from the Calvinist view of salvation that he deliberately presents even those who might appear to have clear grounds for being regarded as elect (Abdiel, for example) as being subject to tests of their faith and obedience. God does not always provide reasons for obeying him, and there are numerous instances of minor trials throughout the poem: for example, when Adam has debated with God the reasons for the creation of Eve, he receives the reply:

> Thus far to try thee, Adam, I was pleased,
> And find thee knowing not of beasts alone,
> Which thou hast rightly named, but of thy self . . .
>   (VIII.437–9)

Adam has passed this particular trial without even knowing that it was there: other trials take place without explanation; George de Forest Lord has written of the humiliation of the good angels during the war in Heaven, suggesting that this indicates, 'as he does with the forbidden fruit, that He will not always provide reasons for obeying Him'.[54]

In composing *Paradise Lost* Milton was drawing upon classical epics by the Greek poet Homer and the Latin poet Virgil, European epics by Tasso (1544–95) and Ariosto (1474–1533), Spenserian epic, the pastoral tradition, dramatic tragedy, the biblical narratives of the creation through to the Last Judgement, and his own capacious theological work. Yet, the most surprising feature about the relation of *Paradise Lost* to its sources is the degree of freedom which the narrative left for Milton's own invention, in Heaven, Hell, and Eden. He decides to invent the character of Abdiel, for example (it is illuminating to ponder the difference which would have resulted from the substitution of the Son for Abdiel in the debate with Satan), to effect the separation of Adam and Eve before Satan's temptation, and to present the exaltation of the Son in the way in which he does. Thus, *Paradise Lost* follows in the tradition of the works by Milton discussed above: it exhibits remarkable innovation and originality whilst working within an established convention. Moreover, the poem is effectively an extended piece of biblical exegesis, explaining at length and in great detail just how the fall of man came to take place. It may be more than coincidence that Milton's major poems should all involve this detailed exposition of biblical texts just as, in his later prose works, biblical citations tend to be more precisely quoted:[55] it is certainly strong supportive evidence for attributing a late date of composition to *Samson Agonistes*.

Adventurous song

Near the beginning of the epic, Milton invokes his Muse in these terms:

> I thence
> Invoke thy aid to my adventurous song,
> That with no middle flight intends to soar
> Above the Aonian mount, while it pursues
> Things unattempted yet in prose or rhyme.
>
> (I.12–16)

This is one of the rare occasions in *Paradise Lost* when 'adventurous' has positive connotations, and it is an appropriate epithet for Milton to apply to his poem, especially in terms of the way in which the narrative is structured.

It is traditional for epics to begin their narrative *in medias res* (in the midst of things), but one could reasonably ask of *Paradise Lost*, what story is being told, and into which narrative are we being plunged? Stanley Fish has written eloquently on the surprise of the reader when first encountering the opening book of *Paradise Lost*:

> In the opening lines of Book I, chronology and sequence are suggested at once in what is almost a plot line: man disobeys, eats fruit, suffers woe and awaits rescue.[56]

However, as Fish points out, this apparently straightforward plot is quickly made more complex by the allusion to Moses:

> Moses is a type of Christ who as the second Adam restores the first by persevering when he could not; as one begins to construct statements of relationship between the three, the clarity of lines 1–3 fades.

An even greater shock is in store, however, when the reader reaches line 54, for the impression of the poem as being concerned with man seems to be destroyed completely. As Fish says:

> I have for some time conducted a private poll with a single question: 'What is your reaction when the second half of line 54 – "for *now* the thought" – tells you that you are *now* with Satan, in Hell?' The unanimous reply is, 'surprise', and an involuntary question: how did I come to be here?

The declared subject of *Paradise Lost* is the disobedience and fall of man, yet the narrative seems to start in the middle of the story of the fall of the angels. There are several obvious advantages in beginning in this way (the implication of a direct causal link, for example, between the fall of the angels and the fall of man; the avoidance, also, of some of the difficulties associated with the passage of time in the unfallen Eden – is it possible to begin in the middle of a story set in an indefinite period of time?), but the principal effect is to surprise the reader and to confront him with the originality of Milton's task. This is a story with no ending, since Christ's second coming has not yet occurred, and with no real beginning, since events can hardly be said to occur in Heaven or in Eden before disobedience has taken place. It is, moreover, a story in which one of the protagonists is the creator not only of all the other characters in the poem, but of the poet himself. It is a story with a circular rather than a linear pattern, in which incidents are so arranged as to make it seem that history, and time itself, can be read in an achronological manner. L.A. Cormican remarks (in a recently reprinted essay), 'The arrangement of the incidents in Milton is determined, not by the desire to tell a good story (as in the *Iliad*) or by the narrative exposition of a theological system (as in *The Divine Comedy*), but by the gradual reinforcing and intertwining of four central themes'.[57] As Cormican himself admits, it matters little what any critic feels these themes to be; what is of significance is that *Paradise Lost* should be seen as a poem which works through reinforcement of ideas and through intertwining. That intertwining might well involve the reader and become, in Stanley Fish's phrase culled from Milton's divorce tracts, 'not so much a teaching, as an intangling'.[58]

Not all of this entangling is evident to the reader on a first reading of *Paradise Lost*, since some of the instances of this process rely upon a realisation on the part of the reader of connections between disparate sections of the narrative. Some examples are, however, striking even on an initial reading: the effect, for instance, of starting in Hell, and thus, apparently, beginning not in the middle of the story of the fall of man but before it has even been contemplated. This is a radical development of epic convention which puts in question traditional notions of narrative plot-lines. Satan's early speeches are also boldly innovative in their apparent anticipation of parts of the narrative which have yet to take place. William Empson pointed out that Satan anticipated the Fortunate Fall of man in the opening book of the poem:[59]

> If then his providence
> Out of our evil seek to bring forth good,
> Our labour must be to pervert that end,
> And out of good still to find means of evil . . .
>
> (I.162–5)

Empson, however, did not appreciate that this is simply one example of a series of instances in the poem when speeches or descriptions ironically foreshadow events elsewhere. Another example occurs a few lines later, when Satan proposes that the fallen angels should

> Consult how we may henceforth most offend
> Our enemy, our own loss how repair,
> How overcome this dire calamity . . .
>
> (I.187–9)

Stanley Fish is puzzled by this passage and wonders

> what Satan could possibly mean or think he means by 'our own *loss* repair'. . . . Milton urges us in another place to 'repair the ruins of our first parents' but the repairing must be preceded by some awareness of what the loss or ruin is, and Satan clearly has no such awareness.[60]

The answer to this puzzle is that Satan is using the expression 'our loss' in one sense, and the reader is being led by Milton to interpret it in quite another sense. Not only does Milton write of the repair of the ruins of Adam and Eve (in *Of Education*), he also has God speak of loss in Book VII:

> I can repair
> That detriment, if such it be to lose
> Self-lost, and in a moment will create
> Another world . . .
>
> (VII.152–5)

What Satan is in fact suggesting in Book I is a conference to discuss how the fallen angels might best make up what they have lost, but the syntax makes it appear that he is talking, as Fish imagines, about the absence of the fallen angels, or their sin in rebelling. Thus, even in this declaration of revenge, Satan is bringing the reader's attention back to the providence of God, and anticipating God's decree on the fate of man: 'Man shall not quite be lost, but saved who will' (III.173).

It is impossible for any character in this poem to speak without somehow referring to God, and passages involving personal possessive pronouns are particularly subject to ambiguity. 'Our loss' could mean what we have lost, or what has been lost for us by someone else, or the loss incurred by someone else by our absence, and a similar multiplicity of meaning is exploited in that passage from Book X, referred to below (p. 149), in which the fallen Adam curses 'his creation' (line 852). This could mean that he cursed the fact that he was created by God, or that he cursed Eve who was created from him, or even that he made the rest of mankind accursed through his sin. The third interpretation is the least obvious, but it is strongly hinted at by the fact that, in the soliloquy which precedes this passage, Adam says:

> both death and I
> Am found eternal, and incorporate both
> Nor I on my part single, in me all
> Posterity stands cursed: fair patrimony
> That I must leave ye, sons . . .
>
> (X.815–19)

Thus Adam, in a single phrase, is able to encompass events which have passed and those to come, just as Satan, in the early books of the poem, creates a fictional history for himself and a fictional future. Like all fallen, rational creatures, Satan imagines himself to be at the centre of his own story, and fashions his own version of history upon which to build this fiction. Since this is a process with which we are all of us familiar, we respond to the fiction and are therefore surprised when it is subverted in the centre of the poem by two separate events: Satan's dispute with Abdiel, and the accounts of their history by Adam and Eve.

Abdiel is present at the conference in Book V at which Satan initiates the rebellion against God, and he counters Satan's claims with the announcement of a different view of history, startlingly at odds with that which the reader has received from Satan. Abdiel presents a true history in which God, the Creator, stands at the centre, and in which Satan is merely one of His creations:

> Thy self though great and glorious dost thou count,
> Or all angelic nature joined in one,
> Equal to him begotten Son, by whom
> As by his Word the mighty Father made
> All things, even thee, and all the spirits of heaven . . .
>
> (V.833–7)

Abdiel accepts that he was created by God through the agency of the Son, and can therefore argue in favour of the exaltation of the Son:

> since he the head
> One of our number thus reduced becomes . . .
>
> (V.842–3)

The exaltation is, in reality, a demotion for the Son, and, at the same time, an opportunity for all the angels to share in his honour. It thus anticipates the further degradation of the Son who must become mortal for man's sake, and the parody of that degradation in the career of Satan (IX.163–6). Abdiel's argument is also remarkably close to that used by Milton in support of Cromwell's Protectorate:

> since, though it be not fit, it may be expedient, that the highest pitch of virtue should be circumscribed within the bounds of some human

appellation, you endured to receive, for the public good, a title most like to that of the father of your country; not to exalt, but rather to bring you nearer to the level of ordinary men . . .[61]

Satan, however, believes Abdiel's arguments even less than the English people believed those of Milton, and, worse still, he refuses to accept Abdiel's account of his creation:

> who saw
> When this creation was? Remember'st thou
> Thy making, while the maker gave thee being?
> We know no time when we were not as now;
> Know none before us, self-begot, self-raised . . .
>
> (V.856–60)

Satan's problem is curiously similar to that of Empson: lacking faith, he cannot accept that there can be any other mode of interpreting history (or the historical narrative) except in a linear sequence. For Satan the argument runs 'we can only remember things as they are now, so they must always have been this way'; for Empson it runs 'narratives must begin somewhere, and so must this one': neither argument holds, since each underestimates the uniqueness of the situation described in the poem.

Adam and Eve, in contrast to Satan, are totally acceptant of their creation, and they place God rather than themselves at the centre of the poem when first we hear them speak in Book IV. Their perfect partnership is based, like Milton's definition of true marriage in the divorce tracts, on the primacy of conversation, rather than the primacy of sexual intercourse leading to the generation of children. Milton says in *The Doctrine and Discipline of Divorce*:

> in God's intention a meet and happy conversation is the chiefest and noblest end of marriage: for we find here no expression so necessarily implying carnal knowledge, as this prevention of loneliness to the mind and spirit of man.[62]

This is precisely the motivation which leads Adam to ask God for a partner, as he tells Raphael in Book VIII, and it is conversation which distinguishes fallen from unfallen creatures. J.B. Broadbent has observed: 'the characters of *Paradise Lost* do not soliloquize until they have fallen; unfallen speech and gesture are directed always to another person, on the supreme model of light inter-reflected by Father and Son'.[63] Thus, in Book IV, we have a description of unfallen conversation alongside that of unfallen love-making, and the subject of that conversation is creation, the acknowledgement of the debt owed to God:

> needs must the power
> That made us, and for us this ample world
> Be infinitely good . . .
>
> (IV.412–14)

Adam's first words are of God as his creator, Eve's are of Adam as hers, thus establishing a pattern of order and a hierarchy which Milton believed essential to the gaining of salvation, mirroring the relationship between God and the Son. Milton's version of this is:

> He for God only, she for God in him
>
> (IV.299)

The doctrine, however, is an entirely conventional one, found in the Bible as: 'The head of every man is Christ; and the head of the woman is the man; and the head of Christ is God' (I Corinthians 11:3). Eve's account of her creation may seem to hint at a potential for self-love, and Adam's conversation with Raphael at the end of Book VIII might seem to indicate that his love for Eve is excessive, but both of them continue to accept the fact of their creation, and of God's providence, up to the fall itself.

God is omnipresent in *Paradise Lost*, and one manifestation of the fall is the delusion that He might not be there, which can lead either to false hope for an amoral, self-centred life, independent of God, or to despair: these consequences are manifest in both fallen angel and fallen man. Satan believes himself beyond the control of God:

> Here at least
> We shall be free; the almighty hath not built
> Here for his envy, will not drive us hence . . .
>
> (I.258–60)

and Belial, in Book II, hopes that God may one day forget about the fallen angels:

> Our supreme foe in time may much remit
> His anger, and perhaps thus far removed,
> Not mind us not offending . . .
>
> (II.210–12)

In a similar fashion, Eve's vain hope immediately after the fall is that God may have failed to see what she has done:

> other care perhaps
> May have diverted from continual watch
> Our great forbidder, safe with all his spies
> About him.
>
> (IX.813–16)

Eve's language becomes satanic at this point, as she imputes negative motives to God ('Our great forbidder'), just as Satan portrayed God negatively in his first speech:

> our grand foe,
> Who now triumphs, and in the excess of joy,
> Sole reigning holds the tyranny of heaven.
>
> (I.122–4)

After the fall, obedience to God's just providence becomes regarded as tyranny and oppression, and the prohibition which had been there as a token of that obedience becomes the tool of the 'great forbidder'. The motives of spite, wrath, vengeance and anger, imputed to God by angels and men after the fall, are themselves indicative of that fallen state.

Ironically, the very syntax used by Belial in the lines cited above reveals the heart of his problem: the lines are capable of imputing to God the title of 'Our supreme foe in time', and it is upon the issue of time that much of the epic turns. The fallen angels, and fallen men, refuse to accept the time-scheme of God and either delude themselves that by living in heavenly eternity they must therefore have been self-generated, or else refuse to believe that Innocence is a dynamic state: 'Innocence, Raphael tells Adam and Eve, far from being static, includes large possibilities for growth as well as the possibility of declining to grow'.[64]

Part of the fall is the desire to accelerate time beyond the pace ordained by God, the temptation to be active rather than to wait. After the fall of the angels, Satan admits that the war in Heaven has been a 'dubious battle' (I.104), an inconclusive encounter, and in their uncertain state in Hell the fallen angels look for a conclusion in time, and wonder if they are capable of death.

Similarly, Adam and Eve are surprised at the effect which the fall has upon them: they do not become more elevated, of course, as the satanic temptation had promised, but neither do they suffer instant death. Throughout the poem, Milton presents angels and men as expecting some remarkable event to ensue from their actions, and this event never comes. After the fall, Adam expects that death will end his miseries, or that the history of the world, as foretold by Michael, will lead to some spectacular and momentous event: he continually interrupts the narrative in anticipation of this, yet the event does not occur.

God is ever-present in the poem, and the fact that some books, in which God does not appear to play a central role, seem to be detachable and capable of independent study is a testimony to Milton's success in implying the freedom of God's creatures within the poem. The sensitive reader will be attuned to the ways in which events within the poem seem to be continually reinforcing one another by the careful parallelism of language. Stanley Fish observes that 'It is pleasant to cross-reference Milton's poem ... finding echoes and anticipations, but this is a synthetic operation performed after the fact and with the aid of a concordance'.[65]

Some instances of cross-reference are perhaps explicit enough to be clear even on a first reading, but, even if we accept Fish's point, there is no reason why it should not be a valuable exercise to consider the implications of deconstructing *Paradise Lost* with or without a concordance.

For example, it must be more than coincidence that Book X ends with the penitence of Adam and Eve, described in these terms: ·

> they forthwith to the place
> Repairing where he judged them prostrate fell
> Before him reverent . . .
>
> (X.1098–100)

In a different poem these lines might seem unambiguous, but in this poem there is extra weight in Milton's use of 'Repairing' which allows it to mean more than simply 'adjourning to', and recalls the process of loss and repair which is at the centre of the poem. The word is given further prominence by being placed at the beginning of the line, and by the fact that this passage echoes a speech by Adam some ten lines previously which had also juxtaposed the concepts of repairing, judgement and fall.

Similarly, Adam's desperate soliloquy in Book X concludes:

> O conscience! into what abyss of fears
> And horrors hast thou driven me; out of which
> I find no way, from deep to deeper plunged!
>
> (X.842–4)

closely mirroring Satan's despair at the beginning of Book IV:

> Which way I fly is hell; myself am hell;
> And in the lowest deep a lower deep
> Still threatening to devour me opens wide,
> To which the hell I suffer seems a heaven.
>
> (IV.75–8)

In each case fear drives the speaker downward: to the abyss in Adam's case, back to Hell for Satan (repeatedly, Satan's soliloquies include the torture of comparison between Hell, Heaven and Eden).

Other critics have commented on the placing of the image of Adam and Eve 'hand in hand' across the poem. G.A. Wilkes suggests that 'the image "hand in hand", acknowledging the responsibility of the future, is retrospective too'.[66] He remarks that it occurs when Satan first sees Adam and Eve (IV.321–2), when Eve leaves Adam to work alone (IX.385–8), and in the closing lines of the poem:

> They hand in hand with wandering steps and slow,
> Through Eden took their solitary way.
>
> (XII.648–9)

Stanley Fish has written at length[67] on the way in which the word 'wandering' comes to acquire the sense it has in these closing lines of 'willingness to go out at the sign of God',[68] and, in the process, drawn attention to the parallel instances within the poem of endless, and therefore inconclusive, activity: from the philosophical speculations of the fallen angels in Book II:

> reasoned high,
> Of providence, foreknowledge, will and fate,
> . . . And found no end, in wandering mazes lost.
>
> (II.558–61)

through the war in heaven:

> Whence in perpetual fight they needs must last
> Endless, and no solution will be found . . .
>
> (VI.693–4)

to the anticlimactic squabbling of Adam and Eve at the end of Book IX:

> Thus they in mutual accusation spent
> The fruitless hours, but neither self-condemning,
> And of their vain contest appeared no end.
>
> (IX.1187–9)

This last example, of course, points the way towards the resolution of this concept of perpetual frustration through the coming of the Son who, according to Michael, will be 'of kings/The last, for of his reign shall be no end' (XII.329–30).

These are merely instances of some of the linguistic parallels which occur across the poem and which allow incidents continually to reinforce one another. The parallels also have the effect both of rendering certain concepts morally neutral and of emphasising the circularity of the narrative.

Thus, the notion of eternity can be presented positively in the poem, as in heaven or in the endless reign of the Son, or negatively, as in the speculation of the fallen angels or the bickering of Adam and Eve: kingship, poetry, love-making, even history are all presented ambivalently within the poem, their moral polarity conveyed by the user.[69] This has the effect of allowing the reader to consider, whilst reading a negative instance of a concept, the positive example which will transcend it. When Satan speaks of repairing the loss of the angels in the opening book, we think of the reparation to occur later (not yet predicted by God) and that the final word spoken in the poem is 'restore'. As Adam and Eve bicker at the end of Book IX the very words in which this activity is described anticipates the second coming of the Son, even before the way for repentance has been cleared.

In a work which is essentially circular, it might seem that the choice of where to start the narrative becomes purely arbitrary, but I should like to draw this section to a conclusion by considering some of the advantages of beginning in Hell.

By starting the narrative in Hell, Milton presents the reader with negative instances of his central concepts, instances which have an attraction for the reader because they are familiar from conventional narratives. The reader attends closely to Satan's account of his history, in which he leads his people bravely against an oppressor who wields invincible might, and watches Satan's apparent heroism as he volunteers to represent his people on the dangerous mission against Eden. Yet the total effect of the opening two books is to establish a false set of values which is quickly overturned by the portrait of Heaven in Book III. Milton is well aware that this second location will inevitably force the reader to look for contrasts and comparisons between Hell and Heaven, and he arranges his narrative (the poet, like God, has knowledge of what is to come) in order to take maximum advantage of this process. In Heaven there is true prescience on the part of God (not shared, even by the Son): God knows what will happen, knows that man will fall, and yet He still provides for man's salvation. This heavenly certainty replaces the insecurity of Hell, which is very evident in Satan's address to the fallen angels at the beginning of Book II. The speech as a whole argues in favour of a return to Heaven and the defeat of its ruler, yet it involves Satan's justification of his own leadership in these terms:

> The happier state
> In heaven, which follows dignity, might draw
> Envy from each inferior; but who here
> Will envy whom the highest place exposes
> Foremost to stand against the thunderer's aim . . .
> Where there is then no good
> For which to strive, no strife can grow up there
> From faction . . .

(II.24–32)

Although the passage above begins by describing Heaven as the place of the 'happier state', it goes on to argue as if Hell were a kind of political utopia, a development of the pastoral tradition, in which ambition is inconceivable. Why then, we might ask, should Satan want to leave? God's true foreknowledge replaces the conspiracy of the debate in Book II in which Satan's plan to ruin man is first voiced by Beelzebub. God knows that the Son will volunteer to save man, even though the Son does not know it: Beelzebub knows that Satan will volunteer to ruin mankind, because Satan has told him beforehand. The openness of God's providential plan replaces and reverses the conspiracies and plottings of Hell.

One significant product of presenting Hell before Heaven is the shift in historical perspective: Satan's viewpoint is inevitably retrospective, grieving for what he has lost, and yet he bases his plans for the future on a total misreading of that history, which breeds his motives of revenge and destruction. God, on the other hand, does not sit gloating in Heaven over his defeat of the fallen angels but is concerned with the future, a future emanating from God's love for man. The cumulative effect of the first three books is to delay the entry of Adam and Eve into the narrative, and, in the process of that delay, to make their entry more significant: they are not merely attractive characters in an idyllic landscape, they are also the focus of the very different attentions of God and Satan, and therefore representatives as well as individuals. By the time we reach Eden, we have been presented with a conventionally heroic figure in Satan, seeking elevation through military action and revenge, and a most unconventional hero in the Son, willing to suffer the degradation of becoming man and suffering death for love. The heroism of the Son indicates very clearly what Satan, for all his initial attraction, lacks: endurance, patience, love, and most of all, faith.

Partial song

After the great debate in Hell, in Book II of *Paradise Lost*, the fallen angels celebrate their own heroism, in a passage already cited above:

> Others more mild,
> Retreated in a silent valley, sing
> With notes angelical to many a harp
> Their own heroic deeds . . .
> Their song was partial, but the harmony
> (What could it less when spirits immortal sing?)
> Suspended hell, and took with ravishment
> The thronging audience.

(II.546–55)

The song of the fallen angels is 'partial' in a number of different ways: it is divided into separate lines of harmony; it presents a biased account of the war in Heaven; and it is an incomplete song, presenting only part of the total story. The preceding section of this book has attempted to demonstrate that all the apparently separate narrative strands of *Paradise Lost* are, in fact, parts of a larger whole, and that they constantly support and reinforce one another. This section will examine the way in which Milton exploits 'partial' narratives.

It is not uncommon for an epic hero to read of his own story during the course of his epic, or to discover that what seemed to be his individual narrative is merely a part of a much large struggle. Beowulf, for example, in the Old English epic, has to listen to a version of his own past from the mouth of the treacherous Unferth at the beginning of the poem; in a more recent instance, Frodo Baggins discovers in *The Lord of the Rings* (1954–55) by J.R.R. Tolkien (1892–1973) that he is not at the centre of the epic at all, that he is not the eponymous hero but merely a subsidiary character in the story of Aragorn, and a character whose significance is likely to be underestimated by future tellers of the story. What is unique about Milton's handling of partial narrative is the extent to which apparently separate narrative strands are ultimately proved to be in harmony (and thus manifest God's providence); the resolution of apparently conflicting accounts into harmony; and the sense that, even after this resolution, we are still left with a narrative which has yet to be completed: we are not left with the impression of a perfected narrative set in time, with a reassuring conclusion; the narrative continues to require an effort from the reader even after the poem has ended, because its component strands have been carefully disposed so as to seem to take place simultaneously rather than sequentially.

Stanley Fish, writing of Eve's dream in Book V, observes:

> The dream is a carefully woven web of echoing and anticipatory detail. Satan's opening 'Why sleep'st thou Eve' is a slightly altered version of his 'earlier' address to Beelzebub . . . (The relationship between the two temptations is confused for us since we have not yet been told of the revolt which has already occurred when Satan squats at the ear of Eve.)[70]

This confusion of time is a deliberate contrivance on Milton's part to prevent the reader from accepting the poem as a conventional sequential narrative. We have seen in the previous section some examples of verbal echoes in the speeches of various characters in the poem, and one of the means which Milton employs to sustain the interest of the reader is continually to shift the narrative perspective by allowing a whole range of characters to act as story-teller: Adam,

Satan, Eve, Raphael, Michael, Sin and God are all given the opportunity to sing their own 'partial' song.

This technique of narrative variety is one which Milton could have found in almost any long poem, and one which is extensively employed by Spenser in *The Faerie Queene*, but Milton transcends Spenser even when he appears to be following his practice most closely. For example, one feature of Spenser's epic is his tendency to delay the naming of characters freshly introduced into the narrative, sometimes for a considerable length of time. The effect is to leave the reader in some confusion as to who is performing a particular action or delivering a particular speech. Milton tends to be much more precise, naming his characters as soon as they are introduced, yet his departures from this precision to a more Spenserian style are carefully contrived.

The Son of God, whose exaltation is at the heart of *Paradise Lost*, is never given a name either in that poem or in *Paradise Regained*: the effect, however, is not confusion on the part of the reader, because the Son is cleary identified whenever he appears. By leaving the Son unnamed, Milton allows for the possibility of a more representative status for this character, thus making possible Abdiel's argument (cited above) that the exaltation of the Son reflects on all of the angels, and giving a basis for Satan's mocking comment in *Paradise Regained*:

> The Son of God I also am, or was,
> And if I was, I am; relation stands;
> All men are Sons of God . . .

> (IV.518–20)

Satan has, too late, discovered a truth: all men are indeed Sons of God, and this unnamed character is, therefore, made more humble, and more human, by the absence of an elevating title.

The Son of God, however, is not the only offspring in *Paradise Lost* whose name is withheld, and the simple choice of naming or leaving unnamed becomes part of a pattern. At the end of the second Book, Satan leaves Hell and encounters Sin and Death. This episode seems to show Milton at his most Spenserian, introducing abstractions who seem to have an obvious allegorical significance, and the whole incident seems reminiscent of the opening Book of *The Faerie Queene* and, in particular, the defeat of Errour in Canto I:

> And as she lay upon the durtie ground
> Her huge long taile her den all overspred,
> Yet was in knots and many boughtes upwound,
> Pointed with mortall sting. Of her there bred
> A thousand young ones, which she dayly fed,

> Sucking upon her poisonous dugs, each one
> Of sundry shapes, yet all ill favoured . . .
>
> (I.i.15)

This description seems a likely source for Milton's Sin:

> about her middle round
> A cry of hell hounds never ceasing barked
> With wide Cerberian mouths full loud, and rung
> A hideous peal: yet, when they list, would creep,
> If aught disturbed their noise, into her womb,
> And kennel there, yet there still barked and howled,
> Within unseen.
>
> (II.653–9)

Moreover, Milton withholds the name of this creature and of her companion for a further hundred lines, and thus the parallel with *The Faerie Queene* seems all the closer. Yet the effect proves on closer inspection to be more of an ironic counterpoint. The reader's expectations are whetted by this incident into anticipating a combat between Satan and the terrible monster, yet this combat never occurs. Satan falls prey to the temptation which besets so many heroes of epic narrative, the temptation to act, whatever form that action may take. Whereas the Redcross Knight, the hero of Book I of *The Faerie Queene*, fought and defeated the obviously monstrous Errour, only to fall prey to the wiles of the shape-changing Archimago, Satan, himself a shape-changer, cannot fight the monster Death, because it proves to be his own son. Lascivious sexuality proves the downfall of Redcross and drives a wedge between the fallen Adam and Eve: its counterpart unites Satan and Sin. Satan does not destroy Death but accommodates him into his intended revenge on man, anticipating and parodying God's employment of his Son, who dies so that man may live.

Milton's holding back of the names and ancestry of Sin and Death allows the reader firstly to form an impression of a brave and heroic Satan, undaunted by these terrible foes, only to have that impression totally destroyed in the realisation that these monsters are not only the progeny of Satan but also the means whereby mankind becomes doomed to mortality. The episode thus underlines the monstrosity of Satan's plan: the final instance of the omission of names completes that plan.

In Book XI, Adam is given a vision of the murder of Abel by Cain, and the incident is explained to him by Michael. Adam's astonishment requires an answer:

> O teacher, some great mischief hath befallen
> To that meek man, who well hath sacrificed;

Is piety thus and pure devotion paid?
To whom Michael thus, he also moved, replied.
These two are brethren, Adam, and to come
Out of thy loins . . .

(XI.450–5)

Alastair Fowler comments that neither brother is named during the description of the vision and suggests that 'The omission of names is no doubt so that Adam will not know which of his sons is to turn out a murderer'.[71]

This cannot be a full and complete explanation: the naming of Cain and Abel might identify the murderer prematurely for the reader, but it can scarcely have that effect on Adam, for whom the names can mean nothing, nor does Fowler's note explain why the sons remain unnamed even in Michael's gloss on the incident. The absence of names helps to associate this crime, the first manifestation of mortal death, with the abstraction of Death encountered in Book II: the child of Adam has now become infected by the child of Satan, and Milton implicitly connects these two incidents from opposite ends of the poem, and links them both with the triumph of the Son of God, who is at the centre of the epic. Adam talks in this passage of the sacrifice of Abel, and Michael assures him:

the bloody fact
Will be avenged, and the other's faith approved
Lose no reward . . .

(XI.456–9)

The death of Abel thus becomes another example of loss turned into reward, and his sacrifice anticipates the sacrifice made by the Son for man. Similarly, in the description of her own creation, Sin recalls:

when at the assembly, and in sight
Of all the seraphim with thee combined
In bold conspiracy against heaven's king,
All on a sudden miserable pain
Surprised thee . . . while thy head flames thick and fast
Threw forth, till on the left side opening wide,
Likest to thee in shape and countenance bright,
Then shining heavenly fair, a goddess armed
Out of thy head I sprung . . .

(II.749–58)

This description not only anticipates the creation of Eve from Adam, but is also placed in time as a direct result of Satan's envy at the elevation of the Son. Once again, one part of the narrative evokes other parts which are widely separated across the poem. Satan and Sin produce Death, just as Adam and Eve produce death, in each case through their descent (their degradation to a lower, fallen state, and the lineal descent of later generations). Only God and his Son produce life, triumphing over the apparent degradation of incarnation and winning salvation for mankind through the ascent of the Son.[72]

Present misery

It should be clear that *Paradise Lost* cannot be read as a straightforward allegory, in which particular characters can be regarded as representative of moral qualities or political positions. On the other hand, the poem would undoubtedly have been very different had it been published some twenty years earlier, and it furnishes ample evidence of the effects which the failure of the English Revolution had had upon Milton's thinking, and also of those aspects of his thinking which had remained constant since his earliest antiprelatical tracts. The poem opens and closes with attacks upon organised religion, and the attendant dangers of ritual, and with praise for private, individual worship:

> chiefly thou O Spirit, that dost prefer .
> Before all temples the upright heart and pure,
> Instruct me . . .
>
> (I.17–19)

> Wolves shall succeed for teachers, grievous wolves,
> Who all the sacred mysteries of heaven
> To their vile advantages shall turn
> Of lucre and ambition, and the truth
> With superstitions and traditions taint . . .
>   What will they then
> But force the spirit of grace itself, and bind
> His consort liberty; what, but unbuild
> His living temples, built by faith to stand,
> Their own faith not another's . . .
>
> (XII.508–28)

These ideas seem very familiar, and can be found throughout the early poems and prose, from 'Lycidas' onwards: Milton is continually arguing for the need to exercise an explicit faith, rather than to resign one's conscience to the care of another. Similarly, the portrayal of the fallen angels in terms of the idols of ritualised religion develops as one of Milton's favourite tactics:

> By falsities and lies the greatest part
> Of mankind they corrupted to forsake

> God their creator, and the invisible
> Glory of him that made them, to transform
> Oft to the image of a brute, adorned
> With gay religions full of pomp and gold,
> And devils to adore for deities . . .
>
> (I.367–73)

We may admire the skill whereby Milton constructs this argument so that falsity and lies lead not only to the fall of man (as we might expect) but to the adoption of a fallen, ritualised mode of religion, but the idea itself is one which can be found widely throughout his earlier work.

In his presentation of monarchy, however, Milton adopts a more radical stance in *Paradise Lost* than would have been possible in the years before the execution of Charles I and the establishment of the Protectorate under Oliver Cromwell, and one which is consistent with his continued support of republicanism, even after the Restoration of the monarchy. It is perhaps surprising that the Licenser of Charles II should have objected to this passage[73] from Book I as potentially subversive when there are more blatant instances of subversion elsewhere in the epic:

> as when the sun new risen
> Looks through the horizontal misty air
> Shorn of his beams, or from behind the moon
> In dim eclipse disastrous twilight sheds
> On half the nations, and with fear of change
> Perplexes monarchs.
>
> (I.594–9)

Monarchy itself first occurs in Hell, where Satan's assumption of control is described in these terms:

> till at last
> Satan, whom now transcendent glory raised
> Above his fellows, with monarchal pride
> Conscious of highest worth, unmoved thus spake.
>
> (II.426–9)

Satan's assumed monarchy is set in contrast with the true monarchy of God (introduced in I.42), and the institution as a whole is relegated in these lines to the status of a mere epithet, a convenient way of describing pride. Nor is the beginning of earthly monarchy described any more positively: at the beginning of Book XII, after describing an idyllic period under the rule of 'virtuous primitive governors',[74] Michael goes on:

> till one shall rise
> Of proud ambitious heart, who not content
> With fair equality, fraternal state,
> Will arrogate dominion undeserved
> Over his brethren, and quite dispossess
> Concord and law of nature . . .

(XII.24–9)

Robert Hodge has analysed in detail the account by Raphael of the war in heaven, concluding that God's proposals are consistently more democratic than those of Satan, who seems to fear a subversion of the old system of ranks and hierarchies. Hodge argues that Milton's presentation of monarchy in *Paradise Lost* is parallel to the views which he expressed in *Eikonoklastes*:

> Indeed, if the race of Kings were eminently the best of men, as the breed at Tutbury is of horses, it would in some reason then be their part only to command, ours only to obey. But kings by generation no way excelling others, and most commonly not being the wisest or worthiest by far of whom they claim to have the governing; that we should yield them subjection to our own ruin, or hold of them the right of our common safety . . . we may be sure was never the intent of God.[75]

Milton's description of kingship, like his redefinition of heroism bears the stamp of his recent experience of a failed revolution. As George de Forest Lord has observed, Milton does not follow Virgil's example in including the suppression of personal desire for the larger good as part of his definition of heroism: his heroes do not submerge their individual identities into a corporate institution, they continue to stand out against these institutions: 'Virgilian obedience means loss of freedom; Miltonic obedience is the basis of freedom'.[76] In making obedience the basis of his definition of freedom, Milton is not only deciding to follow the example of Homer rather than Virgil, he is also rationalising his own experience of recent history.

The difficulty of passing back

Much of this section on *Paradise Lost* has been concerned with the way in which the ideas of the poem relate to those expressed in Milton's prose, and the fact that one popular edition of *Paradise Lost* includes extracts from his prose might seem to reinforce the connection between the two. However, although Northrop Frye suggests that 'Renaissance critics . . . made much less of the technical distinction between verse and prose than we do',[77] the reservation which Douglas

Bush expresses is significant: discussing the connection between *Paradise Lost* and *De Doctrina Christiana*, he writes:

> The poem is not always in strict agreement with the treatise, and, in any case, the poetic and dramatic presentation of such beliefs and principles has for the most part a very different effect from that of expository prose.[78]

It is unlikely that Milton, whose sense of the relationship between writer and audience was so strong throughout his career as a writer of polemical prose, would fail to discriminate between the presentation of verse and prose.

A study of the ideas contained in Milton's prose is of undoubted use in assessing two of the aspects of *Paradise Lost*: the relationship between the epic and contemporary history (discussed above), and the extent to which the marriage of Adam and Eve can be seen as representing Milton's ideal of a perfect partnership (discussed below).

One of the principal difficulties, however, in using the prose as a context for the epic, is that the ideas of the best-known prose tract, *Areopagitica*, seem to be reflected most clearly in speeches by Eve in Book IX, with which we are intended to disagree. How can Milton advocate the purification of virtue by trial in *Areopagitica*, and then expect us to censure Eve for expressing this very same viewpoint in arguing with Adam in Book IX? These lines, as Waldock[79] among others has pointed out, are remarkably close to the arguments of *Areopagitica*.

> what is faith, love, virtue unassayed
> Alone, without exterior help sustained?
>
> (IX.335–6)

Various explanations can be advanced to account for this apparent anomaly, discriminating between Eve's situation in Eden and the situation of fallen men in the real world, as described by Milton in *Areopagitica*, but all of these explanations seem to involve the assumption that Eve has already started to fall, and that her voicing of this argument is itself a test, either for herself, or for Adam. It is difficult to escape from the conclusion that Milton, in attempting to turn his narrative into a circular rather than a linear sequence, gives the impression that Adam and Eve are on their way to being fallen long before they taste the forbidden fruit.

One of Milton's most difficult tasks in the poem is to find the right way to write of Adam and Eve. On the one hand, he wants and needs to portray the beauty of unfallen love, and he is eminently successful in making their partnership before the fall coincide precisely with his own definition of true marriage, found in his divorce tracts (see p. 96

above). The emphasis in this partnership is placed not upon sexuality, but upon conversation: Adam and Eve do have a sexual relationship, but it is Satan and Sin who place prime importance upon sex (failing, even, to recognise one another in conversation). Those critics who, like Empson, worry about whether some change occurs in Adam after the fall which affects his control over his own body[80] are missing Milton's argument: after the fall love becomes tainted and leads to a post-coital shame in man, just as it leads to the production of Death from Satan and Sin. After the fall of Eve, Adam (who has yet to taste of the fruit) describes her as:

How art thou lost, how on a sudden lost,
Defaced, deflowered, and now to death devote?

(IX.900–1)

Eve is lost and has become deflowered, her chastity gone, along with her pastoral innocence and fruitfulness: Adam can perceive all this, and yet he nevertheless eats the fruit and brings about his own fall. Milton, for his part, has portrayed the love of Adam and Eve so beautifully that many readers of the poem have concluded that Adam was right to follow Eve's example, to put his love for her before any other duty. Either that, or they have decided that Adam is somehow already fallen before he tastes the fruit, and that his conversation with Raphael on the subject of Eve is testimony to an excessive admiration of Eve which is potentially sinful.

It is difficult to argue against these conclusions: Milton presents Adam in a classic dilemma in which he must choose between a human and personal relationship immediately evident to him and a duty to a higher abstract cause which is temporarily out of his sight. Adam makes the human choice, which we understand, but he is superior to us, and we must therefore condemn him. Milton does not, however, make that condemnation easy for the reader. As Adam comes to the point where he is prepared to take the fruit, his arguments seem to be based on an understandable devotion for Eve, and cannot leave us unmoved:

How can I live without thee, how forgo
Thy sweet converse and love so dearly joined,
To live again in these wild woods forlorn?

(IX.908–10)

It is hard not to feel that Waldock's summary is correct when he suggests that 'Adam falls through love',[81] and not to feel sympathy with a student of mine who elaborated this suggestion: 'Is Man totally to betray Man, in the interest of remaining blindly obedient to God? Can there be any nobility in Man if he does so?'

We, of course, have heard Eve's self-justification before her meeting with Adam, and may feel that her motives for involving him in her predicament are not altruistic. We have certainly been alerted to the change in Eve by her reference to God as 'Our great forbidder', and we may have noticed other alarming details in her arguments. She speaks to Adam, for example, of trial and equality, terms which were brought into satanic conjunction at the end of Book V:

> Our puissance is our own, our own right hand
> Shall teach us highest deeds, by proof to try
> Who is our equal . . .
>
> (V.864–6)

Milton did not believe that liberty and equality were co-existent,[82] and it is ironic that Satan, like Eve and like Adam, seems to define liberty in terms of his own promotion. Eve wants Adam to fall because she selfishly wants to deny him a future without her, and Adam is persuaded through his own form of self-interest, his fear of losing Eve. Even as we admire the passion of the lines cited above, we can hardly avoid noticing that Eden has already become for Adam 'these wild woods'. Adam is allowing his emotions to come before his reason: for the greater part of the poem he has debated and discussed, and yet here he falls prey to that most fundamental of all temptations, the temptation of precipitate action. Milton has kept God out of Book IX and has allowed the reader to believe that Adam and Eve are acting freely and independently. In this time of crisis, however, Adam was free to involve God, through prayer: he chooses not to do so. We may notice all of these hints which are intended to temper our reaction to Adam's 'love' for Eve. We may even appreciate that Eve's urging:

> O glorious trial of exceeding love.
> Illustrious evidence, example high!
>
> (IX.961–2)

echoes Milton's own poem 'On the Circumcision', in its description of Christ's love for man:

> O more exceeding love or law more just?
> Just law indeed, but more exceeding love!
>
> (lines 15–16)

Thus, even at the moment of Adam's fall, there is a reference to the future redemption. However, despite these hints and nudges from the poet, we are left with as finely balanced a choice as can be found anywhere in literature, a choice for Adam and for ourselves as readers. It is entirely possible that we will feel on one occasion that Adam chose rightly, and that human emotion transcends other obligations;

on another we will feel the force of the contrary argument. *Paradise Lost* is not reducible to neat summaries and paraphrases: it will change in the mind of the reader and in the act of reading, and that is why it is such a great and fascinating poem. Many a lesser work will leave the reader with the paradoxical feeling of having mastered the meaning (sufficiently to file the work away and never need to read it again) and yet of feeling empty and cheated, disengaged now from working with the text. *Paradise Lost* constantly poses fresh challenges, and can never be completely read.

Paradise Regained and *Samson Agonistes*

Milton's two other major poems were published together in 1671, and were accepted without question as his final poems until the 1940s. Since then, however, although *Paradise Regained* is still regarded as having been composed in the late 1660s, a variety of possible dates has been suggested for the composition of *Samson Agonistes*. These arguments are reviewed below, but it should be noted that the overwhelming majority of opinion among Milton scholars is currently in favour of ascribing a late date of composition to the poem.

Paradise Regained

Paradise Regained seems to have been written between 1667, when *Paradise Lost* was first published, and 1670, when the poem was licensed and registered for publication. Milton's nephew Edward Phillips wrote of its composition:

> Paradice regain'd . . . doubtless was begun and finisht and Printed after the other [*Paradise Lost*] was publisht, and that in a wonderful short space considering the sublimeness of it.[83]

and Thomas Ellwood, who found lodgings for Milton and his family during the Plague, claims credit for having suggested the idea of the poem to Milton. Having read the manuscript of *Paradise Lost*, Ellwood claims that the following conversation took place with the poet:

> He asked me how I liked it and what I thought of it, which I modestly but freely told him, and after some further discourse about it I pleasantly said to him, 'Thou hast said much here of Paradise Lost, but what hast thou to say of Paradise Found?' He made me no answer but sat some time in a muse. . . . And when afterwards I went to wait on him . . . he shewed me his second poem, called *Paradise Regained*, and in a pleasant tone said to me, 'This is owing

to you; for you put it into my head by the question you put to me at Chalfont, which before I had not thought of'.[84]

Although this is a pleasant little story, it can hardly be regarded as accurate, since the notion of the regaining of Paradise through the action of the Son is clearly predicted within *Paradise Lost*:

Man shall not quite be lost, but saved who will,
. . . Which of ye will be mortal to redeem
Man's mortal crime . . .

(III.173; 214–15)

God's question, and the Son's reply, indicate the possibility of a further narrative poem to complete the story begun in *Paradise Lost*. However, this second poem, Milton's 'brief epic' (the term which he uses in *The Reason of Church Government*),[85] has not met with the kind of approval which greeted *Paradise Lost*. It is little regarded by modern readers (perhaps because it features so rarely on examination syllabuses), and seems to have disappointed contemporary readers too. Edward Phillips noted that:

it is generally censured to be much inferior to the other, though he could not hear with patience any such thing when related to him. Possibly the subject may not afford such variety of invention; but it is thought by the most judicious to be little or nothing inferior to the other for style and decorum.[86]

However tactful Phillips may try to be, the fact remains that Milton chose to write on this subject, and chose to do so in the form of a four-book short epic. To select the temptation in the wilderness as the central act whereby Paradise is regained may seem an unusual choice, and we need to consider why Milton made this selection rather than, for example, concentrating on the crucifixion or the ascension.

At the age of about twenty, Milton had begun a poem on the crucifixion, which he left unfinished, and which ends after eight stanzas with the note: 'This subject the author finding to be above the years he had when he wrote it, and nothing satisfied with what was begun, left it unfinished'.[87] Louis Martz, however, has suggested that Milton's failure to complete this poem may have had something to do with the fact that it employed the devices of a Catholic meditation upon a subject which was in any case unattractive to Puritans,[88] and there is every reason to feel that the crucifixion became more rather than less unattractive to Milton in the years between 1630 and 1670. Milton's brand of Puritanism would naturally place emphasis upon temptation rather than upon sacrifice, and would suggest that the Son regained Paradise in a manner analogous to that in which Adam and

Eve lost it: through obedience and through resistance to temptation. J.A. Wittreich suggests that 'the emphasis on the Passion is wrong. It illustrates Christ's triumph at the divine rather than the human level'.[89]

Paradise Regained consistently portrays the Son as a human figure, possessed of no divine prescience or strength, and presents his heroism as private and unrewarded. The victory of the Son takes place far away from the public eye, and the poem ends in quietude:

> he unobserved
> Home to his mother's house private returned.
>
> (IV.638–9)

A poem which had emphasised the crucifixion could hardly have avoided presenting the heroism of the Son as a public event. The Son in *Paradise Regained,* however, is heroic in the way that Abdiel and others were heroic in *Paradise Lost,* in patience, humility and forbearance. Wittreich concludes that

> Milton's poem does not end with the epiphanies signaled by the pinnacle scene. Those epiphanies are followed by the most heroic act of all. Having learned of his divinity, Christ instead of passing away into ecstasy returns to humanity. . . . By withstanding the temptation on the pinnacle Christ displays his enormous love for God; by returning home he displays his enormous love for man.[90]

Throughout *Paradise Regained,* the Son has rejected the temptation to act too quickly (the temptation which Adam failed to resist) and, at the end of the poem, when his divinity is evident, he nevertheless remains inactive, content to operate according to God's plan.

Beyond these theological reasons for rejecting the Passion and the crucifixion as the central events for his poem, Milton had also a political motive. The crucifixion had been appropriated by the Royalists as a symbol to represent the suffering of Charles I. The frontispiece to *Eikon Basilike* depicts the penitent Charles kneeling in prayer and rejecting the crown of worldly power in favour of the crown of thorns which will eventually bring him a crown of heavenly glory. This evocative portrait was reinforced by tracts such as the sermon published by the Bishop of Rochester which asserted that Charles, like Christ, 'shall ascend, and for an earthly ignominious Crowne, he shall receive an heavenly glorious one'.[91]

Milton is careful therefore to define the kingship of the Son in *Paradise Regained* in terms very far removed from the sacrificial image associated with Charles.[92] He not only underplays the importance of the crucifixion as a stage in the regaining of Paradise, but also gives to the Son a definition of kingship which overturns the words of Charles which accompanied the frontispiece to *Eikon Basilike*. The Son rejects Satan's offer of earthly kingship:

> I reject
> Riches and realms, yet not for that a crown,
> Golden in show, is but a wreath of thorns,
> Brings dangers, troubles, cares, and sleepless nights
> To him who wears the regal diadem,
> When on his shoulders each man's burden lies;
> For therein stands the office of a king,
> His honour, virtue, merit, and chief praise,
> That for the public all this weight he bears.
>
> (II.457–65)

The Son makes it quite clear that he is not rejecting earthly kingship because its duties are arduous and onerous; a king can expect troubles and sleepless nights. This reads very much like a deliberate charge of cowardice against Charles, who had vigorously complained of the woes he suffered in the verse at the front of *Eikon Basilike*:

> Though clogg'd with weights of miseries
> Palm-like Depressed I higher rise
> . . . That splendid but yet toilsom crown
> Regardlessly I trample down
> With joy I take this Crown of thorn
> Though sharp yet easy to be born . . .

It is remarkable that, even after the restoration of the monarchy, Milton should so continue his attack upon Charles I as to have the Son suggest that kings have no business to complain about the burdens which they are forced to endure.

Paradise Regained can scarcely be said to stand as a poem in its own right, so dependent is it upon the narrative and the themes of *Paradise Lost*. Its opening lines take us back immediately to the issues of the earlier epic:

> I who erewhile the happy garden sung,
> By one man's disobedience lost, now sing
> Recovered Paradise to all mankind,
> By one man's firm obedience fully tried
> Through all temptation, and the tempter foiled
> In all his wiles, defeated and repulsed,
> And Eden raised in the waste wilderness.
>
> (I.1–7)

The wilderness is to replace the pastoral Eden as a central locale, obedience and resistance to temptation are to be the basis of the heroism in the poem, effecting a simple defeat of Satan to match the simplicity of his victory over Adam and Eve. The temptations which the Son encounters in the wilderness are in many respects similar to those which Adam faces in *Paradise Lost* (temptations of appetite, action and ambition, for example), but the differences are perhaps more striking. Obedience for Adam and Eve was, after all, relatively straightforward, since they knew precisely what the nature of the prohibition was. Stanley Fish points out that:

> The tree is always there. . . . The literal physicality of the law – the fact of the tree – merely makes it easier for them to see what the issue is – obedience to God – for no other reason for not eating exists.[93]

The Son does not have the benefit of so specific a prohibition, as Satan himself points out:

> What doubts the Son of God to sit and eat?
> These are not fruits forbidden, no interdict
> Defends the touching of these viands pure,
> Their taste no knowledge works, at least of evil,
> But life preserves . . .
>
> (II.368–72)

Paradise Regained, like *Paradise Lost*, is about the exercise of choice, but the context is more worldly and, without the clear definition of a forbidden fruit, the Son must decide for himself what action is good and what evil, just as we must. *Paradise Regained* operates for the most part in a realistic setting and involves temptations which are powerful and alluring. The Son is placed in the midst of a local political struggle between Tiberius, the Israelites, and the Parthians, and the poem is therefore able to concern itself with the problems of a man placed within real time, and with the temptations which will assail him. This has the double advantage of allowing Milton to allude once again to the political situation of his own time, and of humanising the portrayal of the Son.

The soliloquy in Book II is a good instance of the humanity of the Son, in his lack of foreknowledge and the limitation of his power to overcome hunger:

> Where will this end? Four times ten days I have passed
> Wandering this woody maze, and human food
> Nor tasted, nor had appetite . . .
> But now I feel I hunger . . .
>
> (II.245–52)

and his first words in Book I (line 196) indicate that the memory of the

Son goes back only as far as his incarnation as a human child. He is consistently presented as a man throughout *Paradise Regained*, his sole advantage being an extreme faith in the providence of God. In this respect, the portrayal of the Son is reinforced by the characterisation of Mary and the apostles. They, like the Son, reflect upon the personal history of the Messiah, and compare their expectations with their experience. The Son had harboured ambitions which were conventionally heroic:

>   victorious deeds
> Flamed in my heart, heroic acts, one while
> To rescue Israel from the Roman yoke,
> Thence to subdue and quell o'er all the earth
> Brute violence and proud tyrannic power . . .
>
>   (I.215–19)

These ambitions, however, although presented in such stirring terms, have been replaced by more modest but much more far-reaching aims:

> Yet held it more humane, more heavenly first
> By winning words to conquer willing hearts,
> And make persuasion do the work of fear;
> At least to try, and teach the erring soul
> Not wilfully misdoing, but unaware
> Misled . . .
>
>   (I.221–6)

The balance and alliteration give greater emphasis to this new ambition to conquer willing hearts through winning ways. As an activity this may be less spectacular, but it is of greater significance because it involves a personal commitment by each individual to gain his own salvation. The Son has rejected military action which would win supremacy for one nation over another, in favour of education, which will leave each individual free to decide whether his heart is willing to receive salvation.

Milton presents the Son as having worked out for himself the superiority of education over coercion, and he is equally careful to present Mary and the apostles as ordinary people whose faith is tested by their experience. Mary begins her soliloquy by bewailing her fate, which has brought her more disappointment than honour, and yet she ends that speech in acceptance of the ways of God:

>   I to wait with patience am inured;
> My heart hath been a storehouse long of things
> And sayings laid up, portending strange events.
>
>   (II.102–4)

Nor does Milton elevate the apostles in *Paradise Regained*. They are introduced as simple, ordinary men, confused at what has been going on around them:

> Then on the bank of Jordan, by a creek:
> Where winds with reeds, and osiers whisp'ring play
> Plain fishermen, no greater men them call,
> Close in a cottage low together got
> Their unexpected loss and plaints outbreathed.
>
> (II.25–9)

The apostles become, therefore, almost pastoral figures in Milton's poem, and their faith and patience are first tested and then rewarded. Heroism is thus defined in this poem, as in *Paradise Lost*, in terms of the acceptance of God's providence and the patient endurance of suffering in the belief that a larger plan is being fulfilled. Mary and the apostles manifest this kind of heroism by continuing to believe that they have not been deserted by God or by the Son, even though the withdrawal of the Son to the wilderness is both disappointing and incomprehensible to them.

Milton's principal sources for the poem (in addition to the account of the temptation of Christ in St Luke's gospel) seem to be the trial of Sir Guyon in Book II of Spenser's *The Faerie Queene*, and the Old Testament book of *Job*. Milton described *Job* as the model of a brief epic in his survey of literary genres in *The Reason of Church Government*, and its story of unmerited suffering and trial seems to provide the closest analogy to the narrative of *Paradise Regained*: Job is, moreover, alluded to six times in the course of the poem, as a forerunner of Satan's temptation of the Son.

There are a number of parallels in the narrative construction of *Paradise Regained* and *Paradise Lost*. Each begins *in medias res*, includes a dream which anticipates a later incident, and involves action in three different locations. *Paradise Regained* makes use of the earlier poem to build a much more economical narrative: it is able to encompass all three of its centres of action within the opening book of the poem. In consequence, a rather different impression is given of Satan: he is more confident at the opening of the poem than at the beginning of *Paradise Lost*. Although he is unsure how best to tempt the Son, he has no doubt that temptation is the strategy to be employed, and the uncertainties which the fallen angels express at the beginning of *Paradise Lost* about their own natures and their possible future are entirely absent. The effect is to make this poem far more concentrated, and more exclusively concerned with a single, worldly event. The first meeting of Satan and the Son occurs within the opening book, and Satan's initial approach is brilliantly described:

But now an aged man in rural weeds,
Following, as seemed, the quest of some stray ewe,
Or withered sticks to gather; which might serve
Against a winter's day when winds blow keen,
To warm him wet returned from field at eve . . .

(I.314–18)

This description not only makes Satan seem innocuous, a powerless and pathetic old man, but even invests him with possible positive attributes through its use of pastoral allusion. Satan assumes the guise of a shepherd and becomes a parody of the Christian priest taking care of his flock. Satan, however, like Comus before him, is interested only in maintaining his flock of 'withered sticks': sinful souls of which he can make use. Satan's temptations can be as alluring as those of *Paradise Lost*, especially in the description of the feast which he presents to the Son, a sensuous delight:

In ample space under the broadest shade
A table richly spread, in regal mode,
With dishes piled, and meats of noblest sort
And savour, beasts of chase, or fowl of game,
In pastry built, or from the spit, or boiled,
Grisamber-steamed; all fish from sea or shore,
Freshet, or purling brook, of shell or fin,
And exquisitest name . . .
And at a stately sideboard by the wine
That fragrant smell diffused, in order stood
Tall stripling youths rich-clad, of fairer hue
Than Ganymede or Hylas . . .

(II.339–53)

Like *Paradise Lost*, this brief epic contains disparaging references to earlier, conventional epics, and the debates between Satan and the Son turn on the difference between conventional heroism and the new heroism of the Messiah. At the beginning of Book III Satan attempts to compare the Son with earlier heroes:

Thy years are ripe, and over-ripe, the son
Of Macedonian Philip had ere these
Won Asia and the throne of Cyrus held
At his dispose, young Scipio had brought down
The Carthaginian pride, young Pompey quelled
The Pontic king and in triumph had rode.

(III.31–6)

The point of this ringing list of heroic names is to tempt the Son to political expediency. Satan's error is to assume that the Son is in any sense comparable to these earlier heroes: he fails to appreciate that the Son is not interested in achieving a political or military victory, and is therefore incomparable. It is unfortunate that one of the consequences of this incomparability is that the Son cannot be described in terms of conventional epic simile: he is quite different from all previous heroes and therefore transcends comparison or contrast. Satan's attempts at comparisons are thwarted by the speeches of the Son, which redefine the concepts surrounding heroism. The Son rejects the kind of glory associated with Alexander ('the son/of Macedonian Philip'), Scipio and Pompey:

> They err who count it glorious to subdue
> By conquest far and wide, to overrun
> Large countries, and in field great battles win,
> Great cities by assault . . .

>   (III.71-4)

The glory which the Son seeks is the further glory of God, not the valueless fame sought by conventional heroes. His kingship is not the sovereignty of any individual nation, but the guidance of all men to their spiritual health:

>   to guide nations in the way of truth
> By saving doctrine, and from error lead
> To know, and, knowing worship God aright,
> Is yet more kingly, this attracts the soul,
> Governs the inner man, the nobler part,
> That other o'er the body only reigns,
> And oft by force, which to a generous mind
> So reigning can be no sincere delight.

>   (II.473-80)

Throughout the poem the Son rejects the miraculous, the flamboyant and the public, and offers his teaching openly to Satan, who is clearly allowed freedom of choice:

> Thy coming hither, though I know thy scope,
> I bid not or forbid; do as thou find'st
> Permission from above; thou canst not more.

>   (I.494-6)

Satan, however, fails to learn from the teaching of the Son, although the Son himself profits from their debate and learns the nature of his own divinity. As might be expected from a poem written so late in Milton's career, there is little faith in the behaviour of the people at large:

> For what is glory but the blaze of fame,
> The people's praise, if always praise unmixed?
> And what the people but a herd confused,
> A miscellaneous rabble, who extol
> Things vulgar . . .
>
> (III.47–51)

Fallen man will tend to act rashly, according to Milton, and for this reason cannot be trusted. Milton had felt that the people were fickle for some time: *Eikonoklastes* (1649) had ended: 'an inconstant, irrational, and image-doting rabble; that like a credulous and hapless herd, begotten to servility'.[94] By 1660, this rabble had become so large that Milton was forced to conclude that the majority had no right to choose how they should be governed:

> More just it is, doubtless, if it come to force, that a less number compel a greater to retain, which can be no wrong to them, than that a greater number, for the pleasure of their baseness, compel a less most injuriously to be their fellow-slaves.[95]

In this context, it is perhaps unsurprising that the Son should reject the temptation to effect a victory on behalf of an elect nation, and should work instead for those who, like himself, continually renew their faith through working in the world.

Samson Agonistes

Samson Agonistes is at once an intriguing and an impressive poem. It is intriguing in the number of questions to which it gives rise: should the work be called a poem or a drama? When was it composed? How seriously can the views of the Chorus be taken? Is the work a tragedy? Is it a Christian work? It is impressive in the many individual passages of brilliance, in its inventiveness, and in its concentration upon its central character.

The pathos of Samson's condition at the beginning of the poem is immediately striking:

> O dark, dark, dark, amid the blaze of noon,
> Irrecoverably dark, total eclipse
> Without all hope of day!
> O first-created beam, and thou great word,
> Let there be light, and light was over all;
> Why I am thus bereaved thy prime decree?
>
> (lines 80–5)

This soliloquy is comparable to the laments by Satan and Adam in

Paradise Lost and the opening speech of the Son in *Paradise Regained*, and is all the more effective for its skilful use of repetition (relatively rare in Milton's poetry) and for its placing at the very outset of the work. However, passages of this calibre are not restricted to the opening soliloquy. The description by the Chorus of the approaching Dalila is equally memorable:

> Like a stately ship
> Of Tarsus, bound for th' isles
> Of Javan or Gadire
> With all her bravery on, and tackle trim,
> Sails filled, and streamers waving,
> Courted by all the winds that hold them play,
> An amber scent of odorous perfume
> Her harbinger, a damsel train behind . . .
>
> (lines 714–21)

Throughout the play, Milton discriminates carefully between the sounds of the feet of the various visitors to Samson, in a manner appropriate to a work which has a blind man as its central protagonist, and in this case the image of Dalila floating towards Samson gives rise to this extended simile. It implies not only the splendour of Dalila's appearance, but also her lack of consistency (liable to be moved by any wind that blows), and the attraction of her very smell.

At the climax of the work, Samson's destruction of the Philistine theatre is described by a messenger whose own excitement is evident in the vividness of his report:

> straining all his nerves he bowed,
> As with the force of winds and waters pent,
> When mountains tremble, those two massy pillars
> With horrible convulsion to and fro
> He tugged, he shook, till down they came and drew
> The whole roof after them, with burst of thunder
> Upon the heads of all who sat beneath . . .
>
> (lines 1646–52)

Samson Agonistes is a most inventive work in terms of Milton's expansion of the biblical narrative of Samson, found in *Judges*, chapters 13–16. There is no mention of these visitors to the captive Samson in the biblical account, no source for the possibility of release offered by Manoa and Dalila, no reference at all to the meeting of Samon and Harapha, and little more than the name itself upon which to develop the character of Manoa. *Samson Agonistes*, therefore, perhaps more than any other work by Milton, illustrates the extent of the poet's powers of imagination and invention.

It is also a work of remarkable concentration, so exclusively concerned with Samson and his fate that even when he has left the stage the other characters continue to talk exclusively of him. At times, indeed, the other characters seem to function as reflections of Samson, voicing ideas and even echoing images which Samson himself has used. The effect is to present the reader with a developing appraisal of Samson's career, involving the comparison and appraisal of his past, present, and possible futures. So absorbing is this appraisal, both for the reader and the characters within the poem, that the possibility of God's providence seems progressively to disappear from the centre of the debate, and the climax is all the more startling.

Milton wrote a preface to *Samson Agonistes* in which he explained his choice of form, modelled on the Greek tragedies of Aeschylus, Sophocles and Euripides. The preface contains this teasing sentence: 'Division into act and scene referring chiefly to the stage (to which this work never was intended) is here omitted'.[96] The parenthesis in this sentence raises a minor problem of classification: is this a poem or a drama? Milton does not make a discrimination, even in this preface, for he refers to tragedy as 'the most profitable of all other poems', and to *Samson Agonistes* itself as a 'drama'. Most critics refer to the work as a drama, and, despite Milton's statement of intent, *Samson Agonistes* has been regularly staged over the past three centuries, most recently in an effective adaptation for the 1983 Edinburgh Festival by the Backdrop Theatre Company.

Those who would challenge the long-accepted dating of *Samson Agonistes* as Milton's final work base their arguments on a wide range of different kinds of evidence. There is no extant manuscript for the play, no record of its composition in any of Milton's writings, and, furthermore, although Milton must presumably have dictated the play to an amanuensis, this individual has not been identified. References to the poem in early biographies of Milton fail to ascribe to it any conclusive date of composition, and therefore any attempt at dating the play must rest primarily on conclusions drawn from within the text itself.

William Riley Parker, one of the foremost Milton critics of this century, was perhaps the first to challenge the traditional date of *Samson Agonistes*, ascribing a date 1647–53 on the basis of echoes of prose works from that period, and of the inclusion of rhyme in the play: Milton had condemned rhyme in the second edition of *Paradise Lost* in 1668.[97] A.S.P. Woodhouse, on the other hand, argued that the play must have been composed immediately after the Restoration on the grounds of resemblances between Samson's condition and Milton's own dejection at that time.[98] Almost every piece of evidence advanced by a critic in support of one date has been countered by evidence by other critics who would reject that date, and the debate seems now to have all but died out. Few scholars would disagree that, although the story of Samson may have been in Milton's mind for many years, the composition of *Samson Agonistes* took place after the publication of *Paradise Lost*.

In deciding to write a drama on the model of Greek tragedy, Milton was committing himself to a genre with well-defined conventions. Renaissance interpretation of classical poetic theory dictated that Milton's drama would need to observe the unities of time, place and action. The action of the play would unfold on an unchanging set which represented a fixed location, and there would be a coincidence of dramatic time and real time. Milton's play has a single theme, the fate of Samson, and takes place on a feast day, the catastrophe itself occurring at noon. Further conventions dictated that acts of violence take place off-stage and are reported by observers, and that the structure of the play should be stylised: it opens with a prologue by the main character, and proceeds through a series of episodes in which that character debates with one or two other characters. After the prologue, and after each episode, there is a speech by the Chorus which sums up the action of that part of the play, and the whole drama is brought to a close with a final choric ode.

In *Samson Agonistes* there is an opening soliloquy, which is followed by five episodes leading up to Samson's departure from the stage. The hero is visited in turn by the Chorus, Manoa, Dalila, Harapha, and the Philistine Officer, a sequence of visits which is arranged climactically to bring Samson from his initial desperate and passive state to a position where he can once more believe that God has a role for him to play in his divine scheme.

In the prologue Samson presents himself as physically beaten, although mentally very alert. He is at a low ebb as he seeks rest for his tired body on this holiday which celebrates an alien god. Samson, who is described by the Chorus as lying 'at random, carelessly diffused' (line 118), is aware of the irony of his situation; allowed a holiday from physical labour by a religion which he despises, he is in fact subject to an even greater torment from his own thoughts. The prologue makes clear that Samson feels that he has been betrayed by God, and that the promises of his election, so flamboyantly announced before his birth, have not been fulfilled. Samson describes this announcement with vigour and energy:

> foretold
> Twice by an angel, who at last in sight
> Of both my parents all in flames ascended
> From off the altar, where an offering burned,

As in a fiery column charioting
His godlike presence . . .

(lines 23–8)

Samson's initial response is to blame God for not having allowed him
to fulfil this brilliant promise, and he is unable to accept his share of
the responsibility even though he tries. He admits that he was foolish
to betray his secret to a woman, but immediately goes on to blame
God, firstly for not giving him more wisdom, and secondly for the
terms of the bond made between God and himself:

God, when he gave me strength, to show withal
How slight the gift was, hung it in my hair.

(lines 58–9)

At this stage, at the beginning of the play, Samson appears to believe
that his hair was the literal seat of his strength, and that prohibitions
on its cutting were therefore an indication of God's manipulation of
man: he believes that God set him an arbitrary test merely to enforce
his obedience. Samson's attitude to this temptation, which has
occurred outside of the time-scale of the drama, is therefore comparable
to that of Adam and the Son to their temptations in *Paradise Lost* and
Paradise Regained. The pledge of Samson's obedience like the tree of
knowledge for Adam, may seem arbitrary, but it is also very clear: so
long as Samson retained the secret, he remained the champion of God.
The temptations which Samson has to face in the course of the drama,
on the other hand, are less clearly signposted, and are therefore closer
to those which the Son had to undergo in *Paradise Regained*. To
overcome these temptations Samson has to use both reason and a
renewed faith in God, and, having overcome them, he can not only
move on to further action with a new sense of his own ability, he can
also reach a clearer understanding of the real significance of that
earlier pledge of strength associated with his hair. When Harapha, the
Philistine champion, suggests that this pledge was ridiculous, Samson
can reply in a manner which indicates how much he has learned:

Harapha: Thou durst not thus disparage glorious arms
                        . . . had not spells
And black enchantments, some magician's art,
Armed thee or charmed thee strong, which thou from heaven
Feign'dst at thy birth was given thee in thy hair,
Where strength can least abide . . .
Samson: I know no spells, use no forbidden arts;
My trust is in the living God who gave me
At my nativity this strength, diffused
No less through all my sinews, joints and bones,

Than thine, while I preserved these locks unshorn,
The pledge of my unviolated vow.

(lines 1130–44)

At this stage in the poem Samson can appreciate that the association of his strength and his hair was a symbol, not a fact, and that this pledge did not convey the magical properties of an election which absolved him from any personal responsibility. On the contrary, it was the sign of a contract which obliged him to continue to act virtuously throughout his life. By the time that he meets Harapha, Samson has learned that election carries responsibility, and the fact that he is able to repudiate ideas from Harapha which are very close to those which he himself had expressed in the prologue is typical of the way in which his regeneration is effected in *Samson Agonistes*.

The role of the Chorus in *Samson Agonistes* is unusual and problematic. Milton develops the conventional function of the Chorus so that it includes not only commentary on the action which has taken place, but also involvement within that action, since the Chorus is the first of Samson's visitors. This group of fellow tribesmen is the first in the series of comforters, none of which brings any comfort at all, but act instead as catalysts, enabling Samson to clarify his own thinking. Recent criticism of *Samson Agonistes* has tended to take the views of the Chorus more seriously than was the case in the past,[99] but it is not possible to look to the Chorus for absolute guidance on how the drama should be interpreted. The views of the Chorus develop during the course of the play, but they remain limited and partial, not through folly but because of the perspective from which they are taken. The view of the Chorus is limited because the Chorus cannot be aware, as we are, of the way in which this holiday will end, nor can they appreciate, at the close of the play, the effect that Samson's action will have on the history of their tribe. Our perspective enables us to see the limitations of the Chorus, which is no more ridiculous in its aspirations than are the disciples in *Paradise Regained*: both groups base their hopes on partisan political aims, and we can appreciate the deficiencies in these aims in both cases.

A drama which employs the conventions of Greek tragedy will necessarily involve retrospection and irony. It will be retrospective because it will need to include reference back to those portions of the narrative which have taken place before the beginning of the drama: *Samson Agonistes*, however, is retrospective to a much greater degree than demanded by convention, continually recalling in its first 1200 lines the exciting events of a tale which is regarded by all of the participants as having come to an end long before the play itself started. Tragedies on the Greek model will involve irony because the audience is continually aware of what the ending will involve, and the characters in the drama do not have this awareness. The plots of Greek tragedy were based upon well-known narratives, and the audience is interested not in what will happen at the end, but in the process leading to this climax. There are numerous ironies in *Samson Agonistes* which are revealed in the course of the play, such as the fact that the Philistine holiday brings a Philistine massacre; that Samson's blindness (which apparently renders him harmless) helps him gain the wisdom to be a champion once again; and that Samson's triumph can only be effected at the cost of his own life.

The greatest ironies, however, lie beyond the scope of the play itself, since they depend upon an appreciation of the significance of Samson's story in a larger historical context. The Chorus cannot know that Samson's triumph and its political import are only a fore-shadowing of the triumph which will be effected by Christ, and which will transcend politics and nationhood. Nobody mentions Christ in the course of *Samson Agonistes*, because no character is in a position to anticipate Christ's coming, but Milton could expect his audience to appreciate the connection between Samson's action and the fate of Christ, and to understand the irony of the Chorus's words:

> patience is more oft the exercise
> Of saints, the trial of their fortitude,
> Making them each his own deliverer,
> And victor over all
> That tyranny or fortune can inflict . . .

(lines 1287–91)

Although Samson acts as a hero once again just after this speech, the Chorus is right to feel that each individual needs to find his own path to deliverance. Samson's action at the end of the play is not sufficient to free his people from oppression, nor is Christ's dying for mankind enough to absolve men from responsibility for their own salvation. Milton's play, like his poetry, emphasises the need for everyone to work towards their own salvation, and not to rely upon the efforts of others.

The debate between the Chorus and Samson constitutes the second part of the exposition of the play, which concentrates upon the political dimension of Samson's career. Whereas the prologue had emphasised Samson's personal disappointment at the contrast between his glorious past and his ignominious present, the debate with the Chorus indicates the implications of this fall for the Israelite nation, and forces Samson to defend his earlier behaviour, attempting to justify his errors on the grounds of political necessity. Nevertheless, Samson's principal concern is still with his personal situation, and with the damage which may have been done to his reputation:

> Am I not sung and proverbed for a fool
> In every street, do they not say, how well
> Are come upon him his deserts?
>
> (lines 203–5)

Samson's progress will be indicated in his ability to stop worrying about his personal reputation and to turn his attention instead to the reversal which his God has suffered at the hands of Dagon. That change is begun in the debate with Manoa, the second episode of the play:

> I do acknowledge and confess
> That I this honour, I this pomp have brought
> To Dagon . . .
>
> (lines 448–50)

At this stage in the drama Samson appears to have had a briefly glorious career which has now ended in misery. He has lost the ability which he once had to free his country and has suffered a personal reversal with political implications. He has been a man apart during his earlier career as a hero, and remains so now in his misery for, although his countrymen suffer the oppression of Philistine domination, they have not undergone the physical pain of Samson, who has been literally enslaved by his captors.

In this situation, the temptation implicit in Manoa's visit is particularly attractive, and powerful. Manoa is, after all, no satanic enemy attempting to damn Samson's soul, he is Samson's father and offers only rest and restirement for his son. This temptation is, however, a dangerous one for all men, for it involves the surrender of the individual responsibility for personal salvation. Samson can now appreciate that his own guilt led to his downfall, and that his earlier apparent glory was vain and illusory, yet he harbours the mistaken belief that

> the strife
> With me hath end; all the contest is now
> 'Twixt God and Dagon . . .
>
> (lines 460–2)

If Samson accepted the idea of ransom and retirement offered by Manoa, then he would indeed be moving out of the battle between God and Dagon, but the irony is that he rejects this idea, for the wrong reasons, and thus makes it possible for the providence of God to be manifest. Samson rejects the offer because he cannot believe Manoa's prediction that God has a further use for him, and in a way he is right. Manoa's vision of the future for Samson is limited to a hope that his role as a martial hero will be restored through some splendid miracle:

> God who caused a fountain at thy prayer
> From the dry ground to spring, thy thirst to allay
> After the brunt of battle, can as easy
> Cause light again within thy eyes to spring . . .
>
> (lines 581–4)

Although Samson had himself revealed in the prologue that he still remembered the appeal of these earlier miracles, he does not believe that his sight will be restored, nor that he will win further triumphs in battle. He is correct in these beliefs, although the conclusion he draws (that only punishment and despair remain for him) is wrong. He will indeed 'shortly be with them that rest' (line 598), but only after he has once more acted for God.

Manoa is presented as a very sympathetic character in *Samson Agonistes*. He is genuinely concerned with the well-being of his son, and well aware of his own responsibilities towards Samson. The prologue emphasised Samson's personal crisis, the first episode concentrated on Samson as the Danite champion, but the second is primarily concerned with Samson as the son of Manoa. Beneath all of Manoa's negotiations for the ransom lie his anxieties about the damage which may have been done to his family's reputation. His reference in this second episode to this disgrace:

> Of all reproach the most with shame that ever
> Could have befall'n thee and thy father's house.
>
> (lines 446–7)

is balanced by the kind of consolation which Manoa finds in Samson's fate at the end of the drama. From Manoa's point of view Samson's triumph has restored the good name of the family:

> To Israel
> Honour hath left, and freedom, let but them
> Find courage to lay hold on this occasion,
> To himself and father's house eternal fame . . .
>
> (lines 1714–17)

This concern with family reputation also conditions Manoa's plans for Samson's memorial:

> I . . .
> Will send for all my kindred, all my friends
> To fetch him hence and solemnly attend
> With silent obsequy and funeral train
> Home to his father's house.
>
> (lines 1728–33)

Manoa's aim is a kind of appropriation of Samson, removing from him the dangerous and separating status of national champion in order to accommodate him into the family once more, and he achieves this aim at the end of the play through possession of Samson's body. The audience, however, knows that Samson's place in history depends as little on his having been Manoa's son as it does on his having been a Danite champion. Samson has to transcend family ties and national loyalties, and even the temptation to preserve his own life, in order to effect a triumph which had no immediate political effect. Israel's leaders do not 'find courage to lay hold on this occasion', and the significance of Samson's action is only apparent many years later. The analogy which Milton presumably wished his audience to make is that the long-term consequences of the English Revolution would be a similar ultimate success, reversing the apparent short-term failure.

Like *Paradise Regained*, *Samson Agonistes* is concerned with an alternative version of history, in which those who are politically successful are not those who will ultimately triumph. Manoa's incredulity at Samson's physical situation is comparable to the astonishment feigned by Satan in *Paradise Regained*:

O miserable change! is this the man,
That invincible Samson . . .
(*Samson Agonistes*, 340–1)

Sir, what ill chance hath brought thee to this place
So far from path or road of men . . .
(*Paradise Regained*, I.321–2)

In both cases the physical degradation is only apparent, serving as a platform on which spiritual development can be built.

The debate between Samson and Dalila is central to *Samson Agonistes*. Dalila is a Philistine, Samson's wife, and the source of his previous downfall, and thus represents a potent mixture of divided loyalties for Samson. The temptation which she offers of a future with her involves a more extreme form of abdication of responsibility than that offered by Manoa. If Samson were to submit to Dalila he would not only be resigning his role as a champion but also be renouncing his patriotic duty as an Israelite and his very manhood itself, surrendering himself to the supremacy of a woman. Samson has come to realise the extent to which this vanity has made his former career seem hollow:

Fearless of danger, like a petty god
I walked about admired of all and dreaded
On hostile ground, none daring my affront.
Then swoll'n with pride into the snare I fell
Of fair fallacious looks . . .
(lines 529–33)

The very pride which led Samson to act as champion 'like a petty god', believing himself to be greater than other men, brought about his downfall by making him susceptible to Dalila's blandishments, thus making him weaker than other men. By the time that Dalila herself appears in the play, Samson has already come to see the irony and the bathos of his earlier defeat, and has confessed that, after withstanding battles against his enemies, he eventually gave way to 'blandished parleys, feminine assaults,/ Tongue-batteries' (lines 403–4).

The bitterness of the anticlimax in these images is not merely an index of Samson's feelings for Dalila, it also arises from his developing insight into his own folly, his own culpability, and that makes the debate with Dalila all the more vigorous. Samson can respond readily to Dalila's arguments because they bear a curious similarity to those which he has used himself to defend his own actions. Dalila claims a political motive for her betrayal of Samson, just as he had claimed a political motive for both of his marriages. The fact that he can see through her excuses lays bare the true selfishness of his own past, and the extent to which he has abused the privilege of his election. At the end of the episode, Samson is able to understand that his betrayal by Dalila did not merely make his own reputation ridiculous, it also signalled his willingness to put his personal lusts before his love of God:

> God sent her to debase me,
> And aggravate my folly who committed
> To such a viper his most sacred trust
> Of secrecy . . .

> (lines 999–1002)

As the play continues, Samson becomes progressively aware of the extent of his guilt, and of the true significance of his earlier downfall. Dalila, however, is given a closing speech which indicates her expectations of the way in which history will view her:

> in my country where I most desire
> . . . I shall be named among the famousest
> Of women, sung at solemn festivals,
> Living and dead recorded, who to save
> Her country from a fierce destroyer, chose
> Above the faith of wedlock-bands . . .

> (lines 980–6)

There is a double irony in these lines: on the one hand, Milton's audience would not agree with Dalila's description of her place in history, and would include her in the list of temptresses rather than of heroines; on the other hand, the choice which she is advocating is in part the very choice which Samson has to take. He must choose to put country above 'wedlock-bands', but he must also put love of God before all other motives.

Manoa's visit has helped Samson to clarify his relationship with his captors, and has confronted him with questions about whether retirement from the fray is an adequate response to his situation. Dalila's visit helps Samson to define his relationship with his God, and enables him to see that the excuse of divine guidance can appear questionable when used to defend dubious personal or political actions. Samson has assumed in the past that his own election was sufficient to allow him to act in whatever manner he pleased. That illusion has now been removed, and the contest between God and Dagon has come to seem degraded. By the end of the Dalila episode, the audience has seen this contest described in terms of abortive battles and of sexual blackmail. Samson's efforts to use his strength have brought no positive benefits for himself or for his country, since he has failed to keep his own appetites under control. Having arrived at a point where his entire career has come to seem trivial, and where his own claims of divine inspiration can be countered by rival claims from worshippers of Dagon, Samson is visited by Harapha.

Harapha is more obviously a reflection of Samson's past than even Manoa or Dalila. He is an example of the kind of proud, vain champion that Samson once was, and yet his arrival does not instil fear or despair in Samson, who has learned from his earlier visitors and can counter the taunts and jibes of this antagonist, armed with a greater understanding of what it means to be a champion. Samson can now discriminate between the fact of his strength and the symbol of his hair, and he can appreciate that his previous career was doomed to failure:

> I was no private but a person raised
> With strength sufficient and command from heaven
> To free my country; if their servile minds
> Me their deliverer sent would not receive,
> But to their masters gave me up for nought,
> The unworthier they . . .
>
> (lines 1211–16)

The people are so fickle, so wrong-headed that they cannot be relied upon, and, since no champion can effect a lasting victory entirely through his own efforts, the best that Samson can do is to work towards his own salvation.

Throughout the drama, religion and politics have been intermixed, and religious experience has been primarily defined in terms of the dominance of one people by another. Although the drama takes place on a religious holiday there is little expectation that the day will be observed in worship, as Samson himself admits:

> Lords are lordliest in their wine;
> And the well-feasted priest then soonest fired
> With zeal, if aught religion seem concerned:
> No less the people on their holy-days
> Impetuous, insolent, unquenchable . . .
>
> (lines 1418–22)

Samson's final act is a signal of his willingness to submit himself to the will of God; it is an act of sacrifice and of atonement, and might be considered as the single example of religious experience in the entire play, untrammelled by political associations. Samson's final words, reported by the Messenger, emphasise that Samson is, at last, exercising his free will:

> Hitherto, lords, what your commands imposed
> I have performed, as reason was, obeying,
> Not without wonder or delight beheld.
> Now of my own accord such other trial
> I mean to show you of my strength, yet greater;
> As with amaze shall strike all who behold.
>
> (lines 1640–5)

This speech is a fitting epitaph for Samson's entire career, encompassing as it does early tasks which inspired wonder and delight and culminating in Samson's decision to undertake the ultimate test of the strength of his resolution. It hinges on the comparison between Samson's past deeds and his present life, the kind of comparison which has occurred throughout the play, and has rendered unnecessary any other form of simile to describe its hero. The comparison between past and present changes in the course of the play as the glories of Samson's earlier career are increasingly questioned, but, at the end of the drama, Manoa finds that the best yardstick for evaluating Samson's triumph is the comparison with Samson's own career:

> no time for lamentation now,
> Nor much more cause, Samson hath quit himself
> Like Samson, and heroicly hath finished
> A life heroic . . .
>
> (lines 1708–11)

Sonnets

In addition to exercising his considerable technical skill in mastering the long poem, Milton also wrote a number of fine sonnets which show a delicate and subtle control of this small-scale medium. Three in particular are worthy of close attention.

In the early 1650s Milton composéd the sonnet 'When I consider how my light is spent' (Sonnet XIX), in which a meditation on his blindness leads him to consider the role which he might play in working for his God, and the value which God will place upon that role. The opening line of the sonnet is conventional, and recalls Sonnet 15 in Shakespeare's sonnet sequence, yet the development is uniquely personal and individual. The sonnet becomes a dialogue between the poet and Patience, and, in its plainness and its use of direct speech, it resembles the devotional poems of George Herbert (see p. 45). The dialogue centres upon the kind of service which the blind writer can now offer to God, and his concern that God will be critical of his inability to make full use of the single talent which he has: the talent of writing. The sonnet, therefore, draws upon the Christian parable, from the Bible, Matthew, chapter 25, which emphasises that talents must be fully employed, and that those who do not employ them will be severely punished. The punishment specified has a particular relevance for Milton's situation: 'And cast ye the unprofitable servant into outer darkness: there shall be weeping and gnashing of teeth' (Matthew, 25:30). Ironically, it is the very fact of being cast into darkness which prevents Milton from exercising his talent as he would wish.

The answer provided by Patience, however, is reassuring, and contains in its final line the most celebrated sentiment from all of Milton's work:

They also serve who only stand and wait.

This reply is remarkable not only for its simplicity, in which respect it seems to anticipate the style used by the Son in *Paradise Regained*, but also for its definition of service to God. Service is defined in terms which are typically Puritan, involving no ostentatious display, and also consistent with Milton's portrayal of heroism elsewhere in his work, where patience and inaction are frequently more highly valued than dynamism.

Milton wrote a number of sonnets which were addressed to and concerned with particular individuals, but Sonnet XXII to Cyriack Skinner is clearly taken up with his own situation rather than that of his young friend. It is couched, once again, in the form of a dialogue, although the reply of Cyriack is supplied by Milton himself, and its principal theme is again the poet's blindness. Although he has endured the misery of this state for three years, Milton still finds consolation, a consolation of a somewhat more worldly kind than that in the earlier sonnet. By the time that he came to write this poem, Milton had achieved the celebrity for which he had sought so long, through his defence of the Commonwealth against Salmasius. It is this reputation which now sustains Milton in his blindness, and the tone of this sonnet is less plaintive and less poignant than the earlier sonnet on blindness: indeed, the assurance and self-sufficiency of the final lines come close to arrogance, and the last line might well have provided the title for Roger L'Estrange's pamphlet of 1660, *No Blind Guides*, which attacks Milton's defence of the Commonwealth regime.

The most personal and most affecting of Milton's sonnets, Sonnet XXIII, is written in memory of his wife, although there is, unfortunately, some unresolved ambiguity as to whether it is about Mary Powell, his first wife, or about Katherine Woodcock, his second. The poem records a dream in which his wife returns to him from the grave, only to disappear once more just as she is about to embrace him. Early sonneteers, including Shakespeare, had written before Milton of the pain of separation being dispelled by a dream, only to give way again to renewed and redoubled misery, but this poem is unusual within that tradition. The separation with which it deals is no temporary, worldly separation but the division brought about by death. The poet is, moreover, blind, and the vision of the lady in the dream goes beyond merely reuniting two lovers: it briefly restores to the poet that sense of sight which he has forever lost. The loss, therefore, in the final line is twofold:

I waked, she fled, and day brought back my night.

Despite the pathos of this situation, however, the sonnet is not uniformly solemn or pessimistic. The dream of the revivified wife, brought back from the grave like the legendary Alcestis who, in Greek mythology, gave her life to redeem her husband from death but was saved by Hercules, is invested with Christian allusions which carry with them the consolation that there will be an afterlife in which the poet's sight will be restored, and in which he will be reunited with his wife:

And such, as yet once more I trust to have
Full sight of her in heaven without restraint . . .

Part 3

Characteristics
of Milton's work

THIS PART WILL CONSIDER what the characteristics of Milton's work appear to be, and what is distinctive about his writing in terms of both its content and its style.

One of the most striking features of Milton's work is that his poetry, which ranges so widely in genre and in length, should nevertheless include so many common characteristics. These would include similarities in the use of historical perspective, opening and closing sections which operate to a common scheme, a focus on temptation expressed through the medium of debate, and a consistent definition of the nature of true faith.

It may not seem particularly remarkable to suggest that Milton's poems from 'Lycidas' onwards tend to involve a movement from past, through present, and into the future. This is, after all, the logical way in which time might be expected to be disposed in a narrative. What is unusual in Milton's treatment of historical time is that this process implies not only a movement forward in time, but also a progressive reappraisal of what has happened in the past.

'Lycidas', for example, after the initial *apologia* explaining the circumstances which have led to the writing of the poem, presents a very positive picture of an idyllic past:

Under the opening eye-lids of the morn,
We drove a-field, and both together heard
What time the grey-fly winds her sultry horn . . .
(lines 26–8)

This is replaced by a miserable present with no hope for the future:

Thee shepherd, thee the woods, and desert caves,
With wild thyme and the gadding vine o'ergrown,
And all their echoes mourn.
The willows, and the hazel copses green,
Shall now no more be seen,
Fanning their joyous leaves to thy soft lays.
(lines 39–44)

The poem, as a whole, however, is to move to a view of history which totally reverses this initial pessimism. The loss of Lycidas is demonstrated to have been an illusion, and the future which is anticipated from him eclipses the beauty of his pastoral earlier life:

> So Lycidas sunk low, but mounted high,
> Through the dear might of him that walked the waves;
> Where other groves, and other streams along,
> With nectar pure his oozy locks he laves,
> And hears the unexpressive nuptial song,
> In the blest kingdoms meek of joy and love.
>
> (lines 172-7)

This version of the future of life calls into question the assumptions that have been made about his past, and illustrates a general principle throughout Milton's poetry: that history is more difficult to interpret than might at first appear, and that the obvious patterns which might seem to emerge are not always the most accurate. In *Paradise Lost*, Satan, Adam, and Eve all have moments of retrospection from which they attempt to calculate the form of their futures: in each case the providence of God produces a version of the future which is far beyond their anticipation or prediction. Satan's triumph over man, which he celebrates prematurely in Book X of *Paradise Lost*, is purely temporary. The doom of death which Eve and Adam expect at the end of the poem does not come about as they expect, and the whole of Adam's dialogue with Michael in the last two books of *Paradise Lost* is taken up with Adam's misreading of the pattern of history. The Son, in *Paradise Regained*, begins the poem in some uncertainty about the apparent disparity between his past and his present states, just as Samson does in *Samson Agonistes*: each has learned by the end of the work that God has a plan for his future which transcends conventional heroism.

One aspect of this questioning of traditional readings of history which runs throughout Milton's major works is his exploiting and reversing of our expectations of what is tragic. The fate of Edward King seems a classic instance of the material of tragedy: a young man, whose life was free from blame and full of promise, has suffered violent and unexpected death. It appears that this event has been damaging to the whole world in its disruption of what we might expect of the natural cycle of time, and this apparent damage is emphasised in the early part of 'Lycidas' by the associated imagery of premature death:

> As killing as the canker to the rose,
> Or taint-worm to the weanling herds that graze,
> Or frost to flowers . . .
>
> (lines 45-7)

The poem as a whole, however, argues that the loss of Lycidas is not a tragic event, any more than the poem itself, which has been forced from the unwilling poet, has proved worthless. The apparently premature event has, in the larger time-scheme of God's providence, been to the benefit of the individual and of the human race:

> Henceforth thou art the genius of the shore,
> In thy large recompense, and shalt be good
> To all that wander in that perilous flood.

> (lines 183–5)

After the fall of man in *Paradise Lost*, and the painful vision of the future given to Adam, the poem moves to a conclusion which is far from tragic as Adam realises that the fall has paradoxically been fortunate in allowing God to show his love through the sacrifice of the Son:

> O goodness infinite, goodness immense!
> That all this good of evil shall produce,
> And evil turn to good . . .

> (XII.469–71)

In *Paradise Regained* and *Samson Agonistes*, Milton again calls into question assumptions about the progress of time. The Son is young and vigorous, and is expected to act out the role of the aggressive military leader, Samson is apparently enfeebled and blinded, and is expected to accept retirement. Each must learn to reject these obvious roles, and indeed to take the roles assigned to the other, as part of the manifestation of God's scheme.

The effect of this questioning is to produce passages at the conclusions of Milton's works which are much more optimistic in tone than the gravity of the preceding narratives might have suggested, and which suggest the reversal of previously-held views. Lycidas is 'not dead' but 'mounted high', Samson's death is no cause for lamentation, the Son has quelled Satan and can 'begin to save mankind', and Adam can articulate his own folly and his new knowledge:

> Greatly instructed I shall hence depart,
> Greatly in peace of thought, and have my fill
> Of knowledge, what this vessel can contain;
> Beyond which was my folly to aspire.

> (XII.557–60)

However, Milton does not merely leave the reader with an unambiguously optimistic ending, in which the central character has, through some splendid action, absolved the rest of humanity from the need to act. In each of the major works the conclusion takes the reader back into the world of everyday reality to put into practice the lessons learned from the experience of reading. In 'Lycidas' this movement is represented through the figure of the 'uncouth swain', who is revealed to have been, to the surprise of the reader, the author of the poem:

And now the sun had stretched out all the hills,
And now was dropped into the western bay;
At last he rose, and twitched his mantle blue:
Tomorrow to fresh woods, and pastures new.

(lines 190–3)

The calmness and the contemplative quality of this ending are in contrast with the energy of much of the earlier part of the poem, and yet are strongly suggestive, even at this point in Milton's career, of the need for action to be rational, considered, and undramatic. The 'uncouth swain' embodies Milton's ideal of quiet, steadfast, Christian service.

Paradise Lost ends by returning the poem to the reader, in leaving Adam and Eve to face the struggle of life encountered each day by each of us:

The world was all before them, where to choose
Their place of rest, and providence their guide:
They hand in hand with wandering steps and slow,
Through Eden took their solitary way.

(XII.646–9)

This beautifully simple ending has the effect of both reassurance and of challenge: there is a providential guide for Adam and Eve, as there is for all of us, and yet we are not absolved from the responsibility of continually exercising choice on the hazardous journey through life. The conclusion of the poem, like that of 'Lycidas', does not include solution, but rather a preparedness on the part of a character to apply the lessons of the poem to a life outside. This process is also contained within the endings of *Paradise Regained* and *Samson Agonistes*:

he unobserved
Home to his mother's house private returned.
(*Paradise Regained*, IV.638–9)

His servants he with new acquist
Of true experience from this great event
With peace and consolation hath dismissed,
And calm of mind all passion spent.
(*Samson Agonistes*, lines 1755–8)

Each of these works ends with a movement back to the everyday world, and each emphasises the process of education contained within the work as a whole. This process involves, of course, the education of the reader as well as the education of the characters within the works, and thus Milton's major poems constitute a challenging body of material.

One instance of the kind of challenge offered by Milton's work is the frequent occurrence of suggestively ambiguous opening passages. In 'Lycidas' the first eight lines are, at the same time, an apology for writing and a re-enactment of the death of Lycidas. *Paradise Lost* opens with a line which encourages one interpretation, only to reveal a different meaning as we read the second line:

> Of man's first disobedience, and the fruit
> Of that forbidden tree . . .

The opening line seems to make sense on its own, and to introduce the subject of the poem as disobedience and its direct consequences. However, as we move to the second line, we discover that 'fruit' is not to be linked with 'disobedience', but with the literal fruit of the tree of knowledge. At the end of this introductory passage, Milton defines his purpose in writing:

> That to the highth of this great argument
> I may assert eternal providence,
> And justify the ways of God to men.
>
> (I.24–6)

Even this apparently simple statement is capable of more than one construction: is he justifying to men the ways of God, or justifying the way in which God acts towards men?[1]

The ambiguity in the opening of *Samson Agonistes* lies in the absence of an identified recipient for Samson's opening speech. Although the speech is usually described as a soliloquy, the opening eleven lines seem to be addressed to a particular individual:

> A little onward lend thy guiding hand
> To these dark steps, a little further on . . .
>
> (lines 1–2)

The hand could be that of God, guiding Samson's path through life, or that of a human guide who is dismissed at line 11 by Samson's command 'here leave me to respire': the ambiguity becomes a problem only when the text is played on the stage.

Milton's poetry requires careful and attentive reading, and it is a useful and instructive exercise to attempt to render this poetry into prose, for that will often indicate how little of the richness of the poetry can be retained in a prose translation. Even so acute a critic as

Mary Ann Radzinowicz seems to do less than justice to the subtleties of Milton when she gives this prose version of *Samson Agonistes*, lines 46–51:

> I who could not keep under the seal of silence this high gift of strength committed to me and how easily bereft me and in what part it was lodged but o'ercome with importunity and tears must reveal it weakly to a woman.[2]

It is possible to read these lines with the interpretation:

> I could not keep under the seal of silence who it was who committed to me this high gift of strength and how easily bereft me and in what part it was lodged but o'ercome with importunity and tears must reveal it weakly to a woman.

Milton's original lines are capable of being read both ways, even in such an apparently straightforward a passage as this.

Throughout Milton's poetry there is a constant preoccupation with the meeting and defeating of temptation, and if this is to be successfully presented, then it must involve temptations in which the reader can become genuinely interested. The early poems give a very clear indication of the skill with which the young poet can describe the delights of sensuous temptation:

> When the merry bells ring round,
> And the jocund rebecks sound
> To many a youth, and many a maid,
> Dancing in the chequered shade;
> And young and old come forth to play
> On a sunshine holiday;
> Till the livelong daylight fail,
> Then to the spicy nut-brown ale . . .
>
> (L'Allegro', lines 93–100)

Milton is obviously attracted by these simple pleasures, which are dangerous only to those who devote their lives to enjoyment and nothing else. Temptation through the senses, however, accompanies the other modes of temptation employed by Comus, as he tries to ensnare the Lady:

> first behold this cordial julep here
> That flames, and dances in his crystal bounds
> With spirits of balm, and fragrant syrups mixed.
>
> (*Comus*, lines 671–3)

It is also part of the armoury of weapons used by Satan, as he tempts the Son by presenting for him a sumptuous feast in Book II of *Paradise*

Regained, and, in *Samson Agonistes*, a threat which Dalila seems to discover almost by accident:

Dalila: Let me approach at least, and touch thy hand.
Samson: Not for thy life, lest fierce remembrance wake
My sudden rage to tear thee joint by joint.

(lines 951-3)

Milton has a keen appreciation of the potency contained in the simple touch of an attractive woman, which, in this case, inspires a more passionate reaction from Samson than any earlier temptation in the play. It is this appreciation which makes his description of Adam's excessive devotion to Eve in *Paradise Lost* all the more credible.

However, vivid and alluring as these sensual and sexual temptations may be in Milton's work, his principal attention is devoted to intellectual arguments presented through debate. Debate becomes an increasingly prevalent force in Milton's work as his career develops, but even his earliest poetry shows his interest in argument, perhaps growing from his experience of delivering formal rhetorical addresses as a student. In 'L'Allegro' and 'Il Penseroso' it may appear that Milton's use of debate is at its most academic, and that he is more concerned with the formal presentation of a finely balanced argument than with giving real support to either viewpoint, but a closer reading reveals that the two poems are not arbitrarily ordered and that the superiority of one mode of living to another is being vigorously argued. Elsewhere, in Milton's major poems, debate is employed so extensively and to such consistent effect that the differences in genres seem to be of little consequence: it is arguable that *Samson Agonistes* has more in common with *Paradise Lost* than it has with *Comus*, although *Samson Agonistes* and *Comus* appear to share a similar dramatic framework.

Broadly speaking Milton's use of debate becomes more sophisticated as his career develops. In 'Lycidas' the series of voices which the poet hears is carefully ordered into a climactic sequence as part of the process whereby we learn of the elevation of 'Lycidas'. However, only two of these voices, those of Phoebus and St Peter, are allowed to speak at any length. *Comus* is more evidently dependent upon debate, although the philosophical dispute between the two brothers seems at times peculiarly arid. The difficulty with the debate between Comus and the Lady, which is potentially the most satisfying episode in the masque, is that the viewpoints of the two speakers are too polarised to admit of the possibility that either will be converted by the other. Indeed, the debate itself ends in stalemate, as Comus realises the virtue of the Lady but still knows that his wickedness cannot be altered and thus has to resort to force:

She fables not, I feel that I do fear
Her words set off by some superior power;
And though not mortal, yet a cold shuddering dew
Dips me all o'er . . .

(lines 799–802)

The debate in *Comus* is sterile, not only because the two central
characters have such extreme views but also because neither can be
changed from their standpoint. In *Paradise Lost*, however, there are
debates which seem truly open-ended, in which there is the possibility
of change and action. When the fallen angels debate in Hell their
rhetoric must transcend the formal presentation of an argument, it
must persuade the audience and be part of the formulation of a
strategy for the future. However, the admiration of the reader for the
skills of the speakers in that debate is likely to be eclipsed when, in
Book V, Abdiel enters the debate against Satan. At that point, in the
light of the account of the debate in Heaven before the war, the nature
of the debate in Hell becomes clearer: in Hell the debate appeared
lively, partly because the differences between the speakers were
relatively slight. The fallen angels may disagree about their best plan
for the future, but they are all fallen angels, and therefore their debate
will not include the possibility of God's forgiveness and His mercy. At
the debate in Heaven, however, Abdiel stands alone to make the
unpopular point that Satan's arguments are wrong. The vehemence of
Abdiel's words is impressive, not least for the courage he displays
when surrounded by his enemies, yet he wins no converts from this
assembly. The message seems to be that, whilst the lies of Satan will
find ready popular assent in Book II, truth may well go unsupported
by the majority in public debate: it does, however, stiffen the resolve of
the faithful.

Satan's temptation of Eve through argument is a more complex
temptation than that of the Lady by Comus. Whereas Comus felt the
power of the Lady's purity even though he could not be changed by it,
Satan comes much closer to being changed by the very sight of Adam
and Eve, before he has spoken to either of them:

to heavenly spirits bright
Little inferior; whom my thoughts pursue
With wonder, and could love, so lively shines
In them divine resemblance, and such grace
The hand that formed them on their shape hath poured.

(*Paradise Lost*, IV.361–5)

Yet Satan's success in his debate with Eve is not a result of the
intellectual force of his argument, but rather the outcome of a well-

conceived strategy. Satan tempts Eve by using arguments which she herself has already used and therefore, in contrast to Comus who opposes the views of the Lady, Satan tells Eve what she wants to hear. She has already argued that evil should be confronted and not avoided, and Satan's argument is therefore likely to win her assent:

> knowledge of good and evil;
> Of good, how just? Of evil, if what is evil
> Be real, why not known, since easier shunned?
>
> (IX.697–9)

In *Samson Agonistes* this technique is developed even further, as each of Samson's visitors uses an argument based upon an opinion which Samson himself had voiced earlier. The difference between the use of debate in *Comus* and that in *Samson Agonistes* is very great. In *Comus* we find the collision of opposing arguments and a central character who, although is some physical danger, shows no propensity for spiritual failing. The blandishments of Comus in his lair are easy to resist because he has become so unattractive to the Lady. In *Samson Agonistes*, on the other hand, the central character is not only capable of falling, he has fallen already, and the arguments which he has to counter are not only put by those with whom he is most intimately involved, they are arguments which he has used himself. Thus, whilst in *Comus* the Attendant Spirit has to point out for the Lady and for the audience the moral that divine help will be given to those who actively seek their own salvation, in *Samson Agonistes* that moral needs no pointing up: we have seen it clearly enacted in Samson's own battle to renew his faith in the light of his own doubts.

As one whose Puritanism had led him consistently to oppose the acceptance of orthodoxy and custom, and had resulted in his progressive alienation from any form of organised worship, Milton, not surprisingly, wrote most vividly of those who exhibited a strenuous and disciplined thirst for truth. It was never likely that he would express approval for those who took an easier route:

> Were it not better done as others use,
> To sport with Amaryllis in the shade
> Or with the tangles of Neaera's hair?
>
> ('Lycidas', lines 67–9)

Samson, perhaps more than any other of Milton's central characters, represented for Milton the spirit of the true warfaring Christian, a man prepared to act according to his conscience even in the face of opposition from his closest friends, accepting no form of sovereignty over him except that of his God.

Part 4

The critical debate

ALTHOUGH THE EARLY EDITIONS of *Paradise Lost* sold well, particularly well in comparison with *Poems 1645*, and Milton received royalty payments from his epic, it was not until the publication in 1688 of a lavish, illustrated, subscription edition of the poem that it could be claimed that *Paradise Lost* had achieved the status of an English classic. As W. W. Robson has recently remarked:

> In the twentieth century, when it is rarely read except by scholars and literary specialists, we are likely to forget how popular *Paradise Lost* once was. It stood on the shelves of every respectable household, beside the Bible and *The Pilgrim's Progress*.[1]

This very popularity, however, could be said to have worked against the liveliness of Milton's epic, in that it led to an unquestioning reverence of the poem on the part of the majority of its readers, and to the production of pale imitations of Milton's style by inferior poets, who failed to see that Milton is quite consciously placing himself at the end of a literary tradition, and that *Paradise Lost* in many respects denies the validity of the epic poem. However, Milton has never at any stage been totally beyond criticism, even on the part of his supporters. The essayist, Joseph Addison (1672–1719), for example, wrote a series of papers on Milton for *The Spectator* in 1712 in which he finds the poet 'sublime', and yet this very assertion led Addison to defend and discuss aspects of *Paradise Lost* which he felt failed to meet this criterion. On an even greater scale, the edition of *Paradise Lost* produced in 1732 by Richard Bentley (1662–1742) went as far as to amend those passages in the poem which the editor did not understand or did not like, on the grounds that these sections could not represent what the poet had intended.

It was not merely, therefore, those who disliked Milton (Dr Johnson (1709–84), for example) who could raise queries about *Paradise Lost*; Addison could question the decorum of the Limbo of Fools in Book III, and Bentley, in his emendation of the closing lines of the poem, forces the reader to consider why Milton described Adam and Eve as 'solitary'. The Bentley version reads:

> Then hand in hand with social steps their way
> Through *Eden* took, with heav'nly comfort cheer'd.[2]

replacing not only 'solitary', but also 'wandering', and thus concentrating the attention of the reader upon these key words.

Bentley justified some of his changes on the grounds that Milton's original text was too shocking to have been what the poet intended, and thus ironically emphasised one of the most conspicuous qualities of *Paradise Lost*. Milton undoubtedly intended his poem to shock and to challenge, and however eccentric Bentley's reading of the poem may be, it is arguable that he would have preferred Bentley's active engagement with the text to the passive acquiescence which more traditional readers have accorded it. Milton, after all, continually advocated the need for an explicit faith which was constantly renewing itself by challenge and debate, and the presence of recurring Milton controversies over the past two and a half centuries has ensured that successive generations of serious readers have had their faith in Milton's epic enhanced by trial. As Patrick Murray observes:

> In one important respect, Milton is in a more fortunate position than Shakespeare . . . . Modern Shakespeare criticism is lacking in vigour and excitement . . . Shakespeare has become a dead issue. Milton, thanks largely to his modern 'detractors', is still very much alive.[3]

Sir William Empson (*b.*1906), himself a member of the school of 'detractors', says of Bentley: 'he may only produce a trivial piece of nagging, but he has a flair for choosing an important place to do it.'[4]

Recent attacks on Milton have been almost exclusively concerned with *Paradise Lost* (some critics, indeed, wishing that Milton had continued to write as he did in 'Lycidas') and have done great service to the poem by posing questions and provoking responses which might otherwise never have been explicitly and systematically formulated. These attacks, which have been mounted by some of the foremost writers of the century, have centred, oddly enough, on the very issues raised in Barrow's commendatory verses of 1674 (see p. 78 above): can the reader be expected to enjoy the entire poem, and is Satan presented too attractively?

The language, and readability, of *Paradise Lost* has been the subject of debate from Addison and Johnson onwards. Addison argued that Milton

> has carried our language to a greater height than any of the English poets have ever done before or after him, and made the sublimity of his style equal to that of his sentiments.[5]

He also noted that 'our language sunk under him, and was unequal to that greatness of soul which furnished him with such glorious conceptions.'[6] Johnson, more trenchantly, capped Addison's remark with:

he had formed his style by a perverse and pedantic principle. He was desirous to use English words with a foreign idiom . . . . Of him, at last, may be said what Jonson says of Spenser, that *he wrote no language*.[7]

and of the poem as a whole he wrote:

Paradise Lost is one of the books which the reader admires and lays down, and forgets to take up again. None ever wished it longer than it is. Its perusal is a duty rather than a pleasure.[8]

There can be a variety of reasons which lead a critic to write negatively of a poet, and Johnson's criticisms owe as much to what he believed of Milton the man as to his views on poetry. The poet and critic T. S. Eliot (1888–1965) shared Johnson's antipathy towards Milton the man, and argued that not only had Milton had a bad effect on later English poetry, but that he lacked visual imagination, that his poetry gave priority to sound rather than to meaning, and that his language was remote:

Every distortion of construction, the foreign idiom, the use of a word in a foreign way or with the meaning of the foreign word from which it is derived rather than the accepted meaning in English, every idiosyncrasy is a particular act of violence which Milton has been the first to commit.[9]

In his second essay on Milton, Eliot shifted ground somewhat by claiming that this remoteness was a mark of Milton's greatness, but he was not allowed this recantation: the critic F. R. Leavis (1895–1978) carried on the crusade against Milton which Eliot had begun by declaring that Milton's language was monotonous, pompous, laboured, pedantic and artificial. His attack was uncompromising:

So complete, and so mechanically habitual, is Milton's departure from the English order, structure and accentuation that he often produces passages that have to be read through several times before one can see how they go, though the Miltonic mind has nothing to offer that could justify obscurity – no obscurity was intended: it is merely that Milton has forgotten the English language.[10]

The attack upon Milton's language was based upon several false premises. It tended to portray the 'Grand Style' of Milton's epic as unvarying and unwieldy, incapable of subtlety or delicacy, and incomparably poorer than the style of either Shakespeare or Spenser. The effect of the attack has been to prompt the publication of a number of excellent studies of *Paradise Lost*, each of which has demonstrated new intricacies in Milton's handling of the varied style of his epic. There are, undeniably, occasions upon which the style is complex (a less emotive term than Leavis's 'obscurity'), but always when a complex issue is being presented. Moreover, the reader needs to be alert even in those pasages of the poem which seem to yield an obvious meaning: in Book X, for example, where Milton presents this portrait of the despairing Adam:

> on the ground
> Outstretched he lay, on the cold ground, and oft
> Cursed his creation, death as oft accused
> Of tardy execution, since denounced
> The day of his offence. Why comes not death,
> Said he, with one thrice acceptable stroke
> To end me?
>
> (X.850–6)

This passage appears to be no more than a description of fallen man designed to call up in the mind of the reader the comparable portrait of the fallen Satan at the beginning of the poem: 'So stretched out huge in length the arch-fiend lay/Chained on the burning lake' (I.209–10). Closer attention reveals that the lines are not merely describing Adam's physical condition, but are also giving a clear indication of his mental agony. The creation which Adam is cursing is both God's creation of Adam, and the creation of Eve, made from Adam himself; the execution of which death has been tardy is both the carrying out of a promised plan, and the sentence of capital punishment; and the stroke, which Adam terms 'acceptable', involves a pun on 'axe'. Adam's own confusion is mirrored in the ambiguities of his diction.

As Jonathan Richardson, an early commentator on *Paradise Lost*, observed, the reader needs to be especially vigilant:

> a Reader of *Milton* must be Always upon Duty; he is Surrounded with Sense, it rises in every Line, every Word is to the Purpose . . . he Expresses himself So Concisely, Employs Words So Sparingly, that whoever will Possess His Ideas must Dig for them, and Oftentimes pretty far below the Surface.[11]

Since this remark was made as long ago as 1734 it is odd that critics in this century should continue to describe the language of *Paradise Lost* as mere music, as if Milton were using the sound of the words as an alternative for thought. Leavis's version of this line of attack is at least consistent with his other views on Milton:

> the man who uses words in this way has . . . no 'grasp of ideas', and, whatever he may suppose, is not really interested in the achievement of precise thought of any kind.[12]

C. S. Lewis (1898–1963), however, writing ostensibly in defence of Milton against the attacks of Eliot and Leavis, seems to come very close to finding Milton's language mere music himself:

> The epic diction, as Goethe said, is 'a language which does your thinking and your poetizing for you' . . . . The conscious artistry of the poet is thus set free to devote itself wholly to the large-scale problems – construction, character drawing, invention; his *verbal* poetics have become a habit, like grammar and articulation.[13]

The work of more recent critics such as Christopher Ricks, Stanley Fish and others[14] has demonstrated convincingly that Milton's epic diction is far from being a substitute for thought, and that it was no more subject to habit than his grammar or his use of metre. Although Milton employs impressive catalogues in his epic (for example, in Adam's vision of the future in Book XI), these are not simply there to be magnificent: the scholarship of recent editors has indicated the extent to which Milton carefully constructs these catalogues either to undermine the reader's confidence in the character or situation being described, or to challenge the status of earlier epics. Whatever Eliot, or Leavis, or even Lewis may believe, Milton is never so enchanted by the music of his epic diction that he becomes spellbound, like Marlowe's Tamburlaine, believing that magnificent names can in themselves confer dignity: 'Is it not passing brave to be a King,/And ride in triumph through Persepolis?' (*Tamburlaine* I, 758–9).

The misconception that Milton not only used language to avoid analysis, but also wrote with a syntax and a diction closer to Latin than to English has taken a long time to die out. It has, in part, been challenged by statistical surveys of Milton's language which have compared his usage with that of other writers, but these can provide only a limited insight into Milton's practice in his poetry, where it is impossible to discriminate between a strangeness of word-order arising from the imitation of another language, and the kinds of inversion which are a necessary consequence of the decision to write in verse. The following lyric, for example, from Shakespeare's *As You Like It*, illustrates some of the ways in which conventional word-order changes in the transformation from prose to verse:

> Under the greenwood tree
> Who loves to lie with me,
> And turn his merry note
> Unto the sweet bird's throat,
> Come hither, come hither, come hither:
> Here shall he see
> No enemy
> But winter and rough weather.

There is a considerable difference between the ordering of the words in this lyric and that in a prose passage expressing the same idea, and yet no critic has suggested that Shakespeare was wrenching the English language; nor has anyone complained of the strangeness of the word-order in this passage from *Macbeth*, despite the fact that it includes 'incarnadine', a verb of Shakespeare's own invention, based upon a Latin root:

> this my hand will rather
> The multitudinous seas incarnadine,
> Making the green one red.

We accept that 'incarnadine' has been separated from 'will' for reasons of emphasis and metre, and that, in the final line, 'the green' probably means 'the green sea'. Detractors of Milton's style have too rarely exercised such acceptance.

It would be possible to attempt a statistical survey of certain features of Milton's poetic style which were felt to be un-English, and to compare the incidence of these features in the work of a number of writers; and yet such a survey is likely to prove little. Some instances of disrupted word-order will seem particularly successful, as in the cases from Shakespeare cited above, whereas a different example of precisely the same disruption will seem discordant. Furthermore, it may not be possible in every case to state with certainty whether a normal, or conventional word-order has been followed by Milton or not. For example, Satan's speech at the beginning of Book II includes these lines:

> From this descent
> Celestial virtues rising, will appear
> More glorious and more dread than from no fall . . .
>
> (II.14–16)

If we were looking for examples of adjectives following nouns rather than, as is usual, preceding them, we might feel that this passage yielded no evidence: it seems quite conventional in its use of adjectives. However, it is at least arguable that the first six words in this passage could be read either as 'from this fall the rise of celestial virtues' or as 'from this celestial fall ascending groups of angels': the line can be read to include two instances of adjective-noun inversion, one instance, or none at all. In contrast, Book XI contains a passage which on first reading appears to include a clear instance of this kind of inversion, but which, read more carefully, is capable of quite a different meaning. The passage runs:

> So all shall turn degenerate, all depraved,
> Justice and temperance, truth and faith forgot;

One man except, the only son of light
In a dark age, against example good,
Against allurement, custom . . .

(XI.806–10)

The passage seems straightforward enough, describing the single just man who stands firm in a wicked world. 'Example good' in line 809 seems a classic instance of inversion, and it appears that we need only restore the normal order, 'good example', to bring out the sense of the passage. However, we may perhaps pause and ask why this single upright man should be opposed to good example: there is no doubt that he is, and should be, 'Against allurement', but the very presence of these two phrases side by side draws attention to the peculiarity of 'against example good'. The solution seems to be that 'good' is not modifying 'example' at all, but is describing the man, who is good despite the example of his contemporaries. The reader must be constantly alert to Milton's flexible use of language.

Perhaps the most ironic feature of the debate on Milton's language, apart from the fact that Milton himself criticised others for the foreignness of their diction, is that some of the most fluent attacks upon Milton have many of the qualities of Milton's prose. Leavis, for example, is withering in his treatment of his opponents, and employs Milton's tactic of blackmailing his readers by suggesting that no reasonable man could fail to agree with him: as Christopher Ricks remarks:

> In studying Dr. Leavis's argument, one must first notice that he is not above a pretty blatant bullying: 'It should be obvious at once to any one capable of being convinced at all . . .'; or 'It would be of no use to try and argue with any one who contended that . . .'.[15]

Sir William Empson, too, whose criticism of *Paradise Lost* will be considered below, can, while attacking Milton's account of the fallen angels, write prose which has all the bathos of a Miltonic epic simile. This passage, with its beautifully prepared deflationary ending, is comparable to the extended description of Mulciber (I.740–7), which whets our appetite for his story, only to tell us that it is a lie:

> Critics used to be fond of saying that Milton was gloating in the passage [the close of Book X] over how he had humiliated his first wife, when she begged to return to him, after it had become plain that her royalist family was on the losing side in the Civil War. The idea is probably not false.[16]

Empson is the author of the most provocative book on Milton yet written, *Milton's God*, a book which draws not only upon Empson's own atheism, but also upon his experience of having lived and taught outside of Western Europe, and which therefore raises challenging questions about Milton's portrayal of God, some of which have never satisfactorily been answered.

Interest in the presentation of God, and a fascination with the Satanic element in *Paradise Lost* is no new phenomenon, but it has proved a lively area of recent Milton study, in an age when not only were epic language and epic conventions unrecognised, but faith in God and a knowledge of the Bible could not be taken for granted. The twentieth-century reader provides the ideal test for the validity of *Paradise Lost*.

Satan became, for nineteenth-century readers and writers, 'an obsessive topic'.[17] Following Blake's remark in *The Marriage of Heaven and Hell* in 1793 that 'The reason Milton wrote in fetters when he wrote of Angels & God, and at liberty when of Devils & Hell, is because he was a true Poet and of the Devil's party without knowing it', the character of Satan began to exercise a considerable influence on English fiction, especially through the villains of Gothic novels, who are often recognisable as Satan in all but name. Lorna Sage remarks of the novels of Ann Radcliffe (1764–1823): 'in her Satanic villains the tyrant is unequivocally uppermost. Characters like Montoni in her *Mysteries of Udolpho* (1794) are explicitly condemned (though there remains a residue of unexplained attraction)'.[18]

These qualities of energy, wickedness, and an unexplained attraction can be found in a whole range of fictional characters in novels from *Jane Eyre* and *Wuthering Heights* (1847) to William Faulkner's *Light in August* (1932),[19] and the influence of *Paradise Lost* is particularly notable in Mary Shelley's *Frankenstein* (1818), in which the Monster reads Milton's poem and finds in it the explanation of its problem:

> I often referred the several situations, as their similarity struck me to my own. Like Adam, I was apparently united by no link to any other being in existence; but his state was far different from mine in every other respect. He had come forth from the hands of God a perfect creature, happy and prosperous, guarded by the especial care of his Creator . . . but I was wretched, helpless, and alone. Many times I considered Satan as the fitter emblem of my condition; for often, like him, when I viewed the bliss of my protectors, the bitter gall of envy rose within me.[20]

In many respects Mary Shelley's novel is tantamount to a re-interpretation of *Paradise Lost* and her attempt to translate her reading of Milton's epic into the medium of the Gothic novel is as revealing as the heroic opera (for which Milton gave his permission), *The State of Innocence and Fall of Man* (1678) by John Dryden (1631–1700).

In 1947 the critic A J. A. Waldock systematised the feeling which
had become popular through Gothic interpretations of Milton, that
Satan was an attractive figure, ill-deserving of his fate, in his book
Paradise Lost and Its Critics. Approaching the poem from the
perspective of one well versed in reading novels, Waldock argued that
Milton had been so successful in his description of a powerful and
attractive Satan in Books I and II of *Paradise Lost* that he had been
forced to jettison this character altogether and to replace him with the
degraded Satan who appears in the later books. If all the books and
articles on Milton were burned and we were left only with books
written between 1950 and 1980, future generations might be led to feel
that Waldock's critique of *Paradise Lost* had been outstandingly
influential, because so many later critics have written defences of the
poem against Waldock's attacks, far more than have attempted to
repudiate Empson's attacks in *Milton's God.* The truth is that
Waldock's thesis can be overturned relatively easily, whereas Empson's
charges are much more weighty.

Paradise Lost is neither a novel nor a drama, and Waldock's
attention to speeches (or parts of speeches) and incidents fails to do
justice to Milton's creation of a poetic narrative. Although ostensibly
concerned with the development of the narrative in the poem,
Waldock is not above considering incidents in an entirely different
order from that in which Milton has placed them, or omitting vital
details of their presentation. Writing, for example, of the temptation
of Adam by Eve at the end of Book IX, Waldock describes the
incident entirely in terms of the speeches made by the two characters,
and asks us to judge whether or not Adam should have yielded on the
basis of this dialogue. He fails to point out the effect of the context in
which this exchange takes place and, in particular, the symbolism of
the description of Adam's meeting Eve: he with a garland of flowers
which fade as soon as Eve tells her news, she with a bough from the
Tree of Knowledge. These details are crucial both to our evaluation of
the scene and to Adam's guilt. Similarly, although he censures Milton
for intruding authorial comments about Satan which undermine the
magnificence of his early speeches, Waldock himself attempts to
persuade us by imagining the reaction of the fallen angels to these
speeches: Milton chose when to give us these reactions and when to
withhold them. Waldock, therefore, provides a critique upon a poem
which is not Milton's *Paradise Lost*, and lays charges against Milton
which are quite unfair: for Waldock, Hell is not described in
sufficiently concrete detail, and yet, if it had been, Milton's God would
have been truly vengeful and the debate among the fallen angels in
Book II would have been utterly pointless: the only possible outcome
of being sent to a hell of concrete pain could be the attempt to escape.

In Milton's poem the fall of the angels, like the fall of man, has intellectual as well as physical consequences, and among these is the temptation to believe that a fallen life is not so bad, and that God might have forgotten about the sinners. This is a consequence of the fall which we all suffer: 'Thus we live in danger, our greatest danger being that we should feel no danger, and our safety lying in the very dread of feeling safe.'[21]

The virtues of Waldock's book are that it raised some real questions about what happens in *Paradise Lost* (whether, for example, Eve's fall is of a different order from that of Adam), and that it prompted two detailed defences of *Paradise Lost* from Dennis Burden (*The Logical Epic*, 1967) and Stanley Fish (*Surprised by Sin*, 1967). Neither of these critics disagrees with Waldock's assertion that Milton portrays Satan attractively. What they claim, however, along with other recent critics of the poem, is that Milton does this quite deliberately and that the anti-epic or satanic-epic aspects of *Paradise Lost* are a conscious part of Milton's design.

The Logical Epic takes the reader back to Milton's poem and away from the speculation about issues which may arise from the poem. It may be stimulating to argue about whether God's foreknowledge predetermines the fate of man, but it is more relevant for the student of *Paradise Lost* to investigate, as Burden does, how Milton contrives his description of God to make it seem that man has free will by, for example, making certain decisions about his description of the fall of Eve and Adam:

> In Book IX all is done out of human decision, and the Fall unfolds in a series of human problems. God has already foretold it, but his foreknowledge is here kept apart from the foretold event and is fulfilled . . . without comment.[22]

Burden's approach to the poem, like that of Fish, carefully emphasises the choices which Milton has made in the setting out of his narrative, and discriminates between those parts of the poem which derive from the Bible and those which are of Milton's own invention. The modern reader faces real difficulties in assessing the success of *Paradise Lost*, partly because our knowledge of the Bible is far less detailed than that of our forefathers, and we are therefore liable to make a mistaken assessment of Milton's originality, partly because we have insufficient experience with other epics to be able to recognise anti-epic features in this poem, and partly because we need constantly to remind ourselves that this massive work is the product of human invention, it is not 'given' but came about as a result of a set of choices which Milton made. The work of both Burden and Fish has done much to help the modern reader cope with these problems.

Burden suggests that the poem contains within it a 'satanic epic' of which Satan is the hero, and argues convincingly that Satan constantly thinks of himself in terms of the attributes of the hero of a conventional epic, ambitious, courageous, representing his people against the might of a fierce oppressor. This self-portrait extends beyond the early books in Hell, and is part of his method for tempting Eve, in the guise of a serpent:

> Look on me,
> Me who have touched and tasted, yet both live,
> And life more perfect have attained than fate
> Meant me, by venturing higher than my lot.
>
> (IX.687–90)

Burden says of these lines: 'Satan is claiming to have acted as the typical hero of his own sort of poetry, a satanic epic about "Thir own heroic deeds" (II.549)'.[23] Yet this satanic epic proves to have a disappointing climax for its hero when, as he later reports to Hell, he seems to have effected the downfall of mankind, not through a great military triumph, but with an apple.

Paradise Lost is quite explicitly a poem intended to educate, as Milton declares at the beginning of its first book as he asks for inspiration to 'assert eternal providence,/ And justify the ways of God to men' (I.25–6). Part of the process of education is the rejection of the attractions of the satanic epic, and the exercising of judgement in recognising satanic heroism from its true counterpart. It is at this task Adam fails, responding to Eve's false epic just as Eve had responded to Satan's:

> Bold deed thou hast presumed, adventurous Eve,
> And peril great provoked, who thus hast dared . . .
>
> (IX.921–2)

In *Paradise Lost* to be daring and adventurous is hardly ever right.

Stanley Fish's book is a detailed investigation of the process undergone in reading *Paradise Lost* and the ways in which the reader is tempted by the attractions of the satanic epic. The thesis of the book is substantially in accord with that of Burden, and together these two critics present a lucid case for regarding *Paradise Lost* as a carefully and a remarkably innovative work. A single instance from Burden of Milton's care in presenting the temptation of Eve may be appropriate at this point: 'as Satan presents it, the Tree is tempting and irresistible. But he is telling lies about it: when he leads Eve there, it is left significantly undescribed'.[24] It would be too easy to blame Milton, or Milton's God, for making the Tree too attractive, and not to realise that this attraction came only from the words of Satan.

Good as their defences are, both Burden and Fish find *Paradise Lost* less than totally successful (they agree that the final two books provide less of a challenge for Milton, less opportunity for innovation). Neither critic completely solves all the puzzles of the poem: it is unlikely that any single reading will ever do this. There arc still questions which remain unanswered from Waldock, and from Empson.

Empson's approach in *Milton's God* (1961) differs from that of earlier detractors of Milton, including Lewis and Eliot, in that he has read the poem extraordinarily carefully, in order to establish the precise grounds for his dissatisfaction. His attack is in general far more illuminating, and more entertaining, than, for example, C. S. Lewis's *Preface to Paradise Lost*, which is written in support of the poem yet adopts an unchallenging stance towards it. Indeed, Empson is able to point with justificaton to instances of assertions by Lewis which betray an inaccurate reading of the text: he says, of Lewis's view of Mammon:

> C. S. Lewis treats him as a sensualist fighting down his pangs of shame – 'Honour? Love? Everybody I meet salutes me, and there is an excellent brothel round the corner.' But Milton tells us that one of the chief pains of Hell, as in human prisons, was deprivation of sex, if it may be so called (IV.510).[25]

This may look like an example of pettiness, scoring niggling points against the minor innaccuracies of one's opponent, but Empson's desire for precision of thinking in relation to *Paradise Lost* serves to indicate the fine distinctions being drawn within the poem. Occasionally he breaks his own rules and implies that a statement has been made in the poem which is, in fact, his own invention: writing, for example, of the account by Beelzebub of the creation of man, he observes 'God sounds particularly like Zeus in this devil's account, whereas Raphael reports him later in the poem as saying he is going to create us to spite the devils (VII.150)'.[26] Raphael's account, of course, makes no mention of spite as a motive on God's part.

Sometimes Empson distorts the text of the poem so that the opinions expressed by a character are taken to be the equivalent of Milton's own views, ironically making himself guilty of a fault which John Peter, an earlier detractor of Milton, had derided:

> to wrench the characters and incidents of *Paradise Lost* from their artistic context, and then to consider them as if they were autonomous ... disregarding the significance which has been conferred upon them by the poem.[27]

Commenting on a description of Satan, Empson observes 'If he *endangered* God, the rule of God is not inherently *perpetual*'.[28] Yet the paradox of having these two contradictory terms juxtaposed derives

not from Milton's muddled thinking but from the mind of the
character, Beelzebub, who delivers the line.

In general, Empson's thesis is rigorously and logically expounded: if
God had foreknowledge, and he knew that man would fall even before
the revolt of Satan, then the whole poem presents God in a very bad
light, playing a malicious joke at the expense of his creations. This, for
example, is Empson's interpretation of the angels' reaction to the news
of the creation of man, and the exaltation of the Son:

> We gather that the angels regarded this rumour as a threat to their
> status in the hierarchy, just as they did the promotion which actually
> caused the revolt. The source of a rumour in such a hierarchy on
> earth . . . is usually mysterious; but in Heaven it is hard to see who
> could be the ultimate source but God himself, as part of a war of
> nerves.[29]

> If the Son had inherently held this position from before the creation
> of all angels, why has it been officially withheld from him till this
> day, and still more, why have the angels not previously been told
> that he was the agent of their creation? . . . to give no reason at all
> for the Exaltation makes it appear a challenge, intended to outrage a
> growing intellectual dissatisfaction among the angels with the claims
> of God.[30]

These are serious challenges to the heart of the poem, and have
provoked a variety of answers. It is possible, for example, to claim that
Milton's purpose was to justify God's ways, and not the existence of
God himself, and that, lacking any faith in God, Empson follows the
fallen characters in the poem and is not prepared to be obedient unless
there is some evident reward. The poem includes several examples of
obedience without immediate reward, which are discussed above.

Dennis Burden's argument is persuasive: that God is presented as
loving and just, but without the arbitrariness of affection which pity
would involve:

> To ascribe pity to God . .·. would, since God has created Man's
> world and Man's nature, indict that providence which *Paradise Lost*
> is written to assert. Milton is very insistent on this need to regard
> without pity those episodes representing God's anger and justice.
> One of Raphael's difficulties in recounting the fall of the angels to
> Adam is the necessity for the story to be told and listened to without
> pity.[31]

It may be significant that, although the revised edition of *Milton's God*
includes an appendix on the reaction of other critics to Empson's
argument, it makes no reference to Burden's book.

Burden's description of a just, impartial God is not dissimilar from that of those critics who have attempted to defend Milton's God on the grounds that, unlike for example the God of the Calvinist tradition, God in *Paradise Lost* does not predestine the fall of man, nor does he deny grace to anyone. Milton's God shows neither arbitrary pity nor favouritism, and the poem does not, therefore, include the notion of an elect whose salvation is predetermined by God. God's speech in Book III emphasises that man is responsible for his own fate:

> without least impulse or shadow of fate,
> Or aught by me immutably foreseen,
> They trespass, authors to themselves in all
> Both what they judge and what they choose; for so
> I formed them free, and free they must remain,
> Till they enthrall themselves . . .
>
> (III.120–5)

and that, after the fall, salvation is equally dependent upon individual choice and action:

> To prayer, repentance, and obedience due,
> Though but endeavoured with sincere intent,
> Mine ear shall not be slow . . .
>
> (III.191–3)

Milton's prose and poetry continually asserted the need for faith to be explicit, and his statements on salvation in *De Doctrina Christiana*, his principal theological treatise, reinforce the impression of his commitment to a belief in the need for good works as part of the process of salvation: 'A true and living faith cannot exist without works'; 'Those who persevere, not those who are elect, are said to attain salvation'.[32] *Paradise Lost* also treats salvation in this Arminian fashion, although the issue is somewhat obscured by Milton's use of the word 'elect'. In *De Doctrina Christiana* he defines the elect as those who believe and continue in the faith, and it is used in this sense in most of the instances in which it occurs in *Paradise Lost*. Thus, for example, the angels who remain loyal to God are described as elect:

> Thus while God spake, ambrosial fragrance filled
> All heaven, and in the blessed spirits elect
> Sense of new joy ineffable diffused . . .
>
> (III.135–8)

Milton is careful to present this group of angels as having achieved election by exercising their own free choice in deciding to remain faithful. This usage of 'elect', therefore, corresponds exactly to that of *De Doctrina Christiana*, implying as it does the act of choosing rather than the passive state of being chosen. The difficulty is that Milton also uses the word in its more usual sense twice in *Paradise Lost*: in the final book Michael describes to Adam the flight of the Israelites from Egypt:

> the race elect
> Safe towards Canaan from the shore advance
> Through the wild desert . . .
>
> (XII.214–16)

and in Book III, in the midst of his declaration of the Arminian doctrine of salvation, Milton's God creates an exception to his own rule:

> Some I have chosen of peculiar grace
> Elect above the rest; so is my will . . .
>
> (III.183–4)

This latter passage seems to refer to those individuals who, like Milton himself, had been singled out by God to enact some special role in the divine scheme. Milton continued to believe in his own personal election, as he had once believed in the special favour which God extended to his chosen English nation, but this did not absolve him, and others similarly elected by God, from the obligation to good works on earth. Indeed, since God's chosen nation had decided not to carry through the Revolution to its full course, the obligation for Milton to remain personally firm was all the stronger. D. J. Enright has recently remarked:

> Milton's belief in God marched with a belief in himself. Thus, in *Defence of Himself*: 'Singular indeed is the favour of God towards me, that He has called me above all others to the defence of liberty . . .'; and in *Second Defence of the English People*: 'I have been aided and enriched by the favour and assistance of God. Anything greater or more glorious than this I neither can, nor wish to, claim'.[33]

Milton goes to considerable lengths to portray man as a free creature, with the necessary knowledge to be able to take decisions rationally. Milton's God is remarkably generous in responding to the curiosity of his creatures:

> Divinity, instead of being reduced to eavesdropping or impulsively intervening in the affairs of men . . . has allowed man a breadth of knowledge about himself and his universe and a moral autonomy that are breathtaking.[34]

Milton builds up an extraordinary self-consciousness in his characters about their nature and function and, given also his concern for divine providence, shows how that providence is manifested.[35]

Milton continually contrives his poem in a way which suggests that, although God may know of the outcome of Satan's temptation, the details of the process are left obscured. Thus, for example, in Book III God talks of the future fall of man, but he does not discriminate between the separate falls of Eve and Adam, nor indicate the precise means whereby Satan will bring about this fall. It seems as if the outcome of events is foreseen by God, but motives and arguments which lead to these events are not predetermined, and, in a work which operates to such a large extent through debates, this means that a considerable part of the most interesting intellectual activity within *Paradise Lost* is made to seem to take place outside of God's prediction. E. E. Stoll remarked, over half a century ago, that in the temptation of Eve in Book IX: 'Devil and woman, both, fairly take your breath away',[36] and Empson himself observes that

> Milton regularly presents a fall as due to an intellectually interesting temptation, such that a cool judge may feel actual doubt whether the fall was not the best thing to do in the circumstances.[37]

These intellectually interesting, breathtaking temptations are Miltonic inventions which are made to seem quite independent of God's predestined plan. They are a product of the self-awareness and freedom which Milton (and by implication, Milton's God) gives to his characters, and which, if abused, leads not to a liberation from God but to a new kind of self-enslavement. What God says of man in Book III: 'I formed them free, and free they must remain,/Till they enthrall themselves' (III.124–5) anticipates in terms of the narrative (although in historical terms it succeeds it) the speech of Abdiel to Satan, one of the most significant definitions in the poem:

> This is servitude,
> To serve the unwise, or him who hath rebelled
> Against his worthier, as thine now serve thee,
> Thy self not free, but to thy self enthralled . . .
>
> (VI.178–81)

The choice which is offered in *Paradise Lost* is between obedience to God and faith in His providence, which is true freedom, or a life without God, which gives the illusion of freedom but is, in fact, the servitude of self-enslavement. One of the consequences of the fall is that a new distinction has to be made between 'liberty' and 'licence', the very distinction which was so significant in the debates during the English Revolution. 'Liberty' for Milton involves obedience to God and conformity to His ordered scheme, 'licentious' behaviour is the signal of the attempt to live outside of this divine scheme, and leads ultimately to anarchy. Milton had needed to make this distinction in 1644 in order to establish that his writings on divorce were concerned with liberty and not with licence:

> What though the brood of Belial, the draff of men, to whom no liberty is pleasing, but unbridled and vagabond lust without pale or partition, will laugh broad perhaps, to see so great a strength of scripture mustering up in favour, as they suppose, of their debaucheries; they will know better when they shall hence learn, that honest liberty is the greatest foe to dishonest licence.[38]

Milton's principal difficulty in working this discrimination between licence and liberty into the fabric of *Paradise Lost* is that his definition of liberty is static and therefore potentially less interesting than conventional notions of freedom. Adam, at the close of the poem, says that he has learned

>   that to obey is best,
> And love with fear the only God, to walk
> As in his presence, ever to observe
> His providence, and on him sole depend . . .
>   (XII.561–4)

But it is difficult to place such a definition of liberty at the centre of an epic poem and yet still maintain the interest of the reader. A great many critics have raised their particular version of this problem, which is a variant of the charge that Satan is too attractive to fail. Molly Mahood, taking *Paradise Regained* into her consideration, argues that 'there is little to show how "Heav'nly love shal outdoo Hellish hate" (*PL* III 298), small demonstration of that "unexampl'd love" which compels the Son to suffer such an ordeal'.[39] G. A. Wilkes holds that

> The loss of paradise is powerfully brought home to us; the process of redemption and restoration may seem by contrast a mechanical victory . . . . Certainly the new Eden promised is to be superior to the Eden that has been lost . . . . But the realization of this paradise is outside the scheme of the poem.[40]

and Dennis Burden is driven to defend the overall scheme of the poem as follows:

> the climax of Book XII, the Incarnation, is not reached with any notable growth or development. The promises about the Messiah are not disposed in any significant order, nor do the types of Christ get bigger and better types . . . . Like the account of the war in

Heaven in Book VI, Book XII offers for the most part less logical challenge and opportunity, and the lacklustre response which is all that it arouses in most of its readers shows how important are the logic and tautness of the poem elsewhere.[41]

In the face of these comments it would seem that one need only observe that the decision of examination boards to concentrate study on Books I, II, IV, and IX of *Paradise Lost* might seem to confirm that temptation is described more vividly than redemption and that the poem was most interesting when not presenting God: Empson, Leavis, and their followers seem to have won the day:

> What has it left? There are the first two books, which are of a piece and grandly impressive, and, in the others, numbers of 'beauties' major and minor. But surely, whatever is left, it cannot justify talk about 'architectonic'.[42]

In our discussion of *Paradise Lost* in Part 2 of this handbook, however, we have argued that this sense of disappointment, experienced by many readers of the poem, is deliberately contrived by Milton, is consistent with the reversal of expectation endured by characters within the poem, and is part of a re-working of epic convention which is so radical that further development of the genre after Milton became impossible.

Part 5

Suggestions for further reading

Milton's works

The Poems of Milton, edited by John Carey and Alastair Fowler, Longman, London, 1968. An excellent, compact, annotated edition of the poetry, also available in two volumes in paperback.

Paradise Lost, edited by Scott Elledge, Norton, New York, 1975. A very good student text with helpful appendices and criticism.

John Milton's Prose Writings, edited by K. M. Burton, Dent, London, 1957. An inexpensive anthology of Milton's prose, somewhat marred by errors of typography.

John Milton: Selected Prose, edited by C. A. Patrides, Penguin, Harmondsworth, 1974. An excellent selection of Milton's prose, well annotated and skilfully introduced.

Complete Prose Works of John Milton, edited by Don M. Wolfe *et al.*, 8 vols, Yale University Press, New Haven, Conn., 1953–82. The authoritative edition of the prose, containing not only all the works, but also lengthy introductions to the historical, political, and literary background.

Reference works

HANFORD, J. H.: *A Milton Handbook*, Bell, London, 1926. A fluent and readable introduction to Milton's career.

HUNTER, W. B. (ED.): *A Milton Encyclopedia*, 8 vols, Associated University Press, Lewisburg, Pa., 1978–80. A very useful reference tool, with articles on Milton's life and works, and also on background topics.

LE COMTE, E. S. (COMP.): *A Milton Dictionary*, Peter Owen, London, 1961. A compact work of reference arranged in alphabetical order.

Biography

DARBISHIRE, H. (ED.): *The Early Lives of Milton*, Constable, London, 1932. An anthology of accounts of Milton's life by his earliest biographers.

PARKER, W. R.: *Milton: A Biography*, 2 vols, Oxford University Press, London, 1968. The most thoroughly researched biography of Milton produced to date.

WILSON, A. N.: *The Life of John Milton*, Oxford University Press, London, 1983. A readable and provocative biography.

Introductory works

BROADBENT, J. B. (ED.): *John Milton: Introductions*, Cambridge University Press, London, 1973. An anthology of stimulating essays, introducing Milton's life, career and reputation.

POTTER, L.: *A Preface to Milton*, Longman, London, 1972. A well-produced survey of Milton's works, with some interesting illustrations.

The historical context

BARKER, A. E.: *Milton and the Puritan Dilemma*, University of Toronto Press, Toronto, 1942. A thorough survey of the political and religious significance of Milton's prose.

ERSKINE-HILL, H. and STOREY, G. (EDS.): *Revolutionary Prose of the English Civil War*, Cambridge University Press, London, 1983. An anthology of Civil War prose, including some Milton, with good introductory essays.

HILL, C.: *Milton and the English Revolution*, Faber & Faber, London, 1977. The fullest study to date of the political content in Milton's prose and poetry. Destined to become the touchstone of all future debate in this area.

HILL, C. and DELL, E. (EDS.): *The Good Old Cause*, Frank Cass, London, 1969. An anthology of short extracts, illustrating the variety of political and religious opinion in the mid-seventeenth century.

LAMONT, W. and OLDFIELD, S. (EDS.): *Politics, Religion and Literature in the Seventeenth Century*, Dent, London, 1975. An excellent anthology, which demonstrates the force of propaganda before and during the Civil War.

PARKER, W. R.: *Milton's Contemporary Reputation*, Haskell, New York, 1940. This book includes the various pamphlets written explicitly against Milton during his lifetime.

SMITH, N. (ED.): *A Collection of Ranter Writings*, Junction Books, London, 1983. This anthology includes some of the most extreme writings of the English Revolution.

WOLFE, D. M.: *Milton in the Puritan Revolution*, Nelson, London, 1941. Although this book is arranged in a rather eccentric manner, it remains a stimulating study of Milton's politics.

WOODHOUSE, A. S. P.: *Puritanism and Liberty*, Dent, London, 1938. A very sound introduction to the disputes of the late 1640s.

Milton criticism

The corpus of criticism of Milton's work is large, and the titles listed below are merely a selection of those books which are particularly useful and are likely to be readily available to the student.

BURDEN, D.: *The Logical Epic*, Routledge & Kegan Paul, London, 1967. A lucid account of *Paradise Lost*, presenting the notion of a 'satanic epic' at the centre of the poem.

ELIOT, T. S.: *On Poetry and Poets*, Faber & Faber, London, 1957. Contains two essays on Milton which have provoked debate among later critics.

EMPSON, W.: *Milton's God*, Cambridge University Press, London, revised 1981. An essential text for all serious students of *Paradise Lost*, although its comments on *Samson Agonistes* have provoked much less controversy.

FISH, S.: *Surprised by Sin*, University of California Press, Berkeley, 1967. This stimulating study of *Paradise Lost* is particularly strong on the early books of the epic.

KERMODE, F. (ED.): *The Living Milton*, Routledge & Kegan Paul, London, 1960. A collection of essays by various hands on the range of Milton's poetry.

LEAVIS, F. R.: *Revaluation*, Chatto & Windus, London, 1936. A classic anti-Milton essay is included in this volume.

LEWALSKI, B.: *Milton's Brief Epic*, Methuen, London, 1966. The standard work on *Paradise Regained*.

LEWIS, C. S.: *A Preface to Paradise Lost*, Oxford University Press, London, 1942. This book is essentially a series of lectures, and has valuable material on epic convention in particular.

LOW, A.: *The Blaze of Noon*, Columbia University Press, New York, 1974. A full and detailed discussion of *Samson Agonistes*.

PRINCE, F. T.: *The Italian Element in Milton's Verse*, Oxford University Press, London, 1954. A study of the versification of Milton's shorter poems and of *Samson Agonistes*.

RADZINOWICZ, M.: *Toward Samson Agonistes*, Princeton University Press, Princeton, N.J., 1978. Although centrally concerned with *Samson Agonistes*, this book has much to say on the general development of Milton's ideas in poetry and prose.

RAJAN, B.: *The Lofty Rhyme*, Routledge & Kegan Paul, London, 1970. A survey of Milton's poems from the 'Nativity Ode' through to *Samson Agonistes*.

RICKS, C.: *Milton's Grand Style*, Oxford University Press, London, 1963. An able defence of Milton's language, with extensive and detailed illustration from *Paradise Lost*.

RUDRUM, A. (ED.): *Milton*, Macmillan, London, 1969. A fine collection of essays by various critics on a range of different aspects of Milton's poetry and prose.

TUVE, R.: *Image and Themes in Five Poems by Milton*, Harvard University Press, Cambridge, Mass., 1962. A very good introduction to Milton's earlier poems.

Notes

PREFACE
1. W. L. Chernaik, *The Poet's Time*, Cambridge University Press, London, 1983.
2. T. N. Corns, *The Development of Milton's Prose Style*, Oxford University Press, London, 1982.
3. *Revolutionary Prose of the English Civil War*, edited by H. Erskine-Hill and G. Storey, Cambridge University Press, London, 1983; *A Collection of Ranter Writings*, edited by N. Smith, Junction Books, London, 1983.
4. C. Hill, B. Reay and W. Lamont, *The World of the Muggletonians*, Temple Smith, London, 1983.
5. A. N. Wilson, *The Life of John Milton*, Oxford University Press, London, 1983.
6. *The World of the Muggletonians*, for example, was reviewed by a historian for the *Times Higher Education Supplement* and by a literary critic for the *Times Literary Supplement*.
7. C. Hill, 'History is a matter of taking liberties', *The Guardian*, 30 July 1983, p. 15.

PART 1
1. There is a reconstruction of these arms in the west window of St Giles's Church, Cripplegate, London.
2. John Aubrey, cited in A. N. Wilson, *The Life of John Milton*, Oxford University Press, London, 1983, p. 5.
3. *Second Defence of the English People*, 1654, in *John Milton's Prose Writings*, edited by K. Burton, Dent, London, 1958, pp. 341–2.
4. See A. E. Barker, *Milton and the Puritan Dilemma*, University of Toronto Press, Toronto, 1942, pp. 346–7.
5. See M. Treip, *Milton's Punctuation*, Methuen, London, 1970.
6. The story comes from Aubrey.
7. Sometimes wrongly referred to as Tovell; see W. R. Parker, *Milton: A Biography*, Oxford University Press, London, 1968, p. 724.
8. W. R. Parker, *Milton: A Biography*, p. 723.
9. *CPW*, vol. I, p. 314.
10. *CPW*, vol. I, p. 250. These exercises, in Latin, were delivered orally.
11. See *The Poems of Milton*, edited by John Carey and Alastair Fowler, Longman, London, 1968, p. 75.
12. Milton was later to attack the views of Andrewes in *The Reason of Church Government* (1642).
13. *CPW*, vol. I, pp. 319–20.
14. Carey and Fowler (eds.), *The Poems of Milton*, p. 155.

15. The name *Comus* was used to describe this work as early as 1698, although it was not published under that title until 1738 (Parker, *Milton: A Biography*, p. 789). Milton called it *A Masque presented at Ludlow Castle.*
16. Parker, *Milton: A Biography*, p. 791.
17. The Commonplace Book, edited by Ruth Mohl, is included in *CPW*, vol. I. The dates of its earliest and latest entries are disputed.
18. Parker, *Milton: A Biography*, p. 802, lists the most frequent citations.
19. The letter, dated 13 April 1638, is in *CPW*, vol. I, pp. 340–4.
20. For whom he wrote the poem 'Mansus' (1639).
21. Carey and Fowler (eds.), *The Poems of Milton*, p. 279.
22. Helen Darbishire, *The Early Lives of Milton*, Constable, London, 1932, identifies the Anonymous Biographer as John Phillips. Parker in *Milton: A Biography*, pp. xiii–xv, argues against this.
23. J. H. Hanford, *John Milton: Englishman*, Crown, New York, 1949, p. 26.
24. In *The Reason of Church Government*, in Burton (ed.), *John Milton's Prose Writings*, p. 352.
25. The letter to a friend mentions setting up a house, but that was in 1633.
26. Different conclusions are drawn from the same evidence by Parker, *Milton: A Biography*, p. 806; Barker, *Milton and the Puritan Dilemma*, p. 66; and Christopher Hill, *Milton and the English Revolution*, Faber & Faber, London, 1977, p. 123.
27. Wilson, *The Life of John Milton*, pp. 133–4.
28. Ibid., p. 134.
29. Darbishire, *The Early Lives of Milton*, p. 66.
30. William Prynne, *Twelve Considerable Serious Questions* (1644), cited in W. R. Parker, *Milton's Contemporary Reputation*, Haskell, New York, 1940, p. 73.
31. Daniel Featley, *The Dippers Dipt* (1645), in Parker, *Milton's Contemporary Reputation*, p. 74.
32. Thomas Edwards, *Gangraena* (1646), in Parker, *Milton's Contemporary Reputation*, pp. 76–7.
33. John Eachard, *Grounds and Occasions* (1670) in Parker, *Milton's Contemporary Reputation*, p. 110.
34. Cited in Barker, *Milton and the Puritan Dilemma*, p. 353.
35. Milton may have read Burton in the mid-1630s; see G. M. Ridden, 'Henry Burton and a possible source for 'Lycidas'', *Notes and Queries*, vol. 31, 1984.
36. See *CPW*, vol. II, pp. 142–3.
37. Parker, *Milton's Contemporary Reputation*, pp. 73–4.
38. Keith W. Stavely, *The Politics of Milton's Prose Style*, Yale University Press, New Haven, Conn., 1975, p. 66.
39. See the letter to Philaris, *CPW*, vol. IV, p. 869.
40. See Leo Miller, 'Milton's portraits', *Milton Quarterly*, University of Ohio, Athens, Ohio, 1976, Special Issue.
41. Carey and Fowler (eds.), *The Poems of Milton*, p. 292.
42. D. Masson, *The Life of John Milton*, Macmillan, London, 1871–80, vol. III, p. 456.

43. Wilson, *The Life of John Milton*, p. 154. Wilson also notes the comparative success of the collection of poems by Edmund Waller also published in 1645.
44. Hill, *Milton and the English Revolution*, p. 280. *John Milton: Selected Prose*, edited by C. A. Patrides, Penguin Books, Harmondsworth, 1974, p. 21, gives an extract from a pamphlet by Paul Knell called *Israel and England Paralleled*, (1648).
45. Carey and Fowler (eds.), *The Poems of Milton*, pp. 311–12. The political allusion is noted in *CPW*, vol. v, pp. 431–2, and in *Politics, Religion and Literature in the Seventeenth Century*, edited by William Lamont and Sybil Oldfield, Dent, London, 1975, p. 112.
46. Carey and Fowler (eds.), *The Poems of Milton*, p. 323.
47. Burton (ed.), *John Milton's Prose Writings*, p. 190.
48. See Joan S. Bennett, 'God, Satan and King Charles', *Publications of the Modern Language Association of America*, George Banta Publishing, Menasha, xcii, 1977, pp. 441–57.
49. See G. M. Ridden, 'Winstanley's allusion to Milton', *Notes and Queries*, vol. 31, 1984.
50. Parker, *Milton: A Biography*, p. 962.
51. Parker, *Milton's Contemporary Reputation*, p. 87.
52. *CPW*, vol. vi, p. 471. See also Hill, *Milton and the English Revolution*, p. 186, and *CPW*, vol. iv, pp. 113–14.
53. Printed in full in Parker, *Milton's Contemporary Reputation*, pp. 218–28.
54. Cited in Lamont and Oldfield (eds.), *Politics, Religion and Literature in the Seventeenth Century*, p. 157.
55. Milton's relationship with Cromwell is dealt with in more detail in Hill, *Milton and the English Revolution*, chs. 13 and 14; in Don M. Wolfe, *Milton in the Puritan Revolution*, Nelson, London, 1941, pp. 242ff.; and in Austin Woolrych, 'Milton and Cromwell', in *Achievements of the Left Hand*, edited by M. Lieb and J. T. Shawcross, University of Massachusetts Press, Amherst, Mass., 1974, pp. 185–218.
56. See Hill, *Milton and the English Revolution*, p. 184.
57. For further reading on Milton and Marvell see C. Hill, 'Milton and Marvell', in *Approaches to Marvell*, edited by C. A. Patrides, Routledge & Kegan Paul, London, 1978, pp. 1–30; I. Rivers, *The Poetry of Conservatism*, Rivers, Cambridge, 1973, pp. 73–126; W. Chernaik, *The Poet's Time*, Cambridge University Press, London, 1983; R. B. Waddington, 'Milton among the Carolines', in *The Age of Milton*, edited by C. A. Patrides and R. B. Waddington, Manchester University Press, Manchester, 1980, pp. 338–64.
58. See Wilson, *The Life of John Milton*, pp. 181–3.
59. Mary Ann Radzinowicz, *Toward Samson Agonistes*, Princeton University Press, Princeton, N.J., 1978, p. 82.
60. Burton (ed.), *John Milton's Prose Writings*, p. 233.
61. His *Defence of the English People* and *Eikonoklastes* were banned. *The Tenure of Kings and Magistrates* was not.
62. C. V. Wedgwood, *The Trial of Charles I*, Collins, London, 1964, p. 216.
63. Parker, *Milton: A Biography*, p. 576.

64. Carey and Fowler (eds.), *The Poems of Milton*, p. 423.
65. Ibid., p. xxii. See also Anne Manning, *Deborah's Diary*, Hall, Virtue & Co., London, 1859.
66. Burton (ed.), *John Milton's Prose Writings*, pp. 133–4.
67. See A. W. Read, 'The disinterment of Milton's remains', *Publications of the Modern Language Association of America*, George Banta Publishing, Monasha, XLV, 1930, pp. 1050–68.
68. J. H. Hanford, *A Milton Handbook*, Bell, London, 1926, p. 1.
69. These passages, in *The Reason of Church Government*, *An Apology for Smectymnuus* and the *Second Defence*, are included in Hanford, *A Milton Handbook*, in Burton (ed.), *John Milton's Prose Writings*, and in Patrides (ed.), *John Milton: Selected Prose*. The complete set of autobiographical allusions is contained in John Diekhoff, *Milton on Himself*, Oxford University Press, London, 1939.
70. Based on Helen Darbishire's dating of Aubrey in *The Early Lives of Milton*, which includes biographies of Milton by Aubrey, Anthony à Wood, Edward Phillips, John Toland, and the anonymous biographer. Selections from early biographies are also included in Hanford, *A Milton Handbook*.
71. See Patrides (ed.), *John Milton: Selected Prose*, p. 20, for an account of the friendship, and Hill, *Milton and the English Revolution*, p. 452, for the editing of the list of friends.
72. See Wolfe, *Milton in the Puritan Revolution*, p. 123, and also Barker, *Milton and the Puritan Dilemma*, p. xvii and p. 63. Milton's concern for his reputation after the divorce tracts is described fully in T. N. Corns, 'Milton's quest for respectability', *Modern Language Review*, MHRA, London, LXXVII, 1982, pp. 769–79.
73. F. Kermode, 'Milton in Old Age', *Southern Review*, Louisiana State University Press, Baton Rouge, XI, 1975, pp. 513–29.
74. Parker, *Milton: A Biography*, p. 1162.
75. Ibid., p. 1173.
76. Radzinowicz, *Toward Samson Agonistes*, p. 19.
77. Wilson, *The Life of John Milton*, pp.181–3.
78. Hill, *Milton and the English Revolution*, p. 371. Peter Malekin, *Liberty and Love*, Hutchinson, London, 1981, p. 91.
79. See the entries under 'novels' and 'plays' in the index to Parker, *Milton: A Biography*, and also the article 'Fiction (Biographical)' in *A Milton Encyclopedia*, edited by W. B. Hunter, Associated University Press, Lewisburg, Pa., vol. III, 1978, pp. 102–4. Of related interest is the film *Omnibus: Milton – Paradise Restored*, written and directed by Don Taylor (January 1972).
80. Robert Graves, *Wife to Mr. Milton*, Cassell, London, 1942.
81. See note 65.
82. Hill, *Milton and the English Revolution*, p. 7.
83. There are extensive references to Williams in Wolfe, *Milton in the Puritan Revolution*; Barker, *Milton and the Puritan Dilemma*; and Edmund Fuller, *John Milton*, Gollancz, London, 1944. Fuller, like many writers on Milton, makes the poet famous far too early.

84. Wilson, *The Life of John Milton*.
85. See note 7 for details.
86. See note 26 for details. Hill's approach is challenged by Wilson, *The Life of John Milton*, pp. 159–60, and by A. Milner in *John Milton and the English Revolution*, Macmillan, London, 1981. There is a more temperate reaction in Corns, 'Milton's quest for respectability'.
87. In addition to attacking Hill, Wilson also dislikes academics in general, sufficiently to deride the possibility of Milton's teachers influencing his views.
88. Sonnet IV, Carey and Fowler (eds.), *The Poems of Milton*, p. 94.
89. Malcolm Smuts, 'The political failure of Stuart cultural patronage', in *Patronage in the Renaissance*, edited by G. F. Lytle and S. Orgel, Princeton University Press, Princeton, N.J., 1981, p. 166.
90. *An Apology for Smectymnuus*, in Burton (ed.), *John Milton's Prose Writings*, pp. 68–9.
91. See Corns, 'Milton's quest for respectability'.
92. Hill, *Milton and the English Revolution*, p. 118.
93. Parker, *Milton: A Biography*, p. 317.
94. For a recent resumé of criticism of Milton and women see D. Aers and R. Hodge, 'Rational burning', *Milton Studies*, University of Pittsburgh Press, Pittsburgh, Pa., XIII, 1979, pp. 3–34. This article is reprinted in D. Aers *et al.*, *Literature, Language and Society in England 1580–1680*, Gill and Macmillan, London, 1982.
95. Wilson, *The Life of John Milton*, p. 176.
96. *Second Defence*, cited in D. Burden, *The Logical Epic*, Routledge & Kegan Paul, London, 1967, p. 48.
97. Parker, *Milton: A Biography*, p. 571.
98. L. P. Hartley, *The Go-Between*, Penguin Books, Harmondsworth, 1958, p. 7.
99. These disputes are reviewed by Peter Scott in 'Putting the flesh on the bare bones of history', *Times Higher Education Supplement*, 9 September 1983, p. 9.
100. Wilson, *The Life of John Milton*, p. 27.
101. *Of Civil Power*, in Patrides (ed.), *John Milton: Selected Prose*, p. 309.
102. Wolfe, *Milton in the Puritan Revolution*, p. 8.
103. Hill, *Milton and the English Revolution*, p. 65.
104. Wolfe, *Milton in the Puritan Revolution*, p. 17.
105. Smuts, 'The political failure of Stuart cultural patronage', pp. 175–6.
106. Ibid., p. 182.
107. M. Y. Hughes, *Ten Perspectives on Milton*, Yale University Press, New Haven, Conn., 1965, p. 257.
108. 'Puritanism', in Hunter (ed.), *A Milton Encyclopedia*, vol. VII, p. 74.
109. Wilson, *The Life of John Milton*, p. 29.
110. The lyric by Thomas Carew (1595–1640) in reply to the news of the death of the King of Sweden (1632) is widely cited; see, for example, Lamont and Oldfield (eds.), *Politics, Religion and Literature in the Seventeenth Century*, pp. 21–2.
111. Smuts, 'The political failure of Stuart cultural patronage', p. 168.

112. C. V. Wedgwood, *The Trial of Charles I*, Folio Press, London, 1974, p. 6.
113. Burton (ed.), *John Milton's Prose Writings*, p. 42.
114. 'The rhetoric of radicalism', *Times Literary Supplement*, 16 September 1983, p. 992.
115. Lamont and Oldfield (eds.), *Politics, Religion and Literature in the Seventeenth Century*, p. 70.
116. A. S. P. Woodhouse, *Puritanism and Liberty*, Dent, London, 1938, pp. 179–81.
117. Wolfe, *Milton in the Puritan Revolution*, p. 139.
118. *Revolutionary Prose of the English Civil War*, edited by H. Erskine-Hill and G. Storey, Cambridge University Press, London, 1983, pp. 7–8.
119. Hughes, *Ten Perspectives on Milton*, p. 247.
120. Rose Macaulay, *They Were Defeated*, Collins, London, 1932, p. 45.
121. Cited by Corns, 'Milton's quest for respectability', p. 770.
122. Ibid., p. 778.
123. Erskine-Hill and Storey (eds.), *Revolutionary Prose of the English Civil War*, p. 7.
124. See Wedgwood, *The Trial of Charles I*, ch. VIII.
125. Wilson, *The Life of John Milton*, pp. 158–9.
126. Cited by Bernard Sharratt, 'The appropriation of Milton', *Essays and Studies*, John Murray, London, XXXV, 1982, p. 31.
127. Parker, *Milton: A Biography*, p. 1173.
128. Ibid., p. 653.
129. Sharratt, 'The appropriation of Milton', p. 44.
130. Good outline accounts of the course of the English Revolution can be found in the introduction to Erskine-Hill and Storey (eds.), *Revolutionary Prose of the English Civil War*; in Wedgwood, *The Trial of Charles I*; and in the article 'Puritanism' in Hunter (ed.), *A Milton Encyclopedia*, vol. VII, pp. 71–85.
131. Radzinowicz, *Toward Samson Agonistes*, p. 11.
132. See *On Education*, in Burton (ed.), *John Milton's Prose Writings*, p. 326.
133. Burton (ed.), *John Milton's Prose Writings*, p. 51.
134. Ibid., p. 354.
135. 'The Church Porch', lines 5–6, *The Works of George Herbert*, edited by F. E. Hutchinson, Oxford University Press, London, 1941, p. 6.
136. Burton (ed.), *John Milton's Prose Writings*, p. 356.
137. Ibid., p. 69.
138. *Tenure of Kings and Magistrates*, in Burton (ed.), *John Milton's Prose Writings*, p. 189.
139. *Areopagitica*, in Burton (ed.), *John Milton's Prose Writings*, p. 158.
140. *The Norton Anthology of English Literature*, edited by M. H. Abrams *et al.*, Norton, New York, 4th edn., 1979, vol. I, p. 518.
141. Cited in Sharratt, 'The appropriation of Milton', p. 30.
142. Burton (ed.), *John Milton's Prose Writings*, p. 191.
143. For a concise account of Milton's education as a poet see I. Rivers, 'The making of a seventeenth-century poet', in *John Milton: Introductions*, edited by J. B. Broadbent, Cambridge University Press, London, 1973, pp. 75–107.

PART 2
1. A. Pope, *A Discourse on Pastoral Poetry*, edited by E. Audra and A. Williams, Methuen, London, 1961, p. 23.
2. Ibid., pp. 24–5.
3. Ibid., p. 25.
4. Ibid., p. 27.
5. See W. Empson, *Some Versions of Pastoral*, Chatto & Windus, London, 1935, ch. 1.
6. *The Works of Spenser*, edited by J. Hughes, Tonson, London, 1758, vol. I, page ci.
7. *Hippolytus*, in *Seneca's Tragedies*, translated by F. J. Miller, University of Chicago Press, Chicago, 1907, vol. I, p. 525.
8. Lines 380–96, in *Spenser: Poetical Works*, edited by J. C. Smith and E. de Selincourt, Oxford University Press, London, 1916.
9. *Works*, edited by Spedding, Ellis and Heath, Longman, London, 1857–74, vol. VI, p. 138.
10. See 'Utopia' in J. A. Cuddon, *A Dictionary of Literary Terms*, Deutsch, London, 1977.
11. 'Januarye', lines 23–6, in Smith and de Selincourt (eds.), *Spenser's Poetical Works*.
12. There are good general accounts of pastoral in Cuddon, *A Dictionary of Literary Terms*; Empson, *Some Versions of Pastoral*; *A Milton Encyclopedia* edited by W. B. Hunter, Associated University Press, Lewisburg, Pa., vol. VI, 1979; *As You Like It*, edited by Agnes Latham, Methuen, London, 1975; *The Penguin Book of English Pastoral Verse*, edited by J. Barrell and J. Bull, Penguin Books, Harmondsworth, 1974; P. V. Marinelli, *Pastoral*, Methuen, London, 1971; F. Kermode, *English Pastoral Poetry*, Harrap, London, 1962; and D. Friedman, *Marvell's Pastoral Art*, Routledge & Kegan Paul, London, 1970.
13. E. M. W. Tillyard, *The Miltonic Setting*, Cambridge University Press, London, 1938, pp. 14–28.
14. *The Poems of Milton*, edited by John Carey and Alastair Fowler, Longman, London, 1968, p. 118.
15. Jackie di Salvo, 'The Lord's Battells', *Milton Studies*, Pittsburgh University Press, Pittsburgh, Pa., 1972, vol. IV, p. 58.
16. Sonnet XVII, lines 9–14, in Carey and Fowler (eds.), *The Poems of Milton*, p. 410.
17. R. Havens, *The Influence of Milton on English Poetry*, Russell & Russell, New York, 1961, p. 469, cited in *John Milton: L'Allegro and Il Penseroso*, edited by E. B. Safer and T. L. Erskine, Merrill, Columbus, 1970, p. 5.
18. Safer and Erskine (see above) include a very good selection of criticism on 'L'Allegro' and 'Il Penseroso'. See also A. Burnett, *Milton's Style*, Longman, London, 1981, ch. 1.
19. See C. Hill, *Milton and the English Revolution*, Faber & Faber, London, 1977, p. 43–4.
20. Ibid., p. 90.
21. See M. Heinemann, *Puritanism and Theatre*, Cambridge University Press, London, 1980.

22. See J. C. Demaray, *Milton and the Masque Tradition*, Harvard University Press, Cambridge, Mass., 1968.
23. *John Milton's Prose Writings*, edited by K. M. Burton, Dent, London, 1958, p. 158.
24. Ibid., p. 172.
25. See Hill, *Milton and the English Revolution*, p. 45, and W. R. Parker, *Milton: A Biography*, Oxford University Press, London, 1968, p. 142.
26. Book II, Canto xii, 75, in Smith and de Selincourt (eds.), *Spenser: Poetical Works*.
27. The allusions, for example, to canker (line 45) and taint-worm (line 46).
28. In the allusions, for example, to old Damaetas, and to Camus.
29. Radzinowicz, *Toward Samson Agonistes*, p. 123.
30. William Cowper, 'On the late indecent liberties taken with the remains of the great Milton'.
31. Carey and Fowler (eds.), *The Poems of Milton*, p. 23.
32. Ibid., p. 60.
33. A. N. Wilson, *The Life of John Milton*, Oxford University Press, London, 1983, p. 192.
34. *Tetrachordon, CPW*, vol. II, p. 661.
35. Ibid.
36. *An Apology*, in Burton (ed.), *John Milton's Prose Writings*, p. 70.
37. Ibid., p. 57.
38. See T. N. Corns, *The Development of Milton's Prose Style*, Oxford University Press, London, 1982.
39. Burton (ed.), *John Milton's Prose Writings*, p. 202.
40. *Of Reformation*, in Burton (ed.), *John Milton's Prose Writings*, p. 10.
41. Milton's break from Calvinism is emphasised not only in Hill, *Milton and the English Revolution*, but also by M. Mahood, 'Milton's heroes', in *Milton*, edited by A. Rudrum, Macmillan, London, 1969, p. 249; by D. Bush, 'Paradise Lost', in Hunter (ed.), *A Milton Encyclopedia*, vol. VI, 1979, p. 63; and by D. Danielson, *Milton's Good God*, Cambridge University Press, London, 1982.
42. Parker, *Milton: A Biography*, p. 275.
43. Burton (ed.), *John Milton's Prose Writings*, pp. 149–50.
44. *Paradise Lost*, edited by S. Elledge, Norton, New York, 1975.
45. Carey and Fowler (eds.), *The Poems of Milton*, p. 267.
46. See, for example, *Of Reformation*, in Burton (ed.), *John Milton's Prose Writings*, p. 51.
47. See 'Lycidas', lines 176–80; and *Of Reformation*, in Burton (ed.) *John Milton's Prose Writings*, p. 51.
48. Samuel Johnson, *The Lives of the Most Eminent English Poets*, cited in Elledge (ed.), *Paradise Lost*, pp. 521–2.
49. Cited in P. Merchant, *The Epic*, Methuen, London, 1971, p. 1.
50. Cited in Merchant, *The Epic*, p. 64.
51. Cited in Merchant, *The Epic*, p. 54.
52. Isabel MacCaffrey, cited in S. Fish, *Surprised by Sin*, University of California Press, Berkeley, Calif., 1967, p. 30.
53. Fish, *Surprised by Sin*, p. 188.

54. 'Epic', in Hunter (ed.), *A Milton Encyclopedia*, vol. III, 1978, p. 55.
55. See Corns, *The Development of Milton's Prose Style*, p. 58.
56. Fish, *Surprised by Sin*, p. 32.
57. L. A. Cormican, 'Milton's religious verse', in *New Pelican Guide to English Literature, 3: From Donne to Marvell*, edited by Boris Ford, Penguin Books, Harmondsworth, 1982, p. 228.
58. Fish, *Surprised by Sin*, p. 21. The phrase is taken from *Tetrachordon*.
59. W. Empson, *Milton's God*, Cambridge University Press, London, 1981, p. 39.
60. Fish, *Surprised by Sin*, p. 97.
61. *The Second Defence of the English People*, cited in *Politics, Religion, and Literature in the Seventeenth Century*, edited by W. Lamont and S. Oldfield, Dent, London, 1975, p. 157.
62. Burton (ed.), *John Milton's Prose Writings*, p. 261.
63. J. B. Broadbent, *Some Graver Subject*, Chatto & Windus, London, 1960, p. 80.
64. Fish, *Surprised by Sin*, p. 226.
65. Ibid., p. 131.
66. G. A. Wilkes, 'Full of doubt I stand', in *English Renaissance Studies*, Oxford University Press, London, 1980, p. 278.
67. Fish, *Surprised by Sin*, pp. 132–41.
68. Ibid., p. 141.
69. See Carey and Fowler (eds.), *The Poems of Milton*, p. 752.
70. Fish, *Surprised by Sin*, p. 221.
71. Carey and Fowler (eds.), *The Poems of Milton*, p. 1005.
72. See the comments on 'Incarnate' in Empson, *Some Versions of Pastoral*, p. 165.
73. See Joan S. Bennett, 'God, Satan and King Charles', *Publications of the Modern Language Association of America*, George Banta Publishing, Menasha, XCII, 1977; and Carey and Fowler (eds.), *The Poems of Milton*, p. 497.
74. Carey and Fowler (eds.), *The Poems of Milton*, p. 1029.
75. *Eikonoklastes*, cited in R. Hodge, 'Satan and the Revolution of the Saints', *Literature and History*, Thames Polytechnic, London, 1978, No. 7, p. 29.
76. 'Epic', in Hunter (ed.), *A Milton Encyclopedia*, vol. III, 1978, p. 58.
77. N. Frye, *The Return of Eden*, University of Toronto Press, Toronto, 1965, p. 11.
78. D. Bush, 'Paradise Lost', in Hunter (ed.), *A Milton Encyclopedia*, vol. VI, 1979, p. 56.
79. A. J. A. Waldock, *Paradise Lost and its Critics*, Cambridge University Press, London, 1947, p. 22 and p. 35.
80. Empson, *Milton's God*, p. 169.
81. Waldock, *Paradise Lost and its Critics*, p. 51.
82. M. A. Radzinowicz, *Toward Samson Agonistes*, Princeton University Press, Princeton, N.J., 1978, p. 146.
83. *The Early Lives of Milton*, edited by Helen Darbishire, Constable, London, 1932, p. 75.

Notes · 177

84. J. H. Hanford, *A Milton Handbook*, Bell, London, 1926, p. 57.
85. Burton (ed.), *John Milton's Prose Writings*, p. 353.
86. Hanford, *A Milton Handbook*, p. 54.
87. Carey and Fowler (eds.), *The Poems of Milton*, p. 122.
88. Ibid., p. 119.
89. J. Wittreich, 'William Blake and *Paradise Regained*', in *Calm of Mind*, edited by J. Wittreich, Case Western Reserve University Press, Cleveland, 1971, p. 114.
90. Ibid., pp. 121–2.
91. F. Sandler, 'Icon and iconoclast', in *Achievements of the Left Hand*, University of Massachusetts Press, Amherst, Mass., 1974, p. 180.
92. Ibid., p. 183.
93. Fish, *Surprised by Sin*, p. 160.
94. Burton (ed.), *John Milton's Prose Writings*, p. 218.
95. *The Ready and Easy Way*, in Burton (ed.), *John Milton's Prose Writings*, pp. 238–9.
96. Carey and Fowler (eds.), *The Poems of Milton*, p. 345.
97. W. R. Parker, 'The date of *Samson Agonistes*', *Philological Quarterly*, XXVIII, 1949.
98. A. S. P. Woodhouse, '*Samson Agonistes* and Milton's experience', *Transactions of the Royal Society of Canada*, XLIII, 1949.
99. See Radzinowicz, *Toward Samson Agonistes*; and A. Low, *The Blaze of Noon*, Columbia University Press, New York, 1974.

PART 3
1. See C. Hill, *Milton and the English Revolution*, Faber & Faber, London, 1977, p. 471.
2. M. A. Radzinowicz, *Toward Samson Agonistes*, Princeton University Press, Princeton, N.J., 1978, p. 25.

PART 4
1. W. W. Robson, '*Paradise Lost*: Changing interpretations and controversy', *New Pelican Guide to English Literature 3: From Donne to Marvell*, edited by Boris Ford, Penguin Books, Harmondsworth, 1982, p. 243.
2. Cited in R. Adams, *Milton and the Modern Critics*, Cornell University Press, New York, 1955, p. 127.
3. P. Murray, *Milton: The Modern Phase*, Longman, London, 1967, pp. 11–12.
4. W. Empson, *Some Versions of Pastoral*, Chatto & Windus, London, 1935, p. 163.
5. Cited in B. Bergonzi, 'Criticism and the Milton controversy', in *The Living Milton*, edited by Frank Kermode, Routledge & Kegan Paul, London, 1960, p. 162.
6. Ibid.
7. Cited in *Paradise Lost*, edited by S. Elledge, Norton, New York, 1975, p. 332.
8. Ibid., p. 529.
9. T. S. Eliot, *On Poetry and Poets*, Faber & Faber, London, 1957, p. 154.

178 · Notes

10. F. R. Leavis, *Revaluation*, Chatto & Windus, London, 1936, p. 53.
11. Cited by S. Fish, *Surprised by Sin*, University of California Press, Berkeley, Calif., 1967, p. 54.
12. F. R. Leavis, *The Common Pursuit*, Penguin Books, Harmondsworth, 1962, p. 62.
13. C. S. Lewis, *A Preface to Paradise Lost*, Oxford University Press, London, 1942, p. 23.
14. See, for example, the work of Joseph Summers, Anne Ferry and R. Crosman.
15. Ricks, *Milton's Grand Style,* Oxford University Press, London, 1963, p. 3.
16. W. Empson, *Milton's God*, Cambridge University Press, London, rev. edn., 1981, p. 165.
17. L. Sage, 'Milton in literary history', in *John Milton: Introductions*, edited by J. B. Broadbent, Cambridge University Press, London, 1973, p. 315.
18. Ibid.
19. Robson, '*Paradise Lost*: Changing interpretations and controversy', *New Pelican Guide to English Literature 3: From Donne to Marvell*, p. 251.
20. Mary Shelley, *Frankenstein* (1818). This quotation is from the Everyman edition, Dent, London, 1963, pp. 135–6. See also M. Tropp, *Mary Shelley's Monster*, Houghton Mifflin, Boston, 1977, ch. v.
21. W. Haller, cited in Fish, *Surprised by Sin*, p. 14.
22. D. Burden, *The Logical Epic*, Routledge & Kegan Paul, London, 1967, p. 32.
23. Ibid., p. 143.
24. Ibid., p. 133.
25. Empson, *Milton's God*, p. 53.
26. Ibid., p.56.
27. J. Peter, *A Critique of Paradise Lost*, Longman, London, 1960, pp. 126–7.
28. Empson, *Milton's God*, p. 38.
29. Ibid., p. 48.
30. Ibid., p. 102.
31. Burden, *The Logical Epic*, p. 35.
32. Cited in C. Hill, *Milton and the English Revolution*, Faber & Faber, London, 1977, p. 276.
33. *Times Literary Supplement*, 25 November 1983, p. 1306.
34. W. B. Hunter (ed.), *A Milton Encyclopedia*, Associated University Press, Lewisburg, Pa., vol. III, 1978, p. 51.
35. Burden, *The Logical Epic*, p. 84.
36. Cited by M. Mahood, 'Milton's heroes', in *Milton*, edited by A. Rudrum, Macmillan, London, 1969, p. 242.
37. Empson, *Milton's God*, p. 36.
38. *Doctrine and Discipline of Divorce*, in *John Milton's Prose Writings*, edited by K. M. Burton, Dent, London, 1957, p. 250.
39. Mahood, 'Milton's heroes', p. 245.
40. G. A. Wilkes, 'Full of doubt I stand', in *English Renaissance Studies*, Oxford University Press, London, p. 272 and p. 274.
41. Burden, *The Logical Epic*, p. 180.
42. Leavis, *The Common Pursuit*, p. 27.

Index

Further titles

STUDYING CHAUCER
ELISABETH BREWER

The study of set books is always more interesting, rewarding and successful when the student is able to 'read around' the subject. But students faced with such a task will know the difficulties confronting them as they try to tackle work outside the prescribed texts. This Handbook is designed to help students to overcome this problem by offering guidance to the whole of Chaucer's output. An introduction to Chaucer's life and times is followed by a brief description and analysis of all his works, identifying the major issues and themes. The author also discusses contemporary literary conventions, and Chaucer's use of language.

Elisabeth Brewer is Lecturer in English at Homerton College of Education, Cambridge.

STUDYING SHAKESPEARE
MARTIN STEPHEN AND PHILIP FRANKS

Similar in aims to *Studying Chaucer*, this Handbook presents an account of Shakespeare's life and work in general, followed by a brief analysis of each of the plays by Shakespeare which might usefully be studied as background reading for a set book. Philip Franks then throws a different light on the study of Shakespeare by giving an account of his experiences of Shakespeare in performance from his perspective as a professional actor and member of the Royal Shakespeare Company.

Martin Stephen is Second Master at Sedbergh School; Philip Franks is a professional actor.

AN INTRODUCTION TO LITERARY CRITICISM
RICHARD DUTTON

This is an introduction to a subject that has received increasing emphasis in the study of literature in recent years. As a means of identifying the underlying principles of the subject, the author examines the way in which successive eras and individual critics have applied different yardsticks by which to judge literary output. In this way the complexities of modern criticism are set in the perspective of its antecedents, and seen as only the most recent links in a chain of changing outlooks and methods of approach. The threads of this analysis are drawn together in the concluding chapter, which offers a blueprint for the practice of criticism.

Richard Dutton is Lecturer in English Literature at the University of Lancaster.

ENGLISH POETRY
CLIVE T. PROBYN

The first aim of this Handbook is to describe and explain the technical aspects of poetry – all those daunting features in poetry's armoury from metre, form and theme to the iamb, caesura, ictus and heptameter. The second aim is to show how these features have earned their place in the making of poetry and the way in which different eras have applied fresh techniques to achieve the effect desired. Thus the effectiveness of poetic expression is shown to be closely linked to the appropriateness of the technique employed, and in this way the author hopes the reader will gain not only a better understanding of the value of poetic technique, but also a better 'feel' for poetry as a whole.

Clive T. Probyn is Professor of English at Monash University, Victoria, Australia.

THE ENGLISH NOVEL
IAN MILLIGAN

This Handbook deals with the English novel from the historical, thematic and technical points of view, and discusses the various purposes of authors and the manner in which they achieve their effects, as well as the role of the reader. The aim is to bring to light the variety of options at the novelist's disposal and to enhance the reader's critical and interpretive skills – and pleasure.

Ian Milligan is Lecturer in English at the University of Stirling.

PREPARING FOR EXAMINATIONS IN ENGLISH LITERATURE
NEIL McEWAN

This Handbook is specifically designed for all students of English literature who are approaching those final months of revision before an examination. The purpose of the volume is to provide a sound background to the study of set books and topics, placing them within the context and perspective of their particular genres. The author also draws on his wide experience as a teacher of English both in England and abroad to give advice on approaches to study, essay writing, and examination techniques.

Neil McEwan is Lecturer in English at the University of Qatar.

A DICTIONARY OF LITERARY TERMS
MARTIN GRAY

Over one thousand literary terms are dealt with in this Handbook, with definitions, explanations and examples. Entries range from general topics (comedy, epic, metre, romanticism) to more specific terms (acrostic, enjambment, malapropism, onomatopoeia) and specialist technical language (catalexis, deconstruction, *haiku*, paeon). In other words, this single, concise volume should meet the needs of anyone searching for clarification of terms found in the study of literature.

Martin Gray is Lecturer in English at the University of Stirling.

The author of this Handbook

Geoffrey Ridden is Principal Lecturer in English at King Alfred's College, Winchester, and Course Director of the B.A. English degree programmes. He was educated at West Hartlepool Grammar School and at the University of Leeds, where he wrote a thesis on Milton's *Samson Agonistes*. He has held teaching posts at the University of Ghana, University College, London, the University of Durham, and Westfield College, London. He has also spent some time as Visiting Professor at the University of Wisconsin, Eau-Claire. He is the author of five titles in the *York Notes* series and has published a number of articles and reviews, principally on Milton. His hobbies include music and computers: he is currently combining the two in writing a book on computer-composition.